Through the Geek's Lens
An Autobiographical Exploration of Mental Models and Trade-offs

Marc Magrans de Abril

Last revised 2025-06-10

Contents

to Bego and Pili...

Prologue

It's 2007, and I'm with my wife in the Beijing Airport after a month of backpacking around the country. We do not have kids yet, and we have neither started to think about them. However, we are already aware of how special the trip is. We do not come from wealthy nor poor families, but when we were children, our parents didn't have money to spend on fancy holidays in hotels or campings, and even less on pricey airplane tickets. China is a fantastic country, and we are grateful for our luck: delicious food, surprisingly talkative, almost histrionic, and friendly people, buses with beds, crowded trains and train stations, the Leshan Giant Buddha, the Terracotta Warriors of Xi'an, Shanghai, the Yellow River, the daunting Three Gorges Dam, the smog covering Beijing forbidden city, the 6,000 steps of Taishan, the Great Wall, and Chinese, lots and lots of them. Of course, I forgot we are also in love, and as you can imagine, everything is painted in the romantic fire of the early stages of a relationship.

We're close to checking in, but with an almost infinite queue in front of us. Tired and sweating, my wife exclaims: "We are going to stay here forever. We won't make it." I look at her with my mad scientist face and say smiling: "28 minutes, give or take." Bego looks at me with a combination of a suspicious and loving gaze. To me, the issue is settled, and I chill out thinking that 27 minutes—time flies—is not a big deal anyway. I calculated our expected time at the check-in queue using the famous Little's Law and some simple observations. During my Telecommunication studies, I learned Queueing Theory, but at that time, I never made the connection with the real-life calculation of waiting time in the Beijing Airport or any airport whatsoever. It was after reading the delicious *Programming Pearls* from Jon Bentley that I realized about the many uses of this simple tool. It is intriguing and somewhat depressing to realize that many, in retrospect, obvious practical applications of mathematics, science, and engineering escape my imagination. I do not know if it is the way I learn, my lack of imagination, or the way we all learn, focused on grades, theory, and exercises, we lose the connection with the practical applications of our knowledge.

The minutes passed, and I realized that I could update the estimate and make it more accurate over time because the average servicing time will inevitably converge while the queue size will get reduced to zero. According to Little's Law, I can update the estimate by dividing the current queue length, around 250 Chinese and two Catalans, by the number of people dispatched in the last minute, eleven Chinese per minute; therefore, we should remain in the queue for only 23 additional minutes. Five minutes had passed after my last update, which makes the new estimate consistent with the previous one and surprisingly, Bego, bored and impatient, asks about the new estimate. The answer produces a subtle smile of comfort in her face. Is it just love? Either way, a miracle! And the undeniable proof that we were terribly bored or that the numbers made sense to her. Finally, some scientific knowledge was slightly useful to her. A hallmark of our relationship, an absurd stepping stone that will lead us to our marriage, kids, dog, and finally, to a happy mortgage together.

In the same spirit, this book tries to fill the gap between what we learn from books, schools, and universities, and the daily and down-to-earth observations of their consequences. If you are like me, imperfect, curious, with a desire to discover new thinking avenues in mathematics, biology, economics, history, psychology, and physics, then this book could be for you.

Why additional security is almost always oppressing? How is it that being more efficient and busy leads to trouble? Why trying to achieve perfection and excellence has a dark side? What is the best environmentally friendly policy? How can I lose some kilos and get thinner? How is it that intelligent people say stupid things? Is it fair that CEOs earn so much money? Do we need CEOs anyway? Can you hate and love someone without being inconsistent? What is worst than a micromanager? What is the best way to get lost in a new city or to investigate a difficult problem? Are my children normal? Why the Age of Big Data can be in its dusk? Why shouting to your children is a bad idea?

More importantly, how is it even possible that these questions can be answered, even partially using mathematics and science? If you want to know, you are welcomed, this book could be for you.

I warn you, though. The contents of this book are a hodge-podge of ideas without addressing a specific problem. A highly troublesome premise for a business pitch. But, it is true. The contents are like my life, and most likely as any life, connecting experiences and knowledge across domains of expertise. Our experiences are total; they do not have borders. It is quite a phenomenon that mathematics, science, and engineering are so compartmentalized, while reality overflows across domains and does not have specializations and subjects. The reality of our lives does not care about them. Everything connects with each other opportunistically through evolution and learning. Like species in an ecosystem, analogies in our brains, or a cascade of enzyme reactions inside our cells, things connect to each other naturally. This book tries to describe, as Charles Munger names it in *Poor Charlie's Almanack*, a manifold of mental models and analogies that could be used in our lives.

Thus, dear reader, the decision to continue reading and the final judgment rests with you.

Acknowledgements

This book would not have been possible without the help of Bego, my intelligent friend and loving wife, as well as my mother and sister, whose unconditional support has been invaluable. Special thanks go to my brother, who invited me to CERN for a month—a month that ultimately turned into a lifelong stay in Switzerland—and to Edu, Carlos, Oriol, and Dave for their patient proofreading and feedback. Ignacio Regaida designed a fantastic and professionally looking cover, replacing my initial choice from Amazon's default options. I am also deeply grateful to all the anonymous contributors who, as colleagues, supervisors, friends, and neighbours, have shaped the wholeness of my life reflected in this book.

However, the list above does not cover all the contributors. It is, in fact, a diminutive list of the people required for such an endeavour. Through this book, I am also drawing on the accumulated scientific knowledge of millennia, and through the referenced work, I have tried to give fair credit to a small proportion of such giant thinkers. Most likely, I have missed several crucial references and underappreciated their works. I apologize for that; it is entirely my fault.

Disclaimer

The views and opinions expressed in this book are solely my own and do not necessarily reflect those of my past or present employers, colleagues, or friends. I have made every effort to educate myself, understand the different points of view presented, and study the relevant literature. However, any errors, inaccuracies, or misinterpretations are entirely my responsibility, and I sincerely apologize in advance for any mistakes.

Why Mathematics is so Effective?

The most incomprehensible thing about the universe is that it is comprehensible.

   Albert Einstein, Physics and Reality, 1936.

There is a story about two friends, who were classmates in high school, talking about their jobs. One of them became a statistician and was working on population trends. He showed a reprint to his former classmate. The reprint started, as usual, with the Gaussian distribution and the statistician explained to his former classmate the meaning of the symbols for the actual population, for the average population, and so on. His classmate was a bit incredulous and was not quite sure whether the statistician was pulling his leg. "How can you know that?" was his query. "And what is this symbol here?" "Oh," said the statistician, "this is pi" "What is that?" "The ratio of the circumference of the circle to its diameter." "Well, now you are pushing your joke too far," said the classmate, "surely the population has nothing to do with the circumference of the circle."

   Eugene P. Wigner, The Unreasonable Effectiveness of Mathematics in the Natural Sciences, 1959.

Jero is a tall, street-smart, friendly friend. Unfortunately, after the pandemic our lives have drifted away. He possesses a peculiar knack for posing unsolicited personal questions. Perhaps, it is an intelligent way to avoid someone asking him a personal question. "Which new C++ book do you have in your backpack today?" He asked as he routinely did after realizing that my backpack always contained a textbook, and strangely, a bread baguette. However, he was never genuinely curious about the specifics of the book I carried; rather, my inexplicable addiction devouring science and engineering textbooks seemed to tickle him. That particular day, I had no books, just a couple of scientific articles. I believe such behavior was not entirely unusual in a particle accelerator facility, or so I'd like to believe.

As I met his gaze, I contemplated my options. Reading those articles evoked a sensation akin to savoring coffee with milk and two sugars—not three anymore as I'm in a permanent diet war—after indulging in paella. Like the kind of satisfaction one derives from a chocolate dessert. It wasn't essential for survival, but it was deeply satisfying. Delving into the details would inevitably trigger a meta-conversation, not about the articles themselves from Eugene P. Wigner and Richard W. Hamming, but about my eccentric reading habits. Hardly a conversation I looked forward to.

P. Wigner and Richard W. Hamming in their respective articles about the *The Unreasonable Effectiveness of Mathematics* reflect on its effectiveness[93,242]. For engineers, scientists, and mathematicians, the meaning of the equation $y = ax$ is obvious. For every quantity of x, the equation defines a relationship with a second variable y. The product of x raised by a factor of a is equal to y. It's like a mechanical apparatus. Insert $x = 1$ into the equation, and $y = a$ materializes on the other side. Insert $x = 2$, y becomes $2a$. Always the same.

But, how is it possible that these almost mechanical devices of the mind are able to represent nature so accurately?

In any case, Jero had no intention of poring over these articles and thoughts, and I certainly would have done a poor job conveying the profound epiphanies they inspired.

"It's not a C++ book," I remarked with a hint of irritation in my voice. We burst into laughter because I acted as if the articles were of interest to anyone but me. To this day, I'm not entirely sure why he found it amusing. I just guess that my irritation was somewhat funny, given that nobody around cared about such things.

Thus, my mind wandered, inspired by the musings of Wigner and Hamming: why aren't we hanging in an infinite mental loop of admiration when contemplating the symbiotic relationship between equations and tangible reality[1]? By some serendipitous alignment of neurons, a related epiphany dawned upon me: an equation also embodies the essence of a trade-off. A beautiful trivia, perhaps a deepity[2].

In order to keep the balance of the equation $y = ax$, we need a more units of y for each additional unit of x. This balance can be visualized as a line bridging two points in a bi-dimensional space. Look at your preferred equation in this light. It is a balance, it is a line or a curve in space, it is a mechanical device, and sometimes it is an approximation of reality.

For example, the simple budget constraint $B \leq xp_x + yp_y$ is simply telling us that we cannot spend more than the budget B. We either spend in product x or product y or a combination but always within the budget. But, here it comes the interesting part, the equation, and any equation, can be interpreted as a trade-off, too. Once we reach our maximum budget B, any increment of x entails a reduction of y proportional to p_x/p_y, and viceversa. We buy an extra banana and we should reduce the number of apples bought. There is no free lunch and you have to choose.

The same can be said for any equation. Consider the Pythagoras' Theorem $a^2 + b^2 = c^2$ in the same light. This equation establishes a trade-off between three different variables, the lengths of a right triangle's sides. This three dimensional relation can be portrayed as the surface of an infinite cone in three dimensional space. Hence, an equation integrating four variables can be represented as four-dimensional hyper-surface constraining the movement of the four variables, akin to a particle traveling a specific path in space-time. And so on an equation for five, six, or any number of variables. Essentially, an equation constraints the admissible values of the variables, reducing by one the number of dimensions of the space of possible values. The idea is

---

[1] In fact, the experimental agreement between Quantum Electrodynamics Theory and experimental results is to a part in a trillion, not just "some relation". Imagine that someone asks you to estimate the cost of a project and you give the estimate with a 10 μs error over a 1 year estimate, and then it turns out that you nailed it. It is hard to come to terms with such level of accuracy.

[2] As defined by the philosopher Daniel Dennett a deepity is statement that is apparently profound but actually asserts a triviality [52]. For example, "love is just a word." On one level, it is perfectly true, but on a deeper level is also false; love is an emotion, a strong feeling of affection or kindness, a condition, sexual desire, a mental state, and more. It is not just a word.

beautiful, but does it help?

Regardless, Wigner's ruminations about the uncanny ability of equations to replicate the nuances of reality weren't misplaced. Mathematics is unreasonably effective. It's effectiveness is irrefutable given the inhuman prediction accuracy achieved across science fields including physics (e.g., one part in trillion in the measurement of the electron magnetic moment, the existence of the Higg's Bosson confirmed by the Large Hadron Collider experiments, the existence of gravitational waves observed by the Laser Interferometer Gravitational-Wave Observatory, the one in ten quadrillion match of theory and experiments in time dilation, etc.), chemistry (e.g., Schrödinger equation accurately predicts molecular structures and reaction rates, spectroscopy techniques like NMR or infrared precisely match quantum mechanical predictions of electron energy levels and vibrations in molecules, etc.), biology (e.g., genetic studies confirm predicted allele distributions across generations, the Lotka-Volterra equations predict predator-prey dynamics, etc.), computer science and information theory (e.g., Claude Shannon's mathematical framework for information transmission under noise, real-world communication systems like the Internet operate within the efficiency limits predicted by Shannon's formulas, etc.), earth sciences and climate (e.g., climate models predict global warming trends with impressive accuracy validated by real-world temperature data, the mathematics of fractals and chaos theory explains weather unpredictability, etc.), or astronomy and cosmology (e.g., Friedmann equations from general relativity predicted cosmic expansion before it was observed, the discovery of cosmic acceleration, etc.).

This chapter explores how this remarkable power of equations extends beyond pure mathematics to describe trade-offs that permeate our reality. By constraining variables, equations illuminate the balances and limitations inherent in systems we encounter daily. For instance, it delves into the curious relationship between freedom and security, counter-terrorism policies, and the interplay between team size and communication complexity. A small appetizer for what is to come.

Freedom and Security

In 2010, the calm of our family home in Girona was shattered when a robber stealthily broke in. It was the first time in almost 30 years of living in

Montjuic. My parents faced a dilemma: let the time pass by and potentially feel permanently unsafe, or install some security measures to deter future intruders. Although in some contexts the second choice seems obvious, it is not neutral, as it requires spending a considerable amount of money, including recurrent payments to a security firm, installing metal shutters on all windows, and, more importantly, acknowledging that the neighborhood is not safe anymore. Initially, I disagreed with their decision and voiced my concerns. I believed they were sacrificing their freedom out of fear. However, it wasn't my home, decision, or safety at stake. As Nassim Taleb would say, I didn't have skin in the game. Nassim and my mother are always right. In hindsight, I believe they made the right choice. They haven't been robbed since, even in a neighborhood with periodic incidents.

I see a similar pattern connecting freedom and safety when I compare my childhood with that of my children. I often feel a tinge of guilt realizing that my children enjoy less freedom than I did at their age. My parents set a boundary of approximately 2 km radius around our house for our adventures. We knew venturing beyond Cal Vilallonga or Campdorà was off-limits. Occasionally, we pushed those boundaries without their knowledge. In stark contrast, my children never step out of our neighbor's garden without supervision. In essence, even though I consider myself more modern and open minded than my parents, in practice I'm more conservative than them, with a stronger need to control. It's not just me; I observe similar behaviors among my neighbors and friends. Living in a small village in the world's most secure country doesn't offer enough assurance. My children are not going to climb down an old well using a rotten rope, climb up a 20-meter wall in an ancient fortification without safety gear, be chased by a frenzied neighbor wielding an axe because we hid his tools, explore and get lost inside forgotten iron mines, or go berserk on an abandoned construction site. Although my children should be safer than I was at their age, I don't grant them the same liberties. They won't engage in the risky and sometimes illegal endeavors I once embraced as a child. Do they recognize their limited freedom? Are they genuinely safer for it? Is not the lack of exposure to danger very dangerous, too?

From a mathematical perspective, freedom can be defined as the ability of a variable to change in value. True freedom implies an absence of constraints, an unknown state, a random value of the variables, disorder. Consider the equation $x + y = 3$. It possesses one degree of freedom, representing a one-dimensional object: a line that offers a trade-off between variables. We can change the value of x or y, but not both at the same time. If we assign x a value of 2, then y becomes fixed at 1. Conversely, the equation $x + y + z = 3$ has two degrees of freedom, describing a plane in three-dimensional space. Here again, as in the case of the Pythagorean relationship, two variables must be determined to find the third. Typically, the number of degrees of freedom equals the total number of variables minus the number of independent constraints or equations. Mathematically, an increase in safety, order, or structure corresponds to a decrease in freedom. On one hand absolute freedom can be likened to complete randomness, akin to a thermodynamic endpoint. On the other, being completely constrained is also a thermodynamic endpoint due to the lack of possible movements. Total freedom and total safety or constraint are death states for opposite reasons.

Thus, freedom and safety are inversely related, but they both lead mathematically to death. Imposing more constraints on a variable diminishes its degrees of freedom, confining it safely within the set boundaries. The freedom-safety trade-off in mathematics is always equal to 1. A single equation or constraint curtails freedom by exactly one dimension.

In an interconnected world, where people, animals, plants, and ecosystems affect each other's actions, the unchecked freedom of one entity equates the coercion of all others. Any gains in freedom by one agent seem to constrain the other, a truth familiar to my parents after the robbery, viruses, weeds, and bugs attacking freely across our bodies and plants, and to citizens living under the hopefully-to-be-extinct figure of the dictator.

USA Patriot Act and Spanish Corcuera's Law

I distinctly recall that between 2000 and 2004, I was frequently asked for my identity card by undercover police officers. Out of fear of losing it, I opted not to carry the identity card. Unfortunately, the policeman didn't care about my unusual capacity to lose stuff. This led to a couple of incidents where my possessions were scattered across the floor of the Valencia train station while being questioned about my motives. Perhaps it was because I was young, dressed modestly, and frequently traveling for reasons unbeknownst to the police between Valencia and Castello de la Plana. To them, I might have matched some archetype of terrorist or delinquent. I somewhat took pride in this misperception. Nonetheless, my girlfriend theorized that the root of these searches lay in my somewhat disheveled, vagabond-like appearance-hardly a crime in itself.

In Spain, carrying an identity card was made obligatory by the Citizen Security Protection Law or Corcuera's Law (often colloquially termed the "kick in the door law"). Corcuera's Law was created against the backdrop of the separatist group ETA (Euskadi Ta Askatasuna, translated as "Basque Homeland and Liberty" or "Basque Country and Freedom") and was enacted in 1992. The Law granted police the authority to enter private homes of suspects, mandated citizens to always carry an identity card, and permitted the "retention" (syntactically different than "detention" but semantically similar if not equivalent) of individuals by the police without legal counsel.

A similar thing happened in the US after Al-Qaeda attacks of 2001. One of the disheartening government reactions, in addition to the War of Iraq, was the creation of the USA PATRIOT Act (Uniting and Strengthening America by Providing Appropriate Tools Required to Intercept and Obstruct Terrorism), an Act of Congress signed into law by United States President George W. Bush on October 26, 2001. This Act came as a response to the devastating 9/11 attacks, prompting Congress to hastily pass the legislation to bolster national security.

It's intriguing to pinpoint the parallels in the laws birthed in these disparate nations under comparable duress. The pressing question remains: did these or similar legislative measures genuinely enhance citizen safety? The evidence leans towards the contrary. Systematic reviews analyzing the efficacy of counter-terrorism strategies not only highlight the glaring lack of evaluative research on these interventions but also indicate that certain measures either fell short of the intended outcomes or, at times, inadvertently heightened the risk of terrorism[103,138,182]. These findings mirror the little I've been able to assimilate about Vietnam, Afghanistan, Israel, Palestine, Iraq, and Ukraine. Master Yoda expressed succinctly the idea:

Fear leads to anger. Anger leads to hate. Hate leads to suffering.

Did these laws significantly curtail the freedom of terrorists? or instead, did they increase the freedom of our governments, by giving them amplified powers to surveil everyone and prosecute those deemed potential threats without proof? Ironically, but consistently with the mathematical analogy in the previous section, these legislations conferred greater liberties upon governments, and therefore added constraints to citizens, giving them "safety". This very aspect is likely to be the one that ignited concerns regarding potential encroachments on civil liberties and privacy rights both in Spain and US during these periods.

All Models are Wrong

Essentially, all models are wrong, but some are useful.

George E.P. Box, Science and Statistics, 1976.

For over 10 years, I volunteered as a coach for the Mozzarella runners, a diverse group of enthusiasts who met twice a week during lunchtime to exercise. While I'm proud about my engineering accomplishments and my prowess in 24/7 on-call troubleshooting, I genuinely feel that my most impactful contribution to CERN during those years lay in enhancing the well-being and joy of the Mozzarella runners.

Even if you have limited experience in running, it's clear that fatigue mounts progressively with each uptick in pace. Then at some point, there exists a threshold beyond which one must pause and rest. It is not possible to go faster. The relation between effort and speed is nonlinear; beyond a particular exertion level, there are real risks of injury, nausea, or sudden fainting. Speed goes suddenly to zero after a step by step increase with respect to effort. The proportionality between effort and speed breaks down[3].

Remarkably, this seems intuitive and obvious to most, and the nonlinear aspect of running is easily grasped without fuss. Individuals, including engineers and mathematicians, seldom employ the term "nonlinear" in this scenario. Yet, owing to a blend of recognized technical and enigmatic psychological factors, this perceptiveness often fades when the topic pivots to mathematical modeling.

---

[3]As Anna, a Mozzarella runner and physicist, once told me, given the existence of friction, the relationship between running speed and energy is quadratic, close to the kinetic energy expression, and therefore, nonlinear. In addition, the amount of power our bodies are able to deliver is also finite, depressingly closer to a light bulb. Under these constraints, reaching 10 m/s is extremely challenging because it requires almost 10 times more power than our baseline energy spending. It is hardly a surprise that people do not reach higher speeds.

While countless mathematical formulas can depict the relationship between two variables [4], only one of them is linear. The universe of possible nonlinear equations eclipses the variety found in possible dialogues between two friends, especially if they are Finnish. Although both universes of possibilities are infinite, the former is a countable, while the latter in uncountable. Given this enormous space of possibilities, it remains curious—yet understandable, given its simplicity and tractability—that our scientific and engineering community has a conspicuous—and sometimes blind—predilection for linear models.

Yet, nature, in its intricate design, leans predominantly towards the nonlinear time-varying behaviors.

Herein lies the paradox for those textbook lovers with knowledge in Algebra and Calculus. One might mistakenly believe that linearity is more than just a rough approximation. For individuals of my ilk, it's a challenge to concede that sometimes words capture reality more fittingly than numbers.

Nonlinearity is ever present in our daily routines, including our preferences. For example, in Switzerland, I can always buy two or three additional coffees with $10 without affecting my budget nor happiness, but an additional $10 might mean the world to my son, Corso. He'd lovingly deposit the bill into his unicorn-themed bank, only to promptly use it on Pokémon cards. For me, its value is far less pronounced. While drinking water, a glass at a time, might quench thirst, consuming it in excessive amounts can be lethal and drown us. On the other hand, ingesting apple seeds containing cyanide seems harmless, at least from my several decades of first hand experimental observation.

Going back to our initial example with the Mozarella's, it is absolutely obvious that there's a tipping point beyond which physical activity ceases to be therapeutic or enjoyable. In the same vein, even a tête-à-tête with a cherished friend can occasionally grow tedious or even exasperating, it just depends on the actual friend and the duration of the conversation. This underscores why the domain of a relationship's applicability is as crucial as the relationship itself, most specially for linear relationships. Like inexperienced runners find out, knowing when a linear approximation is appropriate is just as important as understanding the relationship itself.

Recognizing the difference between linearity and reality can make all the

---

[4]John von Neumann said "With four parameters I can fit an elephant, and with five I can make him wiggle his trunk" and it is actually true and shown in [148].

difference.

Team Size and Communication Complexity

"Why didn't anybody tell me? Did you know, Alfredo?" she asked her husband, my father-in-law. Everyone knew, including her husband. Everyone except her. My mother-in-law was simultaneously sad, disappointed, and angry as a conspiracy unfolded before her eyes. "You should improve the communication with your husband," an anonymous voice chimed in, highlighting an unresolved issue that had become a recurrent family joke. Being a family of seven without counting animals from other species and partners, communication becomes complex, often disjointed. Increasingly, you find yourself ensuring everyone shares an understanding of the situation, be it the next birthday party, family dinner, Christmas presents, or one of the siblings being sick, depressed, or unemployed.

This is similar to what I observe in my job. I always feel a twinge of apprehension when the team expands. Naturally, teams grow with increased demands: more functionality, better performance, more users. Such changes often lead to larger teams. However, I can't help but wonder at which point the increased team size will shift from being a blessing to a curse.

As Frederick Brooks pointed out in *The Mythical Man-Month: Essays on Software Engineering* [35], in a team of size n, each individual can potentially communicate with $n - 1$ colleagues. The maximum number of communication channels for a team of size n is therefore $n(n - 1)/2$. As the team size grows, we can expect a quadratic increase in communication needs. A team of size 2 has one communication channel, a team of size 4 has 6 channels, a team of size 8 has 28 channels, a team of size 16 has 180 channels, and so on. My wife's family, with seven members, had 21 communication channels—a multitude of interactions to synchronize just for deciding on a dinner date, time, and place. My current team has 136 channels, an overwhelming number of potential information flows. Is it feasible to have a family or team with this many possible information exchanges? Can the team achieve a shared understanding?

For a team of size n, adding just one more member increases the number of communication channels by n, since the new member might need to talk to everyone else. That is, each new team member potentially creates an additional web of communication channels across the team.

The first time I encountered this model, I was struck by its clarity. However, as I was discussing my observations with my PhD-holding brother, I realized that the model didn't always align with real-world scenarios. How can we explain the existence of companies and organizations with hundreds of thousands of employees? What about armies? What about nations, or even the global economy? There's an undeniable overhead with larger teams, but since the time of the great cities of Mesopotamia, we've devised methods to at least partially mitigate these challenges. The simplest of these methods is decomposing large teams into a hierarchy without horizontal communication between people (e.g., companies, armies, churches, etc.). The Catholic Church, for example, has a pope just after God and its emissaries, who elects for life the cardinals—a kind of board of directors for the Catholic Church. Most cardinals are bishops and archbishops leading dioceses and archdioceses (an archdiocese being a diocese for a metropolitan area, like Barcelona, but unlike Girona, a simple diocese). Bishops and archbishops ordain priests, deacons, and lay ministers, which finally lead the laity, the ones that want to be led at least. This tree-like structure keeps the number of communication channels roughly equal to the number of people in the organization. Unfortunately, the positive side-effects of a rich information flow across people are drastically reduced.

While Brooks' model holds some truth, it's also flawed in certain aspects[5]. Nowadays, I see it as a word of caution whenever I witness the possibility of having a fourth or fifth child or a larger team. At some point you have to change the structure of the communication to keep up with the scale demands.

Brooks' Law, a corollary of the above and part of the programmer's folk wisdom suffers from similar mixed evidence:

Adding manpower to a late software project makes it later.

Or as I have to often remind to my kids: "Please, do not help each other, we are late."

---

[5]Team size seems to negatively affect performance although the relation is not very significant. Other factors like task coordination, task complexity, and national culture (i.e., collectivism) seem to be more relevant [23,143,189].

According to F. Brooks himself, the law is an "outrageous oversimplification," but it captures the general rule: more people, more trouble, especially when the project is late.

However, the corollary does not seem to conform again to the practical and sometimes useful measure of increasing the manpower when a project is late [149]. Specially if you have some trained manpower from non-critical projects to help on.

How is it that the argument from Brooks' Law is not always empirically valid? Brooks' observation most likely suffers from confounding. The possibility of mistaking a correlation with a causal relation of a third factor. Confounding indicates that we confuse the proximate and the final causes of the problem. Like when we take painkillers, anti-inflammatory drugs, or surgery when our back hurts.

Late projects, compared to the whole population of projects and irrespective of the team size, have a higher chance of being even later. Why? That's because projects that fail do so for other reasons (i.e., poor cost and schedule estimation, and the impact of risk and requirement changes on them are the primary proximate causes; these issues are typically exacerbated by larger and longer projects or by projects using new technologies or processes [38,73,75,82]). Obviously, late projects are likely to be part of this infamous group. The factors making a project slip influence at the same time the lateness of the project and the decision to add additional manpower. The confounding does not invalidate Brooks' observation; it is more nuanced, though. Throwing more money to a bad investment is not necessarily a good decision, likewise adding manpower to a project should be done carefully, with an eye on the root causes of the lateness, not just the proximate ones.

It's a Nonlinear World

Nothing is wrong with good metaphors so long as we don't take them as reality.

Claus Emmeche, Aspects of complexity in life and science, 1997.

"We all want to be fast. But no one will remember if you completed four tasks a week instead of two—a 100% increase. However, I guarantee everyone will remember and talk endlessly about you if you accidentally delete the database, introduce a critical security issue leading to a confidentiality breach, or snap at a colleague because you're overworked and stressed." My introductory pep talk to newcomers always emphasizes this theme. It's crucial not to confuse the incremental and almost linear benefits of working more efficiently or more hours with the nonlinear consequences of a major mishap. While it's commendable to excel in the former, it's essential to avoid the pitfalls of the latter.

I observed a similar nonlinear trajectory during my stint as a decathlete. In my early twenties, I consistently improved my scores, even breaking into the ranks of the world's top 100 decathletes. That was a significant achievement for me. Naively, I believed this upward trend would lead me to the Olympic glory. However, my progress plateaued when I was just 23 years old. Even though I managed to improve some individual scores, my overall performance remained unchanged until I retired around the age of 28.

No matter which patterns you observe in your daily life, they're likely nonlinear. Even phenomena as simple as increasing the speed of an object or cooking for a growing number of people have their limits. Don't be fooled by nonlinearity.

This same theme of nonlinear effects permeates many aspects of our world

[65], often manifesting as diminishing returns, saturation, and chaos, and sometimes being mistaken for randomness or, like the weather or our destiny, the acts of fate and gods. In this chapter, we will explore just one of the most famous nonlinearities—the Law of Diminishing Returns—a kind of meta-version of the No Free Lunch Law, and we will leave for later chapters the step-by-step discovery of other nonlinearities permeating our daily lives. So, be prepared to explore the CPU power wall faced by the microprocessor industry at the beginning of the 21st century and the challenges of building ever-bigger accelerators, two topics that are especially close to my heart.

Law of Diminishing Returns

"Can I use your telephone?" Jone asked.

"No."

"Can I use your telephone?" Jone asked again.

"No, Jone."

"Can I use your telephone?" Jone asked again. It's a question she might pose repeatedly, a hundred times a day. Really, a hundred times a day if not more. For a time, we used the telephone as leverage—also known as a cheap bribe—to get her to do homework, wash the dishes, play with her brothers, or tackle any other chore. However, this parenting tactic quickly lost its effectiveness, entering the realm of diminishing returns. Initially, she was easily passing the vacuum cleaner and removing the dishes from the dishwasher, sometimes even playing a bit with one of her brothers, a real miracle. Nowadays, she only asks for the telephone, and the mention of doing any household chores prompts a shriek of Pterodactylus anger flapping his wings around the kitchen.

In economics, the Law of Diminishing Returns posits that as additional resources—whether it be time, energy, money, or effort—are invested in a project, the returns on those investments eventually start to wane. Sometimes we also say that the relationship saturates at a certain point, like water eventually becoming unable to dissolve any additional amount of salt. This relationship can be illustrated by a convex curve, resembling a dome or a hat, which indicates that the benefits from each added unit of resource decline and then plateau.

While the Law of Diminishing Returns is foundational in economics, its definition has been somewhat vague, and many purported "proofs" of the law are either weak or incomplete. Concrete evidence supporting the law is sparse, though the principle intuitively resonates with our daily experience of eating disproportionately and not getting stronger and healthier, having more children and running out of patience, time, or savings, trying to improve a solution beyond its usefulness, or accumulating wealth without a proportional improvement in our happiness. Quantity is not the same as quality, even though a US citizen may disagree given the size of the coffee cups offered and its relatively poor quality.

It's crucial to distinguish the Law of Diminishing Returns from the principles of energy conservation and the ever increasing entropy in thermodynamics, which will be discussed in one of the following chapters. The latter two principles account for the impossibility of growing a plant without sunlight and for the fact that all natural or artificial processes are wasteful, respectively. Instead, the Law of Diminishing Returns accounts for the impossibility of indefinitely growing a plant by adding extra amounts of nitrogen, sunlight, water, or any other nutrient. As we all know, there are no kilometer-high sunflowers or sequoias.

The Law of Diminishing Returns can be viewed as a "meta" version of the No Free Lunch Conjecture—nothing comes without a cost, no matter how hidden or indirect—suggesting that every trade-off comes with its own set of trade-offs. As will be explained later, thermodynamics and the No Free Lunch Theorem in mathematics can be viewed as fundamental justifications for the No Free Lunch Conjecture. In contrast, the Law of Diminishing Returns does not have any equivalent mathematical or empirical evidence supporting it, nor a clear delineation of its application domain. It is not a law of nature, as far as we know. Yet, it seems obviously valid in many cases. Perhaps, it is a nonlinear pattern that often emerges in nature from the existence of bottlenecks in interconnected systems.

Thus, my team's productivity won't keep escalating indefinitely with the size of the team, and there's no everlasting bribe that will persuade my daughter to behave. While certain strategies might yield short-term success, their efficacy is destined to decrease over time and abuse.

The Power Wall

In my youth, I remember the thrill of getting a new game console or computer and marveling at the dramatic leap in graphics, sound, and speed. Transitioning from the Atari to the MSX, from the Sega Master System to the Sega Mega Drive, then to the Nintendo 64, and later shifting to personal computers like the 8086, the 486, and finally, my Intel Pentium. But around 2004, the multi-decade trend of exponential growth in microprocessor clock speed began to plateau[66,218]. What happened?

All exponential growth is destined to decelerate and taper off. Whether it's bacteria in a Petri dish or a bullish stock market, the growth rate eventually plateaus and might even decline. The challenge lies in predicting when and why it will halt. For microprocessor speed, from 1970 to 2000, companies managed to roughly double the density of transistors on a microprocessor, as well as their speed, every two years or so. However, this progression also led to an exponential increase in the chip's power consumption. By 2003-2005, the power consumption exceeded what standard cooling techniques could manage. Although the transistor density and the number of transistors per chip kept growing for some additional years, microprocessors hit what became known as the "Power Wall", where any further increase in the number of transistors per microprocessor or its speed required concurrent improvements in power efficiency. As of Today, the exponential reduction of transistor size has already stagnated and it is unclear if the number of transistors per chip will keep the exponential growing pace for more years[27,162,228].

What's particularly intriguing is that not only did the expected exponential growth pause, but few had anticipated it. This oversight is surprising given that we're discussing a field rooted in physics and engineering, the hard sciences—not the softer ones like economics, psychology, or sociology. Still, most experts were surprised. This is not uncommon, and the collapse of exponential growth periods is easily understood a posteriori but not anticipated a priori. We could easily find examples such as the many stock market crashes, the 2008 real estate bubble, viral trends and fads, or, perhaps, our modern industrialization period of exponential economic growth, saturating the environment with pollution and depleting the Earth's resources. Can it run forever, continuously increasing the planet's average temperatures and the probability of extreme weather events? For example, our bodies cannot operate above 37 degrees Celsius, and we can easily die in sustained temperatures over 40 degrees, while wheat and corn cannot grow above 25–27 degrees (with rice being more resilient but still below the human operating range).

In retrospect, without delving too deeply into the intricacies of microprocessor design and solid-state physics, it might seem reasonable to have anticipated the Power Wall around the 100 Watts mark—akin to a traditional incandescent light bulb and the energy consumption of an adult human. Would consumers have been willing to accept a higher electricity bill for improved microprocessor speed?

Faced with these power constraints, computer manufacturers had to innovate. They began adding more cores to their processors and introduced technologies like hyper-threading and pipelining. Concurrently, as microprocessor speeds stagnated, large cloud companies found ways to maintain an exponential increase in delivered computing power to customers by leveraging the cost efficiency and computing gains of the coordinated and concurrent orchestration of millions of microprocessors in data centers while taking advantage of the network effects of serving millions, if not billions, of users. At the same time, these companies effectively managed at scale the required capital, software and hardware complexity, power consumption, and cooling needs. In a way, extending the exponential trend in delivered computing power for a little longer.

Yet, the exponential increase in microprocessor speed has never returned. The once-democratizing miracle of exponential growth in microprocessor speed eventually saturated, and a new growth pattern emerged.

Exponential growth is, by its very nature, unsustainable in the long run.

Livingston Plot

I spent over a decade working at the world's largest particle accelerator facility, and during that time, concerns about its future frequently crossed my mind. The facility already spanned a vast 27 kilometers, and considering the costs of tunneling, hardware, the feasibility of any international collaboration funding, building, and the maintenance and operation of a 100-kilometer accelerator—the senior management's plan—seemed uncertain.

During the last century, particle accelerators have enjoyed a golden age, akin to the microelectronics industry, experiencing exponential growth in terms of particle beam energies. In fact, the exponential relationship between particle beam energy and time has become a hallmark in the field of accelerator physics, especially after Milton S. Livingston's book, *High Energy Accelerators*[136], highlighted the global advances in high-energy accelerators in 1954 using a simple logarithmic graph. The graph showed on a logarithmic scale, a straight ascending line over time equivalent to the explosive exponential growth of beam energies over time, increasing the energy by a factor of 10 every six years. This engineering feat has reached its peak during the construction of the Large Hadron Collider (LHC) at CERN around 2008-9 and its subsequent upgrades of the following decades.

For the physics community, each new accelerator was like a more advanced game console for a child. Accelerators with higher energies granted the opportunity to delve into uncharted scientific territories. However, according to Andrei Seryi's book, *Unifying Physics of Accelerators, Lasers, and Plasma*[206], the Livingston plot can be viewed from a different perspective. When various technologies are depicted on the plot, we start to see signs of saturation for each of the used technologies.

For instance, rectifiers and static generators faced constraints due to the electrical breakdown limit of air. Cyclotrons could not effectively accelerate relativistic particles. Linear accelerators had restrictions related to space and the electrical breakdown voltage in air. Proton-antiproton and subsequent proton-proton colliders grappled with limitations imposed by size and the synchrotron radiation associated with the accelerator's curvature and the energy of the individual beam particles. Nowadays, the current large synchrotron colliders are facing these later limits due to their massive scale and it is unclear if a 100-kilometer accelerator will be ever built because of the staggering costs.

The modus operandi of future physicists concerning colliders might have to undergo a significant change. Although not impossible, constructing even larger accelerators is becoming an increasingly daunting endeavor. It seems that collider technology has embarked again on a trajectory of diminishing returns, indicating that, in the absence of a new particle accelerator type, there might be a ceiling to the insights these colossal machines can offer[6].

---

[6]In theory, bigger particle accelerators can be built. There are some ideas to build them

---

around the Moon and even around the Solar System [5,17].

Optimizing Their Life is Always Simpler

"Why don't they just rent an apartment in the area, settle down, and then buy something without rushing the decision... if they still want to," I mused. My parents-in-law were eager to buy a new property close to Tarragona, near the beach, after selling their home in Corbera de Llobregat near Barcelona. Still, it seemed more prudent for them to rent while they assessed what they truly wanted.

This situation underscored a nagging habit of mine: offering unsolicited solutions for others' challenges. I often dispense advice with limited insight into the whole picture or understanding of the others' thoughts and feelings about the issue. Recognizing this propensity, especially at this point in my life, is a humbling realization.

Why do I consistently feel the need to optimize the lives of those around me? As my sister Astrid aptly said, "Problems always seem simpler when they aren't yours."

What does it mean to optimize something? Optimization involves picking the best option from a set of possibilities based on certain criteria. This could mean finding the quickest route to Rome, the perfect neighborhood to live in, the most effective education method for children, the most efficient design for a particular software, or the best real estate value for my parents-in-law. A typical optimization problem might aim to maximize or minimize a specific goal by systematically selecting input values from an allowable set to choose the best ones.

Consider this: a sphere is the geometrical object with the minimal surface area for a specific volume. It is minimally optimal. This minimal surface characteristic explains why igloos and yurts are preferred in some climates, and why gas storage tanks in refineries are often spherical to save on construction materials. However, it does not explain why houses are typically rectangular, never spheric. When you blindly optimize a criterion, it is likely you leave other important determinants aside.

In other words, shifting the optimization criteria can alter the optimal outcome. For example, maximizing retirement savings isn't the same as maximizing immediate consumption. Reducing construction costs is not the same as maximizing energy efficiency or ventilation.

What happens when there are several optimization criteria? These naturally lead to trade-offs. When there are conflicting optimal criteria, their respective best outcomes differ. For example, a trade-off can be established between maximizing retirement savings and maximizing current spending. Saving $ 1 today might equate to about $ 4 in 30 years, assuming that initial amount and subsequent returns are invested at a 5% interest rate. Hence, spending $ 1 now means forgoing the opportunity to spend $ 4 in the future. The existence of multiple optimization criteria leads to trade-offs.

If two criteria yield a one-dimensional solution space—a curve—with pairs of outputs as a function of the working point (e.g. saving $ 10,000 more yields $ 40,000 return in the future, consuming 20,000$ more yields an $ 80,000 return, and so on), three criteria produce a surface of potential solutions, and the pattern continues. Adding more goals or perspectives to a problem increases the complexity and the number of potential optimal solutions. Every additional goal introduces an additional dimension to the space of solutions.

Multi-faceted decisions, like choosing a career, planning a vacation, deciding on a meal or a restaurant, or picking a residence when multiple individuals are involved, are inherently multi-objective. The dimensionality of the solution space grows with the number of people participating, and therefore the number of optimizing criteria. This underscores Eliyahu M. Goldratt's wisdom: it's vital to not only understand the problem collectively but also to align on the ultimate objective, otherwise it is not possible to optimize. It's impossible to reach an agreement on a decision when there are multiple goals. Considering a combination of goals leads to a dimensional explosion and renders the problem computationally intractable.

Optimization is at the heart of science and engineering, and this long chapter will sample some related topics that for one reason or another have been a part of my life, including Pareto efficiency, its application to portfolio management, and some of its fundamental limitations; the inversion trick; the difference between trade-offs and compromises; heuristics; the Free Lunch Theorem in Optimization and Search; the paradoxical fragility of highly optimized systems; and finally, the uncertainty introduced to any optimization process when humans know that they are being observed.

Pareto Efficiency

In our daily family routine, either I can go for a run or my wife can, but not both of us at the same time. When I'm writing this book, my wife assumes the bulk of household responsibilities. Well, she typically assumes most of them anyway and I help a little bit. Someone needs to attend to the kids, prepare meals, drop them off at school, assist with homework, read a bedtime story, and more. These duties fall to either my wife, me, or both; at any given moment, at least one of us has to be handling these tasks.

Pareto efficiency or Pareto optimality describes a situation where resources are allocated in such a manner that it becomes impossible to rearrange them to benefit one optimization criteria (mine) without adversely affecting another (hers). The Pareto Frontier represents a trade-off between varying optimal criteria (e.g., balancing my personal hobby time against my wife's, investment risk versus expected profit, savings versus consumption, etc.) It is the magic curve (or surface, or hyper-surface depending on the number of optimization criteria) where all possible optimal combinations reside.

Just as with our time for hobbies, both my wife's and my preferences are equally valid, as long as our duties at work and with the family are fulfilled. They are both part of the Pareto Frontier. On one extreme of the curve, there is the combination where I have the maximum possible free time and my wife the minimum. In this extreme, my wife does all the child care, chores, and logistics required at home, not far from reality, though. In the other extreme, I'll do most of the family-related work, and my free time will be reduced to nil. In between, there is a curve describing all the possible trade-offs. The Pareto Frontier of our respective free time.

That is, when there are multiple criteria, an optimization problem does not have a unique solution, but rather a continuum of possible solutions, with the dimension of the space equal to the number of optimization criteria used. Two optimization criteria or goals lead to a curve of optimal solutions, three to a surface, four to a hyper-surface, and so on. Curiously, in the limit, as the number of optimization criteria increases, the Pareto Frontier loses its practical and fundamental value. Practically, because in higher dimensions, reducing the solution space by only one dimension is a meager gain given the immensity of the Pareto hypersurface. And fundamentally, because as the number of dimensions increases, most of the volume is condensed in the thin shell close to the hypersurface, at the extremes [92]. The solutions of a multi-objective optimization problem are in the extremes.

Risk-Return Frontier

"Are you planning to open a Paddle Club here in Commugny?" I asked Sebastian. He recently moved from Chile with his family after the Estallido Social of 2019-2021. While I don't particularly fancy paddle, I have immense respect for entrepreneurs. They shuffle people, goods, and money in innovative ways that no one has tried before. Sometimes they amass wealth, but every venture juggles on the brink of failure, and 80 to 90% of the time they actually fail. Compared to them, I'm a coward, sitting in front of a computer at a fixed price per hour irrespective of my actual output.

Conventional wisdom posits that investors weigh risk against return. The fluctuation in investment returns, often represented by its standard deviation, serves as a measure of risk according to some textbooks. Since there are two criteria to consider—expected return and risk—an investor should pick from the set of Pareto optimal combinations of expected return and risk. For a defined level of risk, we opt for the investment with the higher anticipated return. Or, inverting the argument, given a certain expected return, we would lean towards the investment posing the least risk.

Common belief also holds that the risk-return frontier is both concave and monotonically increasing, like a cup face down. With greater returns comes greater risk, and eventually, the return on investment plateaus. It's commonly believed that there's a ceiling to the returns one can gain for any given risk level. Returns seem to have diminishing returns with respect to risk.

The above does not mean that you cannot choose a really bad investment with a very low expected return and high risk, like buying as many lottery tickets as possible or spending your money in Las Vegas. It just says that for a given expected return, you are not going to find investments below a given level of risk, or conversely, for a given level of risk you cannot find an investment with an unbounded expected return. So, there is no free lunch.

But how accurate is this notion? How does the risk faced by a white-collar programmer or manager compare to that of a waiter? And how about the CEO of a major corporation with their cushy exit packages and golden parachutes? What kind of returns might an ice cream shop yield? Who earns more? Who is more vulnerable to financial downfall a wealthy individual that can build a bunker in New Zealand or the New York homeless?

Empirical Evidence of the Risk-Return Frontier

"No pain, no gain," Lucero, my trainer in Girona, used to say during one of the extenuating decathlon workouts. However, is the saying true across the board? Where does luck come into play? And how about genetic predisposition or the support from one's family?

The insight from Lucero about the existence of a trade-off for training is equivalent to our previously discussed trade-off between risk and return. You cannot obtain something from nothing, you can mess up as much as you want though. However, after more than half a century since Harry Markowitz published his seminal work *Portfolio Selection*[144], the vast amounts of resources poured on the risk-return research program have not been able to empirically validate the existence of a stable and simple relation between expected return and risk in financial markets. These discrepancies can be attributed to factors like the specific market studied, the time frame considered, the granularity of the data, and the particular models applied. Still a simple relation has not been found. While many reputable experts have found a positive correlation between risk and returns, others have identified a negative correlation or no correlation whatsoever[200]. There is no such simple relationship between financial returns and risk.

Isn't it baffling that such a foundational element of financial theory doesn't consistently align with real-world observations? It's quite possible that one or more of the underlying premises of the theory aren't as obviously true as we believe. For example, the theory presupposes the existence of means, variances, and covariances among financial assets. But is this assumption truly valid?

Does Jeff Bezos, Bill Gates, or Warren Buffet, to name a few random names, face a much higher risk of bankruptcy than my Chilean friend in Commugny? If this is not the case, why do we keep explaining these fictions in our academic literature?

Risk in Fat-tailed Distributions

There I was in the office at 6 PM, after an exhausting day, with my wife and my three-year-old daughter waiting for me at home. Unfortunately, I deleted by mistake all the configuration files for the LHC power converter control system. As I will eventually learn someday, I should never do interventions after noon, on Fridays, and any week before holidays. Except for the unfortunate incident, it was a highly productive day where I fixed a couple of bugs in the codebase and had three productive discussions with several customers. All that went down the drain at 6 PM. To fix the mess required a couple more hours in the office during my on-call week, and then when I got home, I found my autistic daughter screaming like an injured animal and my wife completely drained after a long day trying to find an early intervention program around Geneva while trying to calm down our daughter.

Things can always get worse, and since I was on call that day, an operator called me at 3 AM. By some miracle, I didn't get angry and my physical and emotional exhaustion served me well. Even though my children may not fully appreciate it, I am a mere mortal who does foolish things from time to time, especially when tired. Thankfully, that day didn't happen. As I mentioned earlier, no one would consider the amount of work I accomplished that day or my extraordinary personal circumstances; instead, if I made a mistake or my emotions finally spilled over, they would only consider my lack of professionalism. And you guessed it, they would be right. It's imprudent to risk a major failure in pursuit of minor triumphs. Catastrophic risk, in particular, cannot and should not be equated with petty gains.

We don't require technical expertise to grasp the idea. Let's consider this scenario: being punctual, like consistently arriving on time for school or work, has its advantages. However, if rushing to class one morning results in a car accident, would it be considered that important?

This notion can also be understood from a statistical perspective, taking into account the underlying probability distribution and payoff function associated with success and failure. As Nassim Nicholas Taleb explains, it only makes sense to be oblivious of catastrophic situations when the underlying probability distributions are not "fat-tailed" [226]. Beyond a specific threshold within the hierarchy of probability distributions, conventional measures of variability, like standard deviation, fail to stabilize. As the tail gets longer or more fat, even the average stops being well-defined. Why should we care? Because fat-tailed distributions suggest that disastrous events with unbounded harm remain probable, despite seldom appearing in everyday life. While we don't expect to encounter a five meters tall person, we can expect to witness the stock market tumbling by thirty percent one or more times over our life times (unless, as Nassim could say, you are an economist).

The variation of asset prices in financial markets seems to be fat-tailed, their variance does not converge or converge really slowly. In this case, financial models such as the risk-return frontier, Markowitz's portfolio theory, the Capital Asset Pricing Model (CAPM), Black-Scholes option valuation, Value-at-Risk, and similar ones crumble. Yet, these models continue to be taught and utilized. If the variance does not exist, what can you do with these models?

The same logic applies to the pep talk I give to new hires. If a catastrophic event is possible (e.g., deleting a database, leaking confidential information, losing temper with your boss or customer, etc.), then the probability distribution of our work's output isn't normal, but fat-tailed. Therefore, it is always better to be a bit lazy but rested and relaxed, than more industrious but unreliable and grumpy.

When the domain of the probability distribution is unbounded and can lead to ruin, the decision-making process should focus on the prevention or mitigation of the worst-case scenarios. Nothing is more important than the prevention of a catastrophe like a security breach that bankrupts a company, death from a traffic accident, systemic financial risk, climate change, pandemics, etc. Who can afford the risk of death? What civilization wants to endure its collapse? Which species can afford to gamble with its existence?

I'm not an example to follow in this respect, otherwise I would not have been rescued in the Orinoco river during a swim on one of the largest rivers of the world. Logically speaking, if you expose youself to a catastrophic situation repeatedly, you will end up dead or ruined. How many bikers or professional athletes end up in the operating theater with life-long injuries? How many stock market gamblers happily retire?

Epistemologically speaking, discerning whether a historical variable is fat-tailed proves to be impossible until a catastrophe materializes, revealing itself far too late. Therefore, risk assessment methods should emphasize reducing or eliminating repercussions tied to extremes when the harm is unbounded or very large. The possibility of a large harm should implicitly suggest to us that the probability distribution is fat-tailed. The focus should move away from likelihood and average impact calculations. Should we gamble our survival on the likelihood of a distribution being well-behaved, gaussian, or normal?

Balancing rewards versus risks for various categories of hazards isn't prudent, nor logical. Survival under such circumstances becomes implausible. One should adopt a strategy of winning big and losing small, never the opposite.

Invert, Always Invert

"Invert, always invert," Jacobi said.

Charles Munger, Poor Charlie's Almanack, 2005.

Upon first reading *Poor Charlie's Almanac*[157], I failed to grasp the crux of the matter. But one day, as I delved into the maximum network flow problem and its dual, I saw the light.

A sphere possesses the least surface area for a given volume, and conversely, it has the greatest volume for a given surface area. The void around and within a person is also the same person. The maximum network flow is defined by its minimum cut—the nodes that should be removed to prevent a maximal traffic flow. In a two—player contest, my opponent's adversary is like me, and consequently, as the adage goes, my enemy's foe is my ally. Sound is the vibration of the air happening between silences. Knowing how much I need to save for retirement is equivalent to knowing what income I need during my retirement.

Inverting a problem helps us to see the same problem from a different perspective.

Charlie Munger's concept of inversion seems to echo the broader and multifaceted principle of mathematical duality. This doctrine establishes a bijective relationship between concepts or structures: if A is the dual of B, B reciprocally is A's dual. They relay identical information, albeit through unique lenses. Solving one problem is exactly equivalent to solving its inverse or dual.

But if a problem and its dual convey identical information, what makes inversion a valuable tool? The existence of a dual problem allows us to validate our solutions, as both problems should lead to the same solution, solving the dual helps us to cross-check a potential solution. Sometimes, the dual problem is simpler with fewer variables or constraints. And perhaps, it is also a mechanism to bypass the framing bias popularized by Daniel Kahneman in *Thinking Fast and Slow*[45]. Consider this: you're diagnosed with an ailment, and a treatment is presented that heals 90% of its recipients. Now, envision another scenario where a therapy is suggested, but it doesn't cure 10% of patients. Are these two treatments equally effective? Which one would you choose? Do they feel the same? Most people perceive them as different though they are the same, and they prefer the former.

Likewise, employing diverse mental models to the same problem, examining the issue from various angles, or striving to understand conflicting opinions should enhance the decision-making process.

A Compromise is not a Trade-off

Today, my daughter was deeply upset because the last Nutella sandwich went to my son. It was irrelevant that she had already devoured two while my son had just one. She watched as the final sandwich moved from my skilled hands to my son's eager mouth. Why didn't I simply split the sandwich and give half to each of them? In this Solomonic scenario, both would likely had been equally angry, especially my son with me. Why didn't I give the sandwich to my exasperated daughter after the 10th repetition of the same request? I suppose I deemed the situation unfair.

As explained by Eliyahu Goldratt in his novels *The Goal* and *Critical Chain*

[84,85], the second solution where the sandwich is split is a compromise-
an intermediate political solution with conflicting objectives. Instead, the
decision to give the full sandwich to either child can be represented as one of
the possible solutions arising from different goals, a trade—off derived from
the existence of goals. Choosing the correct goal, a point in the trade-off curve,
should not be born from a political compromise, but from a clarification of
the real goal. I must choose between what is fair or what is less exhausting.
The compromise is not fair, not even half-fair, and it satisfies no one.

The existence of a compromise indicates a failure to identify the correct goal,
and therefore, the solution that maximizes it. A compromise should prompt
further analysis.

At least two related ideas make Goldratt's perspective worth considering.

First, Arrow's Impossibility Theorem states that it is not possible to reach
a rational decision based on individual preferences when there are several
alternatives and people involved[11]. The only methods that are fair are the
consensus and the dictatorship, both with known problems. So, if there are
several goals, there is no correct decision-making method. Each different
method will benefit some people and damage others. Our beloved democratic
voting is not an exception, it is also imperfect and it cannot satisfy everybody.

This mathematical insight was quite revealing to me, as it demonstrates a
fundamental limitation in group decision-making. It is impossible to decide as
a group unless we agree on the goal. In other words, there is no uncontroversial
way to make decisions when multiple people with different goals are involved in
the decision-making process. Compromises seem to circumvent the problem
by not arriving at a genuine decision. However, a compromise generates
always a (bad) decision, but by definition is not optimal, sometimes really
bad.

The second reason why Goldratt's perspective is worth considering is less
fundamental but equally persuasive. As Richard Rumelt observes in *Good
Strategy Bad Strategy*[191], one hallmark of bad strategy is "dog's dinner
objectives" or "café para todos" in Spanish. This entails a long list of "things
to do" that everyone agrees with and no one objects to. A lengthy menu
is provided to guests so that everyone is content until the bill arrives at
the table. Conversely, a good strategy will have positive effects on certain
stakeholders and negative effects on others. It will clearly expose the No

Free Lunch concept, and some people or groups will be unhappy about it. A compromise instead is like the lengthy menu with an unknown bill later.

Optimization versus Heuristics

Today, I rode my bike without a helmet. Sometimes, I return home to retrieve it, but not today. My wife won't be pleased. Surprisingly, it took me less than a second to make this decision. It wasn't optimal by any means, considering that repeated exposure to a low-probability yet potentially fatal risk results in a high probability of a tragic outcome, asymptotically approaching to certainty. Isn't it astonishing how my mind dismissed the fatal scenario almost instantly? Did my mind take into account existing information about the weather, route, time to return home, mood, my wife's preferences, and the asymptotic behavior of the probability? Can our minds handle such complex problems? On the bright side, this proves, to my wife's surprise, that I'm not a robot, at least not a perfect Bayesian robot.

Initially introduced by Herbert Simon and more recently explored in *Simple Heuristics that Make Us Smart*[79], there are fundamental heuristics that outperform more computationally-intensive statistical techniques, especially when faced with high uncertainty and dimensionality. For example, a straightforward sorting of optimization criteria and making a decision based on priority rules can exceed more traditional, resource-intensive methods, even under uncertain conditions. In fact, we typically use this approach. We choose a known restaurant, the cheapest airplane ticket, the beautiful sweater, or the book with the best-looking cover. This might be terrifying for a Bayesian-inclined mastermind, but consider this: why didn't evolution create a perfectly Bayesian brain? Instead, after billions of years of optimization, evolution chose us instead, the sloppy robot.

We constantly employ heuristics. If I must select between two meals of similar price and quality, but one demands a significantly longer commute, I'll decide based solely on location, without considering the marginal differences in price or quality, the cost of fuel, or vehicle depreciation. It is not that during our calculations we realize that these other parameters are not significant, we do not use them at all.

How does this work? In highly uncertain environments, some variables don't offer valuable insights and only introduce a delay to the decision-making process. Over-thinking is a waste in many cases.

The presence of heuristics might explain why street-smart individuals often outdo those with academic intelligence, even if they possess a computer, a PhD, or an economics degree [78]. Especially with an economics degree. These cognitive shortcuts and strategies often outshine optimal procedures, not just in speed but also in overall effectiveness. Intriguingly, these heuristics seem to challenge the well-accepted trade-off between speed and accuracy that we will explore in a later chapter.

Is There a Best Way?

"Why can't I use the knife? I want to chop onions like you do!" Corso shouted enviously at his father, who seemed to be enjoying the best moment of the day. "Because I said so, period," came the reply. The period in the dialogue was not the end of the story, but more like the end of a paragraph in a never-ending tale, as Corso disagreed and continued his untiring proving.

Who am I to judge inappropriate a knife in the hands of a 3-year-old, even if I am his father, you might wonder. For instance, in the movie *Captain Fantastic*, a potentially unreliable source of information, Viggo Mortensen gives a hunting knife to his child. Was it a mistake? It seems not, as the child does not harm anyone and Viggo, as my wife reminds me, seems to be such a good (looking) father.

An analogous situation happened during one of those lively Christmas dinners in Corbera de Llobregat with my wife's family. Alfredo and Asier were laughing alongside their sisters, Bego and Ainoha. They recalled the time their mother had asked them to move the car from the parking lot. This story would be trivial if not for the fact that they weren't even teenagers, obviously lacked driving licenses, and hardly arrived to the pedals. Was it an oversight on my mother-in-law's part? It's challenging, and perhaps unfair, to judge, especially given that all her five children are now alive, thriving, and content. My children should still pass the test of time to congratulate myself about my more conservative parenting skills.

This also reminds me back in 2018, while delving into machine learning articles, I came across the now classic paper by David H. Wolpert and William G.

Macready, *No Free Lunch Theorems for Optimization*[245]. Intrigued as I was by the concept of trade-offs in engineering, this paper resonated.

In their seminal paper they explain a simple idea. One might anticipate that there are pairs of optimization or search algorithms, A and B, where A consistently outperforms B, even if B sometimes surpasses A. For instance, one might expect hill-climbing to be more effective than hill-descending when searching for a maximum in a cost function. Surprisingly, this assumption is mistaken. According to the No Free Lunch theorem, the efficacy of a method depends on the environment and the structure of the problem. Thus, discussing an optimal search strategy without considering these factors is misguided. The theorem might not seem to make sense, as it suggests that in 50% of the cases, hill-descending will find the peak of a mountain as effectively as hill-climbing. But what if we consider any "terrain", especially those "mathematical terrains" without physical constraints?

The theorem provides both a humbling and unexpected insight. It proposes that successful optimization is intrinsically aligned with the optimization domain and is, therefore, delicate. An optimization method will remain effective only as long as the domain's characteristics do not shift. For instance, human cognitive bias might be seen as the optimal solution for a particular path in evolutionary history. A Bayesian decision-maker, faced with similar computational constraints in the same environment, would probably underperform humans; otherwise, evolution would have favored those traits.

This understanding should prompt us to exercise caution when evaluating past decisions made by ourselves or others. Unless you have serious and factual doubts about the mental soundness of these people, those choices were likely the best ones given the environment and the constraints present at the time. We shouldn't berate past errors too vehemently because, under those circumstances, past decisions could have been the best ones.

Similarly, whether some parents allow their young children to handle a sharp knife is contingent upon the environment they inhabit. Some decisions may be suitable in one context but not in another. For instance, permitting children to master the art of knife handling or allowing them to drive before they are legally allowed might be the best choices for a head start on the intricacies of the Haute Cuisine, prep work for a zombie apocalypse, or simply, anticipate the day I have to park but I suddenly lose my eyesight.

Lost in the Swedish Forest

In 2007, I traveled to Sweden to attend a series of lectures on Digital Signal Processing. One day, I decided to embark on an hour-long run along a random path that led into the neighboring forests. To my utter shock, I soon realized I was hopelessly lost.

The forests of Sigtuna were unfamiliar terrain for me, making my usual navigational intuition entirely ineffective. The landscape was marked by a seemingly unending succession of small, indistinct hills with abundant forests, devoid of defining peaks or horizons. Typically, I would rely on landmarks—be they prominent mountains, unique trees, distinctive rocks, long slopes, or notable buildings—to guide my way. Yet, in the midst of these repetitive, rolling hills, I felt a profound sense of disorientation.

Optimization can be likened to navigating specific terrains. When an optimization algorithm operates on a particular function, each progression reveals more of the landscape. The algorithm traverses the function's topography. However, if every kind of terrain is possible, witnessing a segment of it offers no insight into the rest of the expanse (that is, if all functions are plausible). As my experience in Sigtuna illustrated, not all navigational strategies are suited to every kind of terrain.

Have you ever gotten lost? When venturing into uncharted territories, the area explored might appear straightforward at first glance, yet it gives no hints about the challenges ahead. Among the myriad of possible terrains, the efficacy of all navigational approaches, including mine, evens out. Thus, when you tread into unfamiliar forests, mountains, or deserts, you might find yourself adrift.

And adrift I was. Accepting my predicament took a while, and finding my way back to the hotel took even longer.

The lesson, though, was not fully learned, as was proven some years later when Raul and I got lost near Mont Blanc (with no bigger reference point in the entire European skyline).

What I didn't Know During my Master Thesis

Around 1999, I was nearing the end of my engineering studies, working on my master's thesis in signal processing applied to the Spanish stock market. I was young, naive, and why not, eager to become wealthy. During that time, the internet was still in its infancy. I didn't have access to it, and obtaining sample data was a challenge. Fortunately, a friend of my master thesis' director who worked at Merrill Lynch provided me with a substantial sample—a CD containing about 10 years of daily stock market prices for various Spanish stocks. At the time, this seemed like a wealth of data to me.

Armed with this data, a student edition copy of Matlab, and my 486 PC, I spent several months in the basement of my home in Barcelona, studying and implementing time series models for the Spanish stock market. After fitting the data to the model, a question lingered: would I become rich?

I wanted to validate my idea in the real stock market. However, lacking the funds and being risk-averse, I devised a more conservative approach. I could divide the data into two subsets: one for estimating and optimizing the models, and the other for validating them. At that time, I didn't realize I was using cross-validation or out-of-sample testing.

What I also didn't understand was that the performance of a cross-validation method critically depends on how closely the in-sample data matches the out-of-sample or unknown data. Naturally, the validity of the assumptions embedded in the model is paramount. Cross-validation is useful as long as the divided subsets align with the in-sample and out-of-sample distributions. If they don't, the efficacy of cross-validation is compromised. This presents a paradox of the method. On one hand, validating out-of-sample will allow a measure of the robustness of the approach, but it reduces the model fit due to a corresponding reduction of the in-sample size. On the other hand, robustness with respect to an out-of-sample fit might not be indicative of real-world performance because stock markets, like many economic and social systems, change over time.

On a deeper level, the No Free Lunch Theorem posits that no algorithm performs universally well across all possible problem domains, including the algorithm used to select the best model using cross-validation (or the more modern bootstrapping or re-sampling). Thus, by splitting the data, I was, in essence, choosing an optimization method suited to a particular problem structure.

Either by luck or common sense, I didn't waste my money in the real game.

Robust Yet Fragile

I typically wake up at 6:45 AM. I do 15 min of gymnastics, and after taking a shower, I help my kids to get up and get dressed. They eat breakfast and then we head off to school by 8 AM. By 8:30, I begin my workday. My wife picks up the kids, and we have a quick lunch together at 12:30 before returning to work until 5 or 6 PM. My kids have been home since 3 PM, and I take over their care, starting with cooking, while my wife spends some time talking to her family, writing, going for a run, or doing whatever she needs to. Sometimes, I also assist the kids with their homework while cooking, and by 8 PM, we all sit down for dinner. Once the kids are in bed around 9 or 10 PM, my wife and I have some time to chat, and then I read, write, or do a bit of coding. Finally, around midnight, I go to bed, ready to start the cycle again like in Bill Murray's *Groundhog Day*. But in my personal movie, time always moves forward, and I age along with everyone else.

Many small "optimizations" are in place: cooking appliances, a dishwasher, a vacuum cleaner, mobile phones, a washing machine, a watch, organized paperwork and bills, coordinated schedules and plans with my wife, and calendars for the kids' activities. However, this system is quite fragile. If one of my kids, myself, or—God forbid—my wife falls ill, the system breaks down, and life becomes much more challenging.

It's been observed, somewhat paradoxically, that while highly optimized systems demonstrate robustness to random failures, they also reveal fragility when key components are targeted [37,57,119,175]. The Internet, for instance, is notably robust and adaptable, yet is vulnerable to malicious exploitation or hijacking of the very mechanisms that give it these robust properties. Every level of the communication protocol stack can be exploited, with worms, viruses, spam, and denial-of-service attacks being just a few examples. Commercial jet airliners with fly-by-wire controls are extremely resilient against most component failures and atmospheric disturbances but become vulnerable to rare events like total power outages, since they rely solely on electronic control. In contrast, the Wright Flyer isn't a robust system but doesn't face power outage issues because it lacks electrical systems. Diseases can be viewed as another instance of the intrinsic fragility of a highly optimized and intricate systems, we humans.

This paradox can also be fundamentally understood through the No Free Lunch Theorem in Optimization. The presence of optimal or near-optimal systems—even those "designed" via evolutionary processes—implies a lack of optimality in different environments or under different conditions. Adapting optimally to an environment always comes at a price.

In some ways, the term "robust" in the field of Robust Optimization might be misleading because any robust optimization mechanism will inevitably fall short under certain conditions.

Our highly optimized and efficient lives might not be suitable in certain scenarios. Sometimes, being disorganized, flawed, and lazy is more advantageous and really robust. There are situations where these behaviors are optimal, even if they seem counterproductive.

Observer Effect

"Corso is so polite and quiet. He's a fantastic kid," Claire, my son's teacher, said to me. Given the number of children she interacts with, I wondered if she might have confused him with someone else. Corso is far from being a saint. It's astonishing how he can undergo such a behavioral transformation once he steps onto the school grounds.

Imagine if parents could be in the classroom watching their kids. Most likely, it wouldn't result in anything positive. As parents, we need to grant our children some independence.

It reminds me of the times when, by some twist of fate, Corso and Jone played harmoniously together at home. It's a fleeting wonder, akin to a rainbow made of the most fragile crystal. A mere glance seems enough to break the spell. So, I often observe them from a distance, cherishing the rarity of such moments.

In quantum physics, the act of observing inherently alters the observed, too. By pinpointing an electron's position, its momentum changes by the tiny impact of the photons used to observe it; it is said that position and momentum are complementary properties and they cannot be measured accurately at the same time.

Is an observer effect exclusive to the quantum realm or does it also influence the behavior of my children? One famous instance of a similar phenomenon is the Hawthorne Effect. This stems from the notable workplace behavior studies at the Hawthorne Plant of the Western Electric Company in the 1920s and 1930s. In these studies, worker productivity increased with every change in lighting conditions, regardless of whether the light was increased or decreased. Simply put, being observed modified the worker's behavior.

Just as electrons' states can change when struck by photons during observation, human behavior can shift when individuals are aware they're being watched. Though the Hawthorne Effect is fascinating, recent research suggests there might not be as much solid evidence supporting it as initially thought [108,150,240]. An observer effect does exist, but it doesn't always manifest in a predictable manner. In this context, the real observer effect aligns more with the quantum uncertainty principle than the Hawthorne Effect. Observing a human changes its behavior unexpectedly.

Related concepts include Goodhart's and Campbell's Laws, both highlighting the pitfalls of metric-based decision-making. The former addresses how people optimize their actions towards a specific measurement rather than the intended goal. The latter delves into the corrupting pressures that measurement can introduce, potentially skewing the results[155]. Charles Goodhart aptly stated, "When a measure becomes a target, it ceases to be a good measure."

Examples are plentiful. Academia and researchers using the Journal Impact Factor and similar metrics have seen the proliferation of self-citations and citation cliques, reduced reproducibility of findings, and an increased number of retractions and fraudulent and fake research[32]; publicly traded companies focused on stock market prices have seen the rise of stock options compensation; the focus on revenue over risk led to the 2008 Lehman Brothers sub-prime failure; the focus on increasing the number of customer accounts led to the creation of millions of fake bank accounts at Wells Fargo [36,133,158]; standardized test grades and the educator's compensation on student test scores, spurred by the US No Child Left Behind Act, led to the cheating scandals in education[164]; the focus on production quantities during the infamous Soviet Union's five-year plans led to the production of unreliable cars and electronics, homogeneously boring clothes and furniture, and unsafe construction materials to name a few[31]; the UK's attempts to use metrics to enhance public service performance led to a collapse of the UK Health Services [40]; and the New York City Police Department's CompStat process (for "Computer Statistics" or "Comparative Statistics"), a data-driven accountability regime introduced to boost police and law enforcement performance, led to an underreporting of crimes[67]. All these can be traced back to the unintended consequences of metrics-based penalties and incentives. Decision-makers choose a metric to be optimized, and then the metric is misused, gamed, and perverted.

This reminds me of Kalun, a brilliant and unique child at my daughter's school in Meyrin. He once remarked, "I received the top score in our class on the Cantonal exams. Everyone knows that if you score below 3.5, you're not cut out for university and you have to go through the apprenticeship path." At merely 10 years old, he understood the true purpose of these tests: to categorize children early for efficiency and ostensibly protect those deemed less capable from future challenges. Even my autistic daughter had to take the test and, according to the forced standard, fail. While teachers assured me, "The test has no repercussions," it was evident that both parents and children understood the underlying implications more acutely, and that these polite teachers wanted to remove my strange daughter from the Geneva public school system[7].

---

[7]Jone, thanks to my wife's persistence and political savvy, as well as the invaluable support of Didier, an extraordinary schoolmaster in Geneva, was indeed the first autistic child fully integrated into the Geneva public school system. However, three years later, when she was eight, they expelled her, and we had to relocate to the neighboring Canton of Vaud, which was more accommodating and open-minded. It is curious that Geneva, the headquarters of the United Nations and part of a country that, in 2017, acceded to the Convention on the Rights of Persons with Disabilities, struggled so much to integrate my daughter into a primary school classroom. Life is full of contradictions.

True or False

Do or do not. There is no try.

Grand Master Yoda, Return of the Jedi.

As an early teen, my bookshelf housed an eclectic mix of the *Book of Saint Cyprian*, *The Quran*, and *Lisp*, alongside superhero comic books and diaries. My interest in the magical and spiritual always struck me as both curious and somewhat shameful. Is it normal to be intrigued by mathematics, science, magic, and mysticism simultaneously? Newton shared this strange combination of interests, needless to say, times were different and I can't compare myself to him in any other aspect.

Although I keep it a secret, I don't see those interests as contradictory but as a logical consequence of being skeptical. If I'm skeptical about the supernatural, why shouldn't I be about its non-existence?

In addition to the healthy and somewhat exaggerated skepticism, I think that new ideas have always captivated me. I often find myself initially believing something after reading a well-written argument, be it magical, philosophical, or scientific. I recall being fascinated and convinced by Plato's dialogues, only to be equally convinced by the opposing views of the next philosopher I encountered.

One of these enlightening arguments is Yoda's advice to his young apprentice Luke Skywalker: "Do or do not. There is no try." After some reflection and a strech of the imagination, Yoda may seem to refer to the Law of Excluded Middle or the Law of the Excluded Third. This law states that for any logical proposition, either that proposition is true, or its negation is true, but both propositions cannot be true simultaneously. There is nothing in the middle between the two propositions. Yoda, the oldest and most powerful

Jedi, drives poor Luke into a dialectic corner. If you do it, then do it, don't lie to yourself; stating something obviously true, but extremely difficult to accomplish, especially when a multi-ton X-wing fighter and the gravitational pull of Dagobah are involved.

The Law of Excluded Middle is self-evident. Either "these words" are in English or they're not, I have a dog named Patxi or I don't, and I'm married or I'm not. One of two contradictory propositions should always be true, not both, not none.

The Law of Excluded Middle asserts that for every logical proposition p, it is always true that either p or its negation $\neg p$ is true (i.e., p OR $\neg p$ is true). It is one of the three Laws of Thought, with its sibling the Law of Non-contradiction (i.e., $\neg(p$ AND $\neg p)$) and the Law of Identity (i.e., $p = p$).

I am either human or not human; it is evident. Sometimes I can act a bit weirdly, my wife may have a preference for which is the truth, but it must be one or the other regardless of her rightful wishes.

While the Law of Excluded Middle emphasizes that there are no gaps in logic (i.e., a statement is either true or false with no other possibilities), the Law of Non-contradiction conveys that a predicate cannot be both true and false simultaneously (i.e. there are no gluts). Contradictory arguments, true and false at the same time, are also said to be inconsistent. However, according to the Second Law of Thought, there cannot be contradictions in logic. It is not possible to be both human and non-human at the same time (although some people like Kilian Journet, Michael Jordan, Albert Einstein, my daughter, and a chimpanzee might appear to exist in a superposition of states). Yoda could have said: "Do and do not. Possible it is not."

These two laws are deeply ingrained in our culture and it is challenging to differentiate between the two. They seem identical, and once I understand their distinctiveness, they begin to blend together again. In fact, under classical logic using De Morgan's Law, both concepts are equivalent:

$$p \text{ OR } \neg p = \neg(\neg p \text{ AND } \neg\neg p) = \neg(\neg p \text{ AND } p)$$

According to classical logic, if we accept these propositions, any proposition is either true or false, neither both nor neither. The meta-proposition would be: "The Law of the Excluded Middle is either true or false, not both, and not neither."

In a sense, these laws represent the most fundamental trade-offs because the truth of a proposition implies the falsehood of its negation.

Building upon this foundational understanding, this chapter will dive into various extensions of classical logic that address complexities beyond binary truth values including the addition of the unknown state of knowledge used in the SQL language; probability theory as a logic extension to deal with uncertainty; paraconsistent logic to deal instead with paradoxes, and its application to ancient Asian philosophical currents.

In any case and in Luke's defense, it is not easy to lift an X-wing fighter even if the logic is as solid as the Beskar, the Mandalorian steel, and you supposedly possess the gift of the Force.

I Do Not Know

"Will we finish the project stage before the 15th of January?" My supervisor asked as Christmas approached. She was increasingly anxious and senior management persistently inquired about the project progress.

"I don't know," I replied. Undoubtedly, it was a true statement given the unpredictable nature of a project, but it was not the answer he was hoping for.

"What do you mean? Yes or No? If the project isn't completed on time, we'll have to let go of some team members. The project board won't allow it to continue as is," he remarked, as if it was an obvious consequence of the situation. He achieved the desired effect and I got scared.

Here we have two people employing different types of logic. For the manager posing the question, there is no middle ground—the law of excluded middle applies. He had a Yoda-like point of view. However, for the person actually executing the work, the question lacks a certain kind of answer, making it impossible to provide a clear-cut response. Consequently, the conversation is reshaped by increasing the complexity of the logic used. A third value is introduced to the Aristotelian true-false binome, creating a new truth value within the gap between true and false. Is the introduction of the "Unknown" logic value illogical?

The existence of various types of logic is an undeniable reality, whether we like it or not. Around 2004 while working in Valencia under the supervision of my prospective father-in-law, I do remember realizing the significant difference between classical logic and the logic used in the Structured Query Language (SQL)—a language for representing and retrieving data from databases. Years later, after reading Louis H. Kauffman's *Laws of Form: An Exploration in Mathematics and Foundations*[111], I began to further grasp the vast array of logical possibilities.

SQL is the standard language for managing data in Relational Database Management Systems (RDBMS). Developed in the 1970s at IBM by Donald D. Chamberlin and R. F. Boyce, who were inspired by Ted Codd's relational model, SQL was officially adopted as the standard language for RDBMS by ANSI and ISO standard groups in 1986. The Database Language SQL has since achieved remarkable success as a universal language for data modeling and manipulation.

One controversial feature of SQL is the NULL value in its three-value logic. When predicates are evaluated over NULLs, they return a logical value of "unknown" or "missing information" rather than true or false. This feature is crucial for performing outer joins of tables because these combine data from two tables even when there isn't a complete match between the joined columns in both tables. In such cases, the NULL value is used to represent the absence of data or missing information in the resulting dataset.

Both the Law of Excluded Middle and Law of Non-contradiction collapse when the NULL value is used. SQL propositions are not always either True or False, but sometimes NULL.

p	$\neg p$	p OR $\neg p$	$\neg(p$ AND $\neg p)$
True	False	True	True
False	True	True	False
NULL	NULL	NULL	NULL

That is, in SQL the Law of Non-Contradiction is not always True, the logic is inconsistent as sometimes a proposition can be neither True nor False. Yet, the logic is globally coherent and we cannot write propositions that do not make sense within the new logic system. That is, a new Law of Excluded Middle and Non-Contradiction emerge in the context of th SQL Language. There a proposition will be either True, False, or Unknown, one and only one of them, instead of the previous bi-valued True or False of the classical logic formalism.

I Guess

"Will we go to the swimming pool tomorrow?" Corso asked me.

"I guess so. Although, it could rain," I said softly, aware of the uncertain weather forecast for tomorrow and the sensitive mood of my child.

"What!? You promised me!" he exclaimed, his voice filled with increased rage.

"Corso, most likely we will be able to go. But if it rains the whole day, the swimming pool will be closed," I said with the most neutral voice possible.

"You lied to me! Why can't I go to the swimming pool!?" Corso threw himself on the floor and started to scream as if his skin was being torn to shreds by a demon.

Again two people arguing using different kinds of logic. A futile endeavour unless common logical ground rules are agreed upon. My son seems to be thinking in terms of a bi-value logic, yes and no, true and false, good and bad. In contrast, my statement about the future weather is more nuanced. It tries to convey even more information than the "I do not know" we saw in the previous section. However, this conceptual grayness didn't seem to help him; on the contrary, he hated it, or me, for some minutes. It is understandable, especially considering that he was aware of the fact that parents have deity-like powers capable of predicting and controlling the weather at will. In this context, it is normal that the probabilistic guesses were unsatisfying.

What is probability theory anyway? Probability theory is a field that combines set theory, logic, and statistics to convey nuanced information about uncertainty. Although I was aware of the use of probability theory in economics, signal processing, telecommunications, embedded systems, control theory, and machine learning to name a few, I only began to understand probability as a kind of logic after reading Edwin T. Jaynes' *Probability Theory: The Logic of*

Science[106]. It was a revealing perspective to view probability, believe or not, as a way to improve our tools for deduction and induction (the latter missing in classical logic).

For example, in classical logic if I see a person with a mask and diamonds in hand in front of a jewellery store with a broken glass and the alarms ringing, I cannot deduce that the person is a thief. A real thief could have given the diamonds and the mask to a bystander during his escape, or some kids could have broken the glass and the man was just trying to help while using his tie as an improvised bandage after getting hurt with the broken glass, or the guy just bought some diamonds and was going to a costume party at the time the shop was robbed, etc. You get the idea. Unless you are one of the Holmes family, You cannot typically make a deduction using classical logic regarding the real world, it is too complex, there are too many details. However, using probabilistic logic you know that all these other situations are even more unlikely, and therefore, you can inductively reason that given your experience, the most likely hypothesis is that the person with the diamonds and the mask is actually a thief. You have a reasonable doubt though, but it is your best guess for the time being. It is interesting how this intuitive and simple idea has required a bit more than a couple of milenia since Aristotle to develop in the modern probabilistic theory.

The aim of probabilistic logic is to combine the abilities of probability theory to handle uncertainty with the abilities of deductive logic to exploit the structure of formal arguments.

Probabilistic logic can be seen as an extension of propositional logic that enables reasoning with uncertain hypotheses, propositions whose truth or falsity is uncertain. A proposition A is neither true nor false, but it has an associated degree of validity $P(A)$ between 0 and 1. Where $P(A) = 1$ implies certainty that the proposition is true, and $P(A) = 0$ implies certainty that the proposition is false.

The Law of Excluded Middle, stating that something is either true or false, continues to be valid in probabilistic logic:

$$p(A \text{ OR } \neg A) = P(A) + P(\neg A) = P(A) + 1 - P(A) = 1$$

The Law of Non-contradiction, stating that something can not be true and false at the same time, holds, too:

$$p(\neg(A \text{ AND } \neg A)) = 1 - P(A \text{ AND } \neg A) = 1 - 0 = 1$$

That is, the laws of classical logic hold, and the propositions can be either true or false, not both, not none. However, the degree of validity of a proposition $P(A)$ could be anywhere in the interval between 0 and 1.

Sometimes, however, probabilities do not seem to convey enough information to my interlocutors. Especially if they are my children or my bosses. They seem to prefer listening to an Oracle with perfect prediction powers rather than the disheartening numbers of probability theory.

Yes and No

During the year, no matter the season or temperature, I bike or run with my daughter Jone to the shore of Lake Léman to swim—Mies Beach and Coppet Harbor being our preferred spots. Jone seems to ignore the freezing water temperature in winter, and after 10 or 15 minutes, I force her to stop. These last summer, after the bath, Jone was always asking me to go visit the horses in the meadows near our home in Commugny. It turns out that she was not interested in the horses but in the seemingly beautiful electrical towers transmitting electricity across the region. While I sat down and read a book, Jone got close to the tower while jumping and flapping in complete happiness. At some point, I always get tired of reading, and after several persuasive shouts, Jone returns and repeats the same phrase: "If I touch the cables, I will die; If I don't touch the cables, I won't die; If I touch the tower on December 2023, I will die; If I touch the tower on January 2024, I will die; If I do not touch the cables on December 2023, I won't die," and she continues as if the first statement didn't logically entail all the others.

Does Jane fail to understand the everyday use of logic? For some reason, the Law of Non-contradiction is not intuitive to her; two contradictory things can be true at the same time. Can something be true and false at the same time?

This is not as strange as it seems. For example, a bit after starting to date my wife on our late twenties, she asked:

"Do you love me?" Being introvert and emotionally immature, the question disarmed me.

"Yes. . . " I said with an insecure voice. This took me off guard, as she still does with some unexpected question or observation. If I really knew what it meant for her, I could tell with certainty. However, I couldn't, and I can't, feel like her. I wish. More importantly, I was scared of giving the wrong answer. Was it perhaps because I loved her? Should I have said instead that I both loved and didn't love her?

"What do you mean?" she asked again. Making the kind of question that I would like to avoid. I felt trapped again.

"I do not really know." Although I was not completely ignorant about it, I replied like a little kid, close to my thirties.

"What? You don't have a clue, do you?" I guess she referred to knowing something about love or its meaning.

"No, I do know." That was certain, at least a clue, for sure. I knew something about all these questions, although it was not crystal clear as to which one and what exactly I did know.

This conversation was somewhat absurd, real, but more to the point, it was also logical in a certain sense. It was logical to me.

Curiously, as the examples seem to show, classical logic is not used as often as we think. It is not unusual to reason and discuss with a mixture of different kinds of logic, even one where true and false can co-exist at the same time.

Have you ever had problems explaining an intuition that you know is correct, but still contradictory with some seemingly known facts?

"I love and I do not love you" or "it is dangerous and it is not" could be understood as either a contradiction or a dialetheia, depending on the logic used these contradictions are impossible or not. A sentence, A, such that both it and its negation, $\neg A$, are true is a dialetheia. This is a controversial point of view. Do dialetheias exist[179,180]? Jone, my daughter, seems to intuitively grasp the possibility of certain statements being both true and false at the same time and tries to ensure in his inquisitive repetition that there are no gluts and gaps in the statements. Well, I really do not know what she thinks.

Regardless, dialetheias oppose or contradict the Law of Non-contradiction. At first glance, it looks absurd because propositions cannot be true and false at the same time. Is it possible to love and not love? At least it is for humans. Who can claim that we are always consistent? I guess the controversy is not about humans, but about logical systems being partially inconsistent and still being valid.

Dialetheism claims that some inconsistency can be maintained without incoherence (i.e., without fundamental logical flaws). Surprisingly it is possible to build coherent logical systems and mathematical formalisms, also known as paraconsistent, with contradictory statements. Can something be true and false at the same time? If this is the case, can something also be not true and not false at the same time?

One of the most popular arguments in favor of dialetheism invokes the existence of logical paradoxes of self-reference. For example, Russell's and the Liar's paradoxes. Russell's paradox arises when one considers the set R of all sets that are not members of themselves. If the set R is not a member of itself, then its definition dictates that it must contain itself, and if it contains itself, then it contradicts its own definition. This set exists and does not exist at the same time. Is it possible? It is expressible in words anyway. In a similar way, the Liar paradox is the statement of a liar declaring that he or she is lying: "I'm lying" or simply the sentence "This sentence is false". If the sentence is true then it should be false and vice versa. Again, a contradiction that can be expressed.

Given that these paradoxes lead to contradictions, it has been argued that they are incorrect or invalid statements. However, a second solution proposed by paraconsistent logicians is to allow for propositions to be true and false at the same time.

However, it is not possible to reconcile the paradoxes with formal logic unless we drop one of the fundamental axioms of logic. A paraconsistent logic is a formal system that allows certain contradictions by dropping the necessity of the Law of Non-contradiction or the Law of Excluded Middle.

The simplest way of generating a paraconsistent logic is to use a many-valued logic as we saw in the previous sections for SQL, the Structured Query Language for databases. However, it is also possible to build a four-valued logic containing true, false, both (true and false), and neither (not true not false at the same time) values.

In the universe where this logic applies, Jone will be electrocuted after not touching the cable of the electrical tower and at the same time she won't be, as if her consciousness observed the quantum multiverse where all possibilities happen at the same time.

Dialetheism in East Asian Philosophy

I find myself living amidst a constant stream of contradictions. Our planet is overpopulated, yet I have three children. I worry about climate change, but I own a car, consume meat, and desire a home near the ocean. I yearn for a just world, but I benefit from a high salary in one of the richest countries in the world. I love my family, yet I reside in Switzerland, far away from them, and I hardly speak with my brother. When I'm with my family during Chrismas or other holidays, I sometimes become irritable and frustrated during our conversations as well. I cherish moments with my children, but I long to travel solo with Bego, my wife and best friend.

Are these genuine contradictions, or merely artifacts of imprecise language usage? Am I alone in experiencing these inconsistencies? Am I a monster for not speaking to my brother, having three children, or eating meat? Language and life seem prone to generating contradictions, at least in the way I employ them. Classical logic seems to be ill suited to address these concerns.

Contradictory statements are not only prevalent in our lives (particularly in mine), but also in Eastern philosophy. For example, more than 2,000 years ago in the *Tao Te Ching*, we find:

> *The Way that can be spoken of is not the true Way [. . .]*

This statement in itself is paradoxical, as it refers to the True Way while simultaneously claiming that it cannot be spoken of. Yet, for over two millennia, such statements have resonated with people across various cultures.

When Buddhism and Daoism merged to form Zen, a philosophy emerged that embraced contradiction as a central tenet. Shunryu Suzuki, in *Zen Mind, Beginner's Mind*[219], offers thought-provoking paradoxes that still ring true:

> *Each of you is perfect the way you are [. . .] and you can use a*

little improvement.

Calmness of mind does not mean you should stop your activity. Real calmness should be found in activity itself. We say, "It is easy to have calmness in inactivity, it is hard to have calmness in activity, but calmness in activity is true calmness".

The advent of paraconsistent logic enables us to interpret Eastern philosophy literally, not as mystical rhetoric but as genuine discussions about reality using logical arguments.

Either A or B

"Would you like to read for a bit or play a board game with Corso? It's your choice," I suggested to Jone, weary of hearing her energetic leaps and bounds throughout the kitchen.

"I'll play with Corso."

Being an innocent child, Jone had fallen into a ville parenting trap. Most likely, she would have preferred to relax on the sofa, watch videos on my smartphone, or continue jumping and flapping around the house like an hybrid between Kangaroo and Butterfly. All viable options, but not the ones I desired.

It's not only that we play this game with others; we also tend to favor clear-cut, black-and-white choices like when I confided to my five-year-old son Corso:

"As a child, I would occasionally get in trouble at school, too." As I said these words, my wife shot me a piercing look of profound disapproval. Later, she explained with her saintly patience, "Children need clear-cut ethical guidance. You have to draw a distinct line between right and wrong, or they'll become confused." I trusted her argument, but it left me wondering if this binary mentality could be harnessed for nefarious purposes, too.

Between any two options lie countless others. Regardless of what your parents, teachers, or boss may tell you. Real-world situations are rarely binary. True or false, yes or no, A or B, fight or flight, stay or leave, my way or the highway, heaven or hell—these dichotomies rarely capture the finer details and complexities of reality. Accepting the given options, assessing the consequences, and selecting the best course of action is just one possibility. Optimizing your options is a lesser strategy than creating new ones. Analysis, being so valued nowadays, does not create value like synthesis does. Analysis and synthesis mirror the exploitation-exploration trade-off: analyzing and remaining within the known, or venturing out and discovering the unknown.

Reject the notion of dichotomies. Do not believe them.

Sampling

"We haven't spoken with them in quite some time, and I can't help but wonder if they're going through a difficult phase." I said this as my wife and I discussed how Carlos and Vanessa disappeared from our radar for a long time. Occasionally, we realize that we haven't seen or communicated with certain friends or family for an extended period. This might be due to either ours or theirs busy and stressful life. Discerning meaning from silence is quite similar of drawing conclusions from a mountain of information. What causes the silence? Silence or lack of data seems to also convey information[135].

A similar observation can be made about history textbooks and the press. These media often focus on wars, murders, the overthrowing of monarchs, rising inflation, unemployment, and other such events. Historians rarely document the repetitive cycles of seasons or the lives of families and tribes during peaceful eras. Who will notice in a thousand years from now my afternoons doing homework with Jone, the meals I prepare for my kids, the trendy jeans of this season, or the next hot summer? While reporting on change is efficient as it minimizes repetition, it also leads to a skewed perception of a perpetually changing world. The approach of highlighting information changes fails to establish a baseline.

In the case of my friends, their silence conveyed information, but does the silence has the same power over historical scales. Does it signify peaceful, uneventful spans without war, famine, or plagues, or does it simply reflect our ignorance?

Given our limited time, attention, and memory, it makes sense to focus on the most useful aspects of reality while discarding some others. But, is it possible to understand the whole by just observing a portion of it? One of the most renowned responses to this question is the Shannon-Nyquist

Sampling Theorem. I first encountered this theorem around 1995 while pursuing my degree in Telecommunications Engineering. The Theorem posits that a continuous signal can be reconstructed from a discrete set of its points. To accurately reconstruct an analog, time-varying signal from a finite sample of points, we must sample the signal at twice its maximum frequency or bandwidth. This means that by examining a continuous signal at specific intervals, we can reconstruct it flawlessly. It is astonishing that we can recreate an intricate curve, regardless of its complexity, from a limited number of points. For any signal, as long as we sample it at an adequate rate, the points between the samples can be perfectly estimated. It seems almost magical.

How can we reconstruct a continuum from a discrete collection of values? How does a purely mathematical expression reveal certain properties of the physical world? Is it feasible to gain a realistic understanding of history or global affairs through a finite number of observations? Can we know a person by just talking with them from time to time?

I do not have answers to all these questions, but this chapter will delve into several subjects that are, somehow, surprisingly related to the seemingly dull subject of sampling including human hearing and compact disks, friendship and long-term relationships, management supervision styles, usability tests, the Bible, and why some people might think that engineers are bad communicators.

Human Hearing Range and Compact Disks

As my father aged, his hearing gradually deteriorated. Losing one's hearing can create a sense of disconnection from others. It is true that my father was an introspective person though, surprisingly considering his successful career as salesman for Pfizer, the pharmaceutical company. Initially it was not obvious that he was not hearing well. My father's hearing loss began subtly but became increasingly distressing over time. However, he never lost the ability to hear my mother's high-pitched voice. We couldn't help but laugh every time he exclaimed, "Don't shout at me; I'm not deaf!" It seemed as though my mother's voice occupied a unique and privileged frequency band on my father's hearing hardware.

As the range of audible frequencies decreases, so does the amount of information received. The typical hearing range for humans spans from 20 Hz to 20 kHz. We can't detect sounds below 20 Hz like whales or elephants, nor can we perceive sounds above 20 kHz, like dolphins, cats, or mice. In his final days, what sounds could my father hear and comprehend? He gradually lost his ability to process incoming information. Did this relative isolation affect his mental state? I believe so. Have you ever talked with a lonely individual? It feels as if the person exist on a different plane of reality. They hear you but they do not understand you.

How does the information content of our spoken words relate to the voice or hearing bandwidth[8]? This concept becomes apparent when considering the storage requirements of a signal. How many samples are needed to perfectly reconstruct a human voice? The higher the pitch, the more samples are necessary to recreate the signal. For instance, to reconstruct a typical human voice with a maximum frequency of 20 kHz, you need, according to the Nyquist-Shannon Sampling Theorem, $2 \cdot 20$ kHz $= 40k$ samples/s. How many "samples" of information per second did my father receive instead?

Another way to intuitively understand the relationship between hearing range and information content is further illustrated by examining dolphins or bats, whose auditory abilities enable them to reconstruct their three-dimensional surroundings from the high frequency echoes of their chirps and clicks. Quite a feat compared to our limited hearing capabilities. All this enabled by the subtle changes of the high frequency echo signals. Lower frequency signals, having less information density, could never enable such capability.

The Wagon-wheel Effect, Aliasing, and Noise

When observing a car's wheels during initial acceleration, there's a moment when the wheel appears to rotate counter-clockwise, or even seem to freeze for a fraction of a second. This is known as the Wagon-wheel Effect, an optical illusion in which a wheel appears to rotate at a different speed and direction than it actually is. Wheels can seem static, rotating more slowly, or even

---

[8]Information in this context is related to data rather than to meaning. The former is related to the amount of signal transferred across a channel, while the latter is related to the impact of the message on the receiver. While the latter is more interesting, there is no sound scientific model for it, and therefore, during this chapter I focus on the perhaps less interesting of the two acceptations of the word.

moving backward. This effect results from the limited sampling rate of human vision, which can be influenced by artificial factors (e.g., television or video frames, fluorescent lights) or natural factors (e.g., related to brain function).

During my student days, I failed to understand the connection between the Sampling Theorem and the Wagon-wheel Effect. It wasn't until a random and mundane day spent observing a car that the realization finally dawned on me. It's always humbling and somewhat embarrassing to acknowledge the limits of one's understanding. How is it that the obvious applications of knowledge don't easily transfer from one domain to another? Merely knowing a theorem doesn't guarantee understanding its implications. Why did it take so long for me to connect the Sampling Theorem and the Wagon-wheel Effect? How many other connections am I missing? Am I truly maximizing my existing knowledge and expertise? Chances are, I'm falling short by a significant margin[9].

The Wagon-wheel Effect is an unintended consequence of sampling images at a rate below the threshold set by the Nyquist-Shannon Theorem. In the domain of signal processing, this effect is known as aliasing. fig. 1 illustrates the ambiguous reconstruction of a fast sinusoidal signal when the frequency falls below the Nyquist-Shannon limit. In this scenario, the same sampled points can be derived from two distinct signals—one below the limit and another above it.

A similar aliasing phenomenon happens to my mother when she calls me between 6 and 9 PM. "You are always busy, you never have time to talk," she claims as she observes a seemingly static situation derived from the fact that she calls during the time I do homework with my kids and prepare dinner. The same unfortunate accident can happen if you take coffee always at the same time your boss happens to pass by. This, of course, could be solved by sampling at random intervals with an average sampling rate above the Nyquist-Shannon limit, either taking the coffee at random moments during the day or telling our bosses to change their agenda to improve serendipity and information gathering.

---

[9]Although we congratulate ourselves by being part of humanity during an exceptional period of exponential growth, it is nevertheless surprising to observe the lag between the invention of the wheel and its generalized use in travel suitcases, or the invention of the screw—turned with a wrench for 300 years—and the screwdriver, an advanced application of the lever.

Thus, regardless of the signal-to-noise ratio of the situation at hand and even in the absence of noise, we could be perceiving a distorted reality simply because we're measuring it too slowly.

Consider a one-year software project with a continuously changing status. However, now imagine that the project manager only checks the status just the week before the monthly release of the new software version. He or she will always feel that the project is in a frenzy fixing last minute issues with everybody fully occupied. Now imagine instead that our project manager checks the status only at the beginning of the release cycle, he will feel that people are not focused, without a clear understanding of the requirements and goals. To avoid this observational bias, the project manager must review the status more often.

What is the appropriate approach? If the project status changes daily, the project manager, according to the Nyquist-Shannon Theorem, should be checking at least twice a day. However, does this make practical sense? It's improbable that any rational project manager or supervisor would request a comprehensive project status update twice a day. Why not? Shouldn't they closely monitor projects according to the Nyquist-Shannon Theorem? The reality is that the measurement noise of the project status signal would be quite high, rendering consecutive samples within a day virtually useless. In a year-long project, the status undoubtedly changes between every morning and afternoon. But, can we provide our boss with an accurate progress update between these two points in time? While we're interested in reconstructing the status signal, it is unfortunately so noisy and expensive to acquire that attempting daily measurements proves to be impractical.

Sampling is therefore affected by the structure of the signal (especially if it is periodic), its rate, but also by the noise mixed in.

What is Worst than a Micromanager?

My wife and I have differing opinions on how to approach cooking recipes. Surprisingly, my wife, the more creative of the two, sees a recipe as a strict set of instructions to follow. For me, the more analytical, a recipe is more like a guideline to achieve a desired outcome, which can be reached in various ways without necessarily following the recipe. I find adhering exactly to the

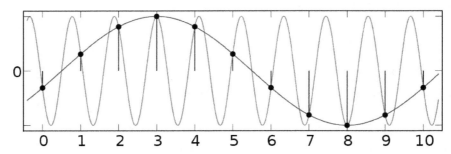

Figure 1: Aliasing of two sinusoidal signals. Unless we assume a limited bandwidth, a set of samples can be interpreted in multiple ways. In other words, if the sampling frequency is too slow, a signal above the Nyquist-Shannon limit can be interpreted as a lower frequency one.

steps to be dull, while she deems it essential. She could get mildly annoyed realizing that I was cooking lamb curry without reading the actual recipe or using the expected ingredients, except for the curry.

I find this reaction akin to the one of a micromanager or a three-star chef expecting their subordinates to follow precise instructions.

Naturally, in specific scenarios such as baking a dessert, landing an airplane, or conducting open-heart surgery, adhering to precise instructions is of utmost importance. In these instances, following detailed guidelines, a detailed checklist, or even having someone verify your work can be critical. If you need evidence of this, just ask my children about my first and, until further notice, last attempt at creating a mutant black forest cake.

So, is micromanagement inherently negative? Or is there something worse than a micromanager? The sampling and control theory offers an interesting perspective on this question.

According to the Nyquist-Shannon theorem, reconstructing a signal from digital samples requires a minimum sampling frequency. Similarly, the digital control of a process is determined by its control bandwidth or, more simply, by the required rise time of the system. Classic control theory texts by authors like Astrom and Landau recommend sampling rates 10 to 30 times above the control bandwidth or 4 to 10 times the rise time of the output[13,130]. Sampling at higher frequencies leads to increased computational costs and measurement noise, while lower frequencies can render the system unstable.

Consider again the project manager's job of controlling a one-year project. The typical rise time is around 6-10 months, so to effectively control such a system, you would need to assess progress and make decisions about once or twice a month—a reasonable expectation. However, if the project's duration is one month, you would need to monitor progress every two or three days.

Longer sampling periods might result in instability due to delayed action, while shorter ones (e.g., several times a day) can lead to inefficient and noisy micromanagement.

From a sampling standpoint, the opposite of a micromanager is not an ideal manager. A hands-off or macro-manager only inquires about the project's status when it is completed or fails, especially when it fails.

As a starting point, we can use the back-of-the-envelope calculation of sampling frequency from feedback control theory to determine if our managers strike the right balance in between.

Whack-a-Mole Friendship and Sampling Jitter

I have a few charming friends who exhibit some frustrating behavior. At times, I mentally reclassify them from friends to good acquaintances. We occasionally go through periods when we keep in touch on a weekly or even daily basis. It's like a positive feedback loop, with our stories, interactions, discussions, and jokes all growing in number. However, inexplicably, they vanish for a month or two, akin to playing whack-a-mole. I can't help but wonder if I behave similarly with some people. On average, I meet these friends more frequently than others, but the issue lies in the inconsistency. Over time, our interactions are marked by periods of frequent contact and periods of silence. This irregularity generates uncertainty and, eventually, distrust, despite our actions and words reflecting our genuine friendship.

In sampling and control theory, a comparable phenomenon is called jitter. The process of sampling a signal assumes the existence of a regular clock to space the samples. But What if the clock is imperfect, not regular, and the ticks aren't evenly spaced? What if samples are sometimes taken slightly earlier or later than expected? In these cases, we say the clock has jitter.

Jitter introduces additional noise, proportional to the rate of change of the signal, into the samples. Imagine a signal constantly growing at a given rate, if we sample always with a fixed interval, the measurement will always increment by the same proportion. However, if the sampling period has jitter, sampling earlier will get a smaller increment, while sampling a bit later we will get a bigger increment. The difference between the actual measurements with jitter and ideal ones with a perfect clock will be proportional to both the signal increment rate and the sampling time error.

Jitter derived noise isn't caused by the source, communication channel, or measurement method, but by samples taken at irregular intervals due to an imperfect clock.

Signal reconstruction is not only limited by the sampling rate or the noise but also by the irregularity of the clock. As the sampling rate increases and noise level decreases, the requirements for the clock become more stringent. I wonder if this is one of the reasons why my whack-a-mole friends create a feeling of distrust in me. The timing irregularities reduce the flow of information by introducing additional uncertainty, and this reduction contributes to mistrust.

Consider a project manager who requests monthly status reports, but these reports sometimes arrive a week early or late. What is the impact of this jitter? The reports will naturally have an additional noise level of around 25% of the signal (i.e. one out of four weeks per month). Timely reports don't reduce noise, but irregular reports introduce it. This applies to the moments when the status is measured, reported, and most importantly, when an action is taken based on the report (with the last being the worst case).

In other words, it's not a big issue if my friend doesn't communicate regularly, as long as they respond promptly or reach out when something important arises (e.g., birthdays, parties, or less positive events). It seems that the most crucial aspect is consistency in response time, rather than the interval between interactions. Reducing uncertainty in response time enables us to better predict the result of our actions, even in the midst of uncertainty in the measurement. How does it feel when a friend doesn't respond or react promptly to a personally important matter? This phenomenon also occurs in control systems, where the worst case is not the irregularity of the loop, but the inconsistency between the measurement and the action. A friend who responds whenever they please ceases to be one.

Hallway Usability Tests and Statistical Sampling

Close to my thirties, I began my career as a proud software developer. However, when it came to evaluating the effectiveness of user interfaces, I was at a loss. Joel Spolsky's *Joel Test: 12 Steps to Better Code* provided a valuable solution[213]:

> *A hallway usability test is where you grab the next person that passes by in the hallway and force them to try to use the code you just wrote. If you do this to five people, you will learn 95% of what there is to learn about usability problems in your code.*

While I doubt that 95% is an exact figure, this approach is not only practical but also embodies a fundamental truth about statistical sampling. It demonstrates that it's possible to estimate certain aspects of reality by obtaining a random, and often small, sample [10].

In this context, sampling refers to gathering information from a subset of the total population. This subset of measurements can be used to approximate certain metric (e.g., estimating the average of a random variable X using a series of samples x_i as $1/N \sum_{i=1}^{N} x_i$).

Unlike the Nyquist-Shannon Theorem, the goal here isn't perfect signal reconstruction, but rather estimating a specific metric with a certain degree of statistical confidence or probable error. Obviously, larger sample sizes yield lower errors and more statistical confidence in the estimate.

However, depending on the statistical properties of both the sample and the total population, estimates may not be particularly robust. For instance, if we always discuss with similar people and read the same newspaper, we may face sampling bias, experiencing a filter bubble. This is why Joel recommends a random sample by suggesting, "grab the next person that passes by in the hallway."

The sampling method significantly impacts the statistical validity of the

---

[10]This argument is similar to the one made in the fantastic book *How to Measure Anything* where the author shows how to measure disparate things like IT and obsolescence risk, the value of a human life or public health, the future demand for space tourism, value of information. its availability, and more [104].

gathered information (e.g., randomly selecting people from the hallway versus choosing office mates).

In some cases, sampling, even if totally random, can also be uninformative due to the fat tails of the underlying distribution. This is a particular characteristic of stock prices, engineering project cost overruns, pandemic impacts, financial risks, and similar phenomena with non-independent random events. Nassim Taleb, in his *Incerto* book series[220–224,226], explains the concept of fat tails by comparing the statistical properties of two distinct samples. Imagine sampling from two different populations: one close to Gaussian, and the other fat-tailed. The first sample could be the weights of 10 randomly chosen people (around 1 billionth of the world population), and the second could be the Dow Jones index for 30 random days within the past 100 years of daily variations (approximately 1 part in a thousand of the total population). The first sample size is nearly a million times larger, relatively speaking, but where would you expect more information and less uncertainty? The uncertainty of both samples doesn't correspond to their relative sample sizes. Two different samples with relative sizes diverging by over six orders of magnitude exhibit completely opposite uncertainties. The distribution of human weight is close to normal, whereas changes in the Dow Jones index have fat tails.

Another way to interpret the Joel's Hallway Usability Tests is to realize how the uncertainty of the average is reduced after the first few samples. As the table below shows, with a single sample the uncertainty of the sample average is infinite, but just after the second sample the remaining uncertainty is proportional to the standard deviation, and after 10 samples we can only further reduce the uncertainty by 30%. When the distribution is not fat-tailed a very small number of samples, even less than 10, gives most of the information.

Samples	Uncertainty	Uncertainty Remaining [%]
1	∞	∞
2	σ	100
10	$\frac{1}{\sqrt{9}}\sigma$	30
100	$\frac{1}{\sqrt{99}}\sigma$	10
10000	$\frac{1}{\sqrt{9999}}\sigma$	1
∞	$\ldots$	0

Sampling Knowledge

Donald Knuth in *3:16 Bible Texts Illuminated*[122] suggests studying a large collection of information (The Bible) by selecting and examining small quasi-random portions in depth. However, instead of using a random sample, he used a stratified sample, selecting a verse from each of the Bible's books. This technique works best when the population can be divided into distinct, non-overlapping subgroups or strata (e.g., the Bible's books, each from a different author), strata are internally homogeneous but externally heterogeneous, and there are clear criteria for assigning population units to strata. Using this simple method, he shows how it is possible to gain a global understanding of a subject through deep knowledge of a very narrow subset of the whole. While the truth of this proposition is debatable, it offers an appealing approach to combat the current information explosion.

This book, the one you are reading, also adopts a sampling approach. Instead of conducting an extensive investigation of a small number of subjects, it carries out a shallow random walk through various personal, mathematical, engineering, and scientific topics offering a glimpse into subjects that have captured my interest and fascination.

I once had a similar conversation with Eduardo regarding my previously discussed obsession about reading C++ books. How many C++ books do I need to read and study? How many programs should I write to become an expert? My supposed obsession seemed irrational to them, but was it useful? As Eduardo wisely observed, how many user manuals does one need to read to use an axe?

Bombers and How to Look at Your Beloved

Just because nobody complains does not mean all parachutes are perfect.

Benny Hill

During the Second World War, statistician Abraham Wald was tasked with examining the distribution of damage in aircraft to advise on how to minimize bomber losses to enemy fire. The military initially leaned towards providing greater protection to parts that sustained more damage, but Wald made the assumption that damage was more uniformly distributed and that the aircraft returning from missions were hit in less vulnerable parts. He observed that the study only considered aircraft that had survived their missions, while the bombers that had been shot down were not available for damage assessment. The holes in the returning aircraft represented areas where a bomber could sustain damage and still return home safely. Wald proposed that the Navy should reinforce the areas where the returning aircraft were unscathed, as those were the areas that, if hit, would result in a lost plane.

The initial military point of view was biased towards the surviving cases. This statistical phenomenon is named attrition or survival bias and also occurs in medicine and engineering practice when some subjects or samples are lost, and therefore, the full population is not sampled, just the surviving subgroup. The same can be said for machines or systems in general, broken systems tend to vanish, so in the long run, we typically observe failures of mostly successful systems, giving importance to minor issues. Catastrophic failures are often absent in the current population of systems, especially when considering safety and security incidents. The impact of serious security and safety incidents is so massive that people, systems, and organizations involved sometimes disappear, rendering them unobservable. Nobody is around to criticize the team and system that caused a significant security breach because everyone got fired after the incident and the system was replaced. Similarly, we may spend hours discussing uneventful flaws in systems that do not have major risks or problems[11].

On a more philosophical note, consider the people close to us—family members, loved ones, long-standing colleagues, or neighbors. Should we view the flaws of our most cherished ones as signs of weakness or strength? Is it possible that the imperfections we observe are, in fact, outlines of their qualities? Are these flaws akin to the hits sustained after long and successful battles? As time goes by and we get closer to our beloved ones, we are more likely to notice the wounds and imperfections in them, rather than the qualities that have made them stand out above the rest of our acquaintances. Almost magically, the qualities of people, things, and systems around us are taken for granted, and our focus falls on the remaining issues to be perfected, whether

---

[11]This aligns surprisingly well with C. Northcote Parkinson's 1957 Law of Triviality, also known as the bikeshedding effect. The law attempts to explain the recurrent situation where people in an organization spend a disproportionate amount of time on trivial issues, such as what materials to use for the staff bicycle shed [170].

relatively important or not.

Make your list.

Why Engineers are Bad Communicators and My Hot Couple is Crazy

Am I? Are we? Let's assume that a recruitment process is capable of selecting programmers who are both good coders and communicators. As shown in fig. 2, the recruitment process has created a bias inside the organization. Even if the traits were not correlated, people inside the organization might infer that good coders are bad communicators. However, no such trade-off exists in the entire population but in the organization after the selection process.

Berkson's paradox occurs when there is a selection based on more than one trait.

It is possible that engineers may be poor communicators, or that good developers tend to be bad architects, or even that good technical leads tend to be poor team leads. However, as a first-order approximation, any combination of traits is less likely than each individual one.

Don't we usually choose the most attractive and smart people as our partners? Does that mean hot boyfriends and girlfriends are a bit crazy, while the intelligent ones aren't that good-looking? It's a tough question, and I wouldn't advise anyone to seek an answer, especially with the person you live, sleep, and raise kids with.

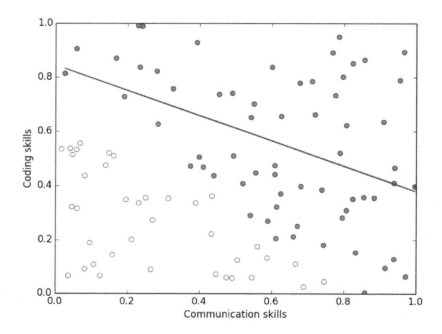

Figure 2: Candidates are initially evenly distributed across coding and communications skills. However, a selection process creates a fake trade-off. The recruitment process selects the candidates with the best combination of both skills. The solid line shows the post-recruitment bias (which becomes a real observation inside the company or organization although a fake one outside.)

Normality

The casino is the only human venture I know where the probabilities are known, Gaussian (i.e. bell-curve), and almost computable.

Nassim Nicholas Taleb, The Black Swan, 2007.

I do not typically read bestsellers. Instead, I prefer spending my free time on textbooks. I admit it is a hobby of questionable value. I tell myself that textbooks provide a vast amount of knowledge per page, especially when I am unfamiliar with the field. However, I have to also admit that the information density of Nassim Taleb's best-selling books is outstanding. Thanks to him, I started to be more cautious about the use of the Gaussian distribution.

The Gaussian, Central, or Normal Distribution is ubiquitous in all fields of science and engineering. Although little is known about the real probability distribution of several natural phenomena (e.g., ages, height, IQ, electrical noise, customer request response time, etc.), the Gaussian distribution is nevertheless used. In many cases, especially in the physical sciences, it is used for good reasons.

This probabilistic distribution is known to emerge when several random and independent phenomena are aggregated. It is explained as the result of the so-called Central Limit Theorem. If N identically randomly distributed variables with an average μ and variance σ^2 are added, then the resulting random variable distribution will tend to a Gaussian of average $N\mu$ and variance $N\sigma^2$.

As explained by Edwin T. Jaynes in *Probability Theory: The Logic of Science*[106], the Gaussian distribution is also the most uncertain distribution when the average and variance are known (i.e., it is the probability distribution that maximizes the information entropy constrained to a known average and variance). For this reason, if those two moments exist and are known and whether our inferences are successful or not, and there is no additional information at hand, there is no justification to use a different distribution. In other words, if we know the average and the variance, and nothing else, we could safely assume that the underlying distribution is Gaussian, as this is the distribution that will allow us to perform the best possible inferences.

Therefore, departing from the Gaussian distribution requires good reasons, and sometimes there are very good reasons for it [12].

In this chapter, we will therefore start by exploring the Gaussian distribution, the central limit theorem, and the law of large numbers, and then gradually we will move away from it by discussing the exceptionality of normality, the lesser-known law of small numbers, the diminishing returns faced by large physics experiments and machine learning models, the maximum entropy principle, our first contact with fat-tailed distributions, and finally, why the intuitions of my mother are more resilient than my own rationalizations.

Computation Accuracy or Why Don't We Arrive Later

"If I drop the kids off school 15 minutes late and continue to run behind schedule, could I end up being 45 minutes late for Jone's appointment with the psychotherapist?" We settled into bed after a typical day packed with our regular activities. For some reason, the day's schedule had Bego trapped in a loop, overwhelmed by appointments she never wanted to schedule, haunted by the terrifying scenario of falling further and further even though she felt like she was on a treadmill.

---

[12]It is not emphasized and reiterated frequently enough that the maximum entropy distribution is quite sensitive to the underlying assumptions. Although it is well-known that a known mean and variance will result in a Gaussian distribution, what happens if we further constrain our assumptions? If it is a positive random variable and we only assume a known average, then the maximum entropy distribution is the exponential. If we further constrain our knowledge to the average of the logarithm, then the maximum entropy distribution is the Pareto. If we assume that we only know its range, then it is the uniform distribution. As we assume less and less, the maximum entropy distribution becomes flatter. How is it that we typically assume a known average and standard deviation? How should we decide about one distribution or another given the sensitivity of the final distribution to our assumptions? When should we assume one distribution or another?

Although possible, is it likely? Probability theory has an answer. Counterintuitively, if both the average and the standard deviation of a probability distribution are known, the sum of several random variables can be determined with greater precision than each individual one. The Law of Large Numbers, a mathematical cousin of the Central Limit Theorem, holds the answer to this paradoxical mistery. Every time we quadruple the number of variables being added, we halve the uncertainty of its sum. The errors with respect to the average value cancel out and the uncertainty gets smaller with each additional variable being added.

This suggests that my wife shouldn't be so apprehensive about the worst-case scenario, where the delay is proportional to the number of appointments. As the number of appointments increases the Law of Large Numbers tells us that the overall uncertainty should decrease by the square root of the number of appointments. Is her intuition misguided?

It turns out that two conditions must be satisfied for this averaging out of uncertainties to occur.

First, both the average and standard deviations of each variable must exist, meaning approximately that the uncertainty of each variable should be bounded. For instance, the length of a doctor's appointment can be 1 hour or even two or three if his car broke, but it will never be a week or a month long. While this is evident in the case of my wife's schedule, it isn't always the case for tasks within any of the projects I work with. Have you ever seen these unfinished houses sold below the market price? Some were unfinished personal projects where time, dreams, and money were buried—projects with an unbounded construction duration. This is the reason why the mortgage risk premium is higher for construction and full house renovations than for the purchase of a ready to live house or terrain. Stock market prices, the number of causalities in wars, flooding levels, and the duration of software projects, to name a few, behave qualitatively different than the duration of a doctor appointment. Their uncertainty is fat-tailed. Do not try to reduce the uncertainty of these by aggregating them, you will just make a fool of yourself. An aggregate of a fat-tailed distribution is equally fat-tailed [13]

---

[13]While it is well-known that the sum of random variables with finite mean and variance converges to a Gaussian distribution, it is less commonly known that when the random variables lack finite variance—such as fat-tailed distributions—or even lack a finite mean, their sum still converges to a stable distribution. Examples of such stable distributions

However, it is not enough for the variable to be thin-tailed. In addition, the random variables should be independent with respect to each other. In simpler terms going back to my wife over-crowded agenda, the length of each subsequent appointment should not be influenced by the previous one. The time taken for a doctor's visit shouldn't correlate with the duration of a school meeting, nor with the duration of the next psychotherapist's appointment. As you can imagine this is not going to happen unless there's a widespread traffic jam, Corso or Galo adamantly refuse to enter the car, the car breaks down, or the doctor has precisely three lovers the schoolteacher, the psychotherapist, and the dentist. Obviously, not my wife though.

So, if we have about four consecutive appointments in a day, we could likely arrive more or less on time to the last one if certain probability conditions are met: thin tails and independence.

In any case, in the grand scheme of things most of our routines and chores do noy really matter and if they matter we can not do much about it. As Epictetus already find out 2,000 years ago:

> *The chief task in life is simply this: to identify and separate matters so that I can say clearly to myself which are externals not under my control, and which have to do with the choices I actually control. Where then do I look for good and evil? Not to uncontrollable externals, but within myself to the choices that are my own.*

I'm Not Normal, Nobody is Normal

When I think intensively I do not hear anyone, I zone out. My hair grows creating a conical shape over my head, too. Bego thinks in pictures. Manolo cannot drink in a glass as it tastes glassy. Galo cannot stand the water dripping over his head. Jone started to use the spoon at the early age of nine months, but she was unable to operate the faucet until she was six years old. My sister has read several encyclopedias worth of information but rarely gives

---

include the Pareto, Lévy, and Cauchy distributions [197]. These stable distributions will still lack variance and/or mean like the distributions of the individual random variables that generated them.

her opinion. There is all kind of people. Tall, medium, and short, fast and slow thinkers, introverts and extroverts, interested in dinosaurs, butterflies, computers, soccer, or germs. Any combination of traits is possible.

Still we could take a sample of all these people and compute the average for the height, intelligence, eye or skin color, etc. How is this average person?

It turns out that there is an answer to this question, but not the one that conforms to certain expectations.

In the 50s a study of the USAF showed that none of the 4063 pilots in the study were close to the "average" pilot in the ten physical dimensions believed to be most relevant for the design of cockpits including height, chest circumference, and sleeve length [46]. Although the average existed in all these dimensions, none of the pilots were close to the "average" pilot. Thus, the optimal design of the cockpit was an adjustable one, perhaps a precursor of our adjustable car seats.

This surprising phenomenon is mathematically inevitable. As the number of variables increases (e.g., height, intelligence, memory, sensitivity to hearing noise, arms length, skin color, etc.), its dimensionality, certain characteristics of the multivariate probability distribution change qualitatively. This phenomenon, first described by Richard Bellman in 1961 as the "Curse of Dimensionality," causes the data points within a high-dimensional space to be maximally far apart from each other, mathematically orthogonal[19]. As the number of characteristics or dimensions taking into consideration increases, the distance between each of the individuals grows to its maximum possible distance[4,56]. This dispersion is analogous to the varied idiosyncrasies we observe among humans, making the grouping and classification of individuals challenging, if not impossible. No one is normal.

This seems counter-intuitive given our prevalent use of simple classification schemes for people, communities, and nationalities. Is this person white or black? Does he supports right or left wing policies? Is this person from a Least Developed Country? Is he intelligent or not? What is their income? and their height? Although we love to classify based on low-dimensionality characteristics, it turns out that considering all possible human characteristics (aka dimensions), every single person is unique and maximally dissimilar than the rest. I'm not talking about a very respectable well-intentioned positive-thinking perspective about diversity and inclusion. It is an unavoidable diversity derived from the many characteristics or traits a human being can have. We are all completely different. Not just a bit, but as far apart as humanly possible. We believe that our neighbour is similar to us given his income, house, and car, but when you consider the whole person, then we are strangers to each other. Finding similar people is extremely difficult when considering all possible human idiosyncrasies. No two humans beings are equal. It is a mathematical fact and it is a good thing.

I know it seems impossible given our usual classifications, but consider one of my favorite still sad statistics, the one of rare diseases, a disease that affects a small percentage of the population, let's say 1 over 2,000 or less. These diseases are rare. However the number of people with a rare disease is around 5 to 10% of the population. This is huge. Somehow there are so many rare diseases that the overall probability of having one is quite large. This large fraction of the population are all already unique without counting the other characteristics.

A similar example is what you can observe in our children's education (although I'm likely biased given my particular experience attempting an inclusive path with my special daughter). It seems that all children should follow the same pattern: to read and write as early as possible, excel in sports, be charming and communicative, learn the alphabet and the multiplication tables at a certain age, and so forth. There is more and more pressure to conform to a normality that does not exist and never existed. How are we going to cultivate future gardeners, cooks, dentists, engineers, writers, drivers, farmers, explorers, just to name a few, if we insist on a one-size-fits-all approach?

An average person is an extraordinary person, unique, never seen. It is believed that this person will fit perfectly in our society. He will be boring though, and unemployable, too.

The Law of Small Numbers

In one of these rainy days when boredom and laziness confabulated to keep me in the sofa, I watched a documentary about homelessness in US. Like a pandemic, homelessness has spread over the wealthiest cities of the world's wealthiest country. Seemingly a paradox, except for some of the documentary commentators that considered the people in the streets to be addicts, lacking will power, or a positive and hard working attitude. Although this situation is paradoxical from an emotional perspective, it is not from a statistical one. The Law of Large Numbers, as the name indicates, does not apply to small samples, especially not to the individual sample. An individual sample is by no means similar to the average of a large population. A person can be poor in the richest city in the world, too. The personal path of a person does not necessarily follow the sample average (i.e., income and wealth are not ergodic, like many other things).

It is like when I ask myself why my daughter is autistic. At the individual level luck and randomness play an incredibly important role. Our attempts to control our lifes are dwarfed by the natural surrounding chaos.

That shocking unequal situation is not unique to US. Homelessness is present in various degrees across the world, being more severe in certain Asian and African countries where the lower average income makes the situation more likely.

How is it possible that the average wealth, income, or growth is not reflected on most of the individuals? According to the documentary, US economy during 2023 was booming, still a million people didn't have a home and had to sleep in the streets. Although this problem has its roots in economics and politics, from a probabilistic perspective it reflects the counterintuitive difference between the Law of the Large Numbers and the actual fat-tailed variability of the individual outcomes.

Likewise, I'm not millionaire eventhough I live in Switzerland, I don't sleep a siesta eventhough I'm Spanish, and I've not been through a midlife crisis eventhough I'm close to my fifties.

The same paradox or fallacy is at play when we believe that we will likely draw tails after drawing five or six consecutive heads. The different throws are independent random events and therefore the next throw is not influenced by the previous ones, ever. However, human beings tend to see patterns on these small samples, our minds cannot stop the predictive and pattern matching machinery.

This curious difference between the behaviour of small and large samples also entails a trade-off between large and small populations as studied in evolution and economics. For example, a new genetic trait with marginally better fitness can easily disappear from the population after its creation because its host could die by accident before giving birth to its offspring. New traits, having by definition very small population sizes, have to escape a stochastic well like the rockets requiring a minimal escape velocity to reach space an escape from Earth gravity well. This stochastic well is also faced by start-ups when launching new products (also known as the chasm in entrepreneurship[153]) or low income individuals trapped in poverty. On the bright side, a especies with smaller populations are more easily altered by random mutations and sexual combinations, and a small startup can revolutionize the market. This is much more difficult on a large population or company.

That is, the survival challenges faced by individuals with new genetic mutations, start-ups trying to launch new products, or people trapped by poverty have also a relative advantage. Larger population struggle with the identification of marginally better traits or ideas. The larger scale entails a natural variability between individuals and therefore these new mutations can be hidden in plain sight. For example, imagine a big company with different software development teams. The performance of each team will change as a function of individual skills, the business domain, the technology used, the practices and processes of the team, or simply by luck. In this situation, how can the decision makers identify the best practices? It could be impossible to significantly distinguish the best practices from the natural variability of the other factors. Perhaps, this is one of the main reasons behind the "Innovator's Dilemma" faced by well-established companies failing to innovate and adapt to disruptive technologies.

Diminishing Returns in Physics Experiments and Machine Learning

During the time I worked at a particle accelerator, I learned about a fundamental challenge shared by certain scientific experiments exploiting the accumulation of data. At some point after the discovery of the Highs Bosson, a mere two years after starting the operation of the LHC, physicists started to plan for a series of experimental upgrades. Why such a hurry? It turns out that the acccumulation of scientific evidence faces diminishing returns. The Law of Large Numbers, which explains how uncertainty is reduced as a function of the sample size, presents a challenge for science.

Why? Consider that we wish to measure a rare phenomenon s with high precision. Assume each measurement x_i comes with an additive noise n_i. Thus, we can't observe s directly but only indirectly from each x_i measurement:

$$x_i = s + n_i$$

The Law of Large Numbers states that the uncertainty in estimating s decreases proportionally to $1/\sqrt{N}$, where N is the number of measurements. The function $1/\sqrt{N}$ is concave, like the slope of a mountain arriving to the sea. This implies that while uncertainty decreases as N increases, the rate of reduction slows for each additional sample. Thus, the uncertainty reduces by a factor of 10 with 100 measurements, a factor of 100 with 10,000 measurements, and only a factor of 1,000 with 1 million measurements. We need an accelerating number of measurements to reduce the uncertainty by each additional factor of 10, a boomer.

Returning to the LHC physics experiments: imagine that, after investing several billions in cutting-edge technology, infrastructure, software, and personnel, the experiment has accumulated 2 years of data between the start of operation in 2010 and the Highs Bosson discovery in 2012. This effort has yielded thousands of peer-reviewed publications in prestigious scientific journals, even a Nobel Prize. But after just two years, the leaders of the project convene and ask: "What do we work on next?" They could continue running the experiment, but to what end? If they aim for a tenfold reduction in uncertainty, they'd need 100 times more samples requiring 200 additional years (i.e. 100 times 2 years). This prospect is hardly enticing, even for an early-career physicist. So, they need to keep upgrading the machine at the fastest pace possible until they run out of money or out of technology options to keep the exponential rhythm of improvements.

This dilemma reflects a fundamental life-cycle challenge of contemporary particle physics experiments. It also explains the exponential growth in their scale and budget. Soon after launching a new experiment and reducing uncertainty, the only viable path forward is to create an even bigger and more sophisticated experiment.

This situation is not just faced by scientific experiments. Interestingly, it is also understood by other organizations that use the exponential accumulation of data and computing power for more chrematistic goals. During the last 50 years, society and especially some companies and organizations, technology giants, have been blessed by the exponential growth of the computing capacity derived from Moore's Law and the accumulation of large corpora of data derived from the expansion of the Internet, digitalization of information, and the development of Cloud Computing. These exponential growths have led to the possibility to train and operate exponentially bigger models counting trillion of parameters and doubling its size every year or less [234]. The accumulation of data including the digitalization of companies, books, scientific papers, and even personal communications has also led to an exponential increase in the data available for these models[193].

However, the performance of these models suffers from the same performance limitations as a function of sample size due to the Law of Large Numbers that scientific experiments face [14]. Therefore, their performance will continue to grow as long as computing power and data availability keeps its exponential growth, or new breakthroughs in machine learning algorithms are discovered. As a result, these giants are subject, with respect to the performance of the machine learning models, to similar life-cycle and exponential growth demands for knowledge, computing power, and data, hoarding and utilizing increasing amounts of them.

Log-normal Distribution

"What are the assumptions of these delivery estimates?" I asked after reviewing a document.

"There are no assumptions. The application performs a Monte Carlo simulation based on the past history, and you get the estimates from there at

---

[14]In the context of statistical learning theory, the Universal Convergence Theorem, also known as the Universal Consistency Theorem, establishes a bound on the difference between the empirical risk (training error when the model is trained or tuned) and the true risk (expected test error after training in the real world). This bound determines how fast the generalization error decreases with an increasing sample size N and it is proportional to $1/\sqrt{N}$. It provides a measure of how well the algorithm is expected to generalize from the training data to new, unseen data, as the training data size N grows [207]. Interestingly, from an empirical perspective, this last theorem seems overoptimistic. Current data scaling laws are closer to $N^{-0.1}$ or $N^{-0.3}$. That is, reducing the error by half requires between 10 and 1000 times more samples, instead of quadrupling them as stated by the Universal Convergence Theorem.

different levels of confidence. Look at the graphic."

"I see. Still, some statistical assumptions have been made. You see, this graphic superimposed to the simulation results looks like a Gaussian, and these numbers seem like the average and the standard deviation. Are we assuming that the task duration is Gaussian or that its sum is Gaussian?"

"No, there are no assumptions. It is a simulation. If you want, you can choose another distribution."

"..."

People like the Gaussian distribution so much that they also use it for positive domains. However, the maximum entropy distribution for a positive random variable (instead of both positive and negative) with known mean and variance is not the Gaussian but the log-normal distribution. A completely different beast. These two distributions are quantitatively and qualitatively different. Many users of statistical tools do not seem to realize or care about this.

One of the most interesting and surprising facts about the log-normal distribution is its adaptability. As a function of its variance, the log-normal can be either close to the Gaussian or to a fat-tailed distribution. The distribution is consistent with the stylized uncertainty found in the estimation of prices, task/project durations, and the like. It should be the first-order approximation or de facto standard for such types of data. However, it is not, and more often than not, people assume Gaussian probability distributions for positive variables.

Pili Knows Better

As N. Taleb might have said, Pili, my mother, knows best. She would be genuinely saddened by hundred people dying in a plane accident. However, she would be truly frightened if a similar number of people suddenly died from a mysterious disease anywhere in the world.

In other words, imagine that one day you wake up and half the world's population is dead. What kind of event could have led to this situation? A systematic crash of planes? From a probabilistic perspective, plane crashes and pandemics have different qualitative behaviors.

As explained by Benoit Mandelbrot in *The (Mis)Behavior of Markets* [141] and later by Nassim Taleb in the *Incerto* book series[220–224,226], there are many practical situations where the variance and even the average do not converge, converge extremely slowly, or where the variables are not completely independent and cannot be blindly aggregated. In these cases, the Gaussian (especially in the tail of the distribution) should not be used. More importantly, if the practical consequences of tail events are catastrophic (e.g., pandemics, climate change, nuclear war, etc.), then it is not mathematically sound nor ethically admissible to use the Central Limit Theorem as an approximation of reality. In fact, when certain events have fat tails, the tail of their aggregation is equally fat-tailed and therefore diversification does not prevent catastrophic events (e.g., Wall Street Crash of 1929, Black Monday of 1987, and the Financial crisis of 2007-2008, etc.)

In the light of the above, risk management should focus on eliminating the consequences of catastrophic events, not merely reducing their probability to an acceptable level. The project management practice of multiplying the probability of a risky event by its cost (i.e., probability x impact) is fundamentally unsound. In other words, repeated exposure to a catastrophic but unlikely events has a certain catastrophic outcome (with probability 1). In catastrophic cases, it is equally invalid to limit the probability of a certain loss (also known as Value at Risk). Does any economic loss truly matter if it means the end for your family, company, country, or even the entire species?

If your team engages in project work constantly subject to tight plans, you will fail. It is certain unless you can somehow prevent the recurring risk.

Markov and Chebychev

"How long will it take to finish?" she asked. My boss always looked for estimates. To her credit, she didn't confuse completion time with effort. Yet, providing an estimate for work is riddled with both human and technical uncertainties. It is no simple feat.

When you possess limited knowledge about the outcome, like the average effort for a task, Markov's Inequality can shed light on the degree of uncertainty. With added details, such as variance, Chebyshev's Inequality can offer a more precise estimate. It's astounding how just the average and variance of a probability distribution can give details about the entire distribution of outcomes. Sadly, this mathematical marvel often goes unnoticed.

Like any other mathematical equations, inequalities are also a representation of a trade-off. In this context, the inequalities represent a balance between the probability level in the tail of the distribution and certain deviations from the mean.

Markov's Inequality, using only the distribution's average, sets an upper limit on the probability that a positive random variable X exceeds a certain threshold $a\mu$:

$$P(X \geq a\mu) \leq \frac{1}{a}$$

Here, the average of the random variable X is represented by μ[15]. The Markov

---

[15]It is typically forgotten that the average does not always exist for all probability distributions. Although it is always possible to calculate the sample average, it does not mean that it is close to real one, if it exists. On an epistemological level, every random variable with unknown distribution and an unbound domain is a potential candidate for not

Inequality expreses the fact that most of the probability is near the average. Knowing the average, the inequality suggests that the tail of the distribution shrinks at a rate of at least $1/x$. Thus, the remaining probability in the tail is inversely proportional to the threshold. For instance, if a task averages 5 working days, I can assure my boss of a likely completion within two weeks ($>50\%$ chance) or, more confidently, within four weeks ($>75\%$ chance). These estimates might not please my boss, but data-driven estimates are.

Can we further refine these uncertainties? If we know the variance of the random variable X, denoted by σ^2, then the Chebyshev's Inequality provides a more stringent probability boundary:

$$P(|X - \mu| \geq a\sigma) \leq \frac{1}{a^2}$$

When the variance of the probability distribution exist, then the tail probability diminishes at least quadratically. For example, let's continue with the previous example of estimating the duration associated with some task. If the average of the task duration is 5 working days and the task's standard deviation is also 5 days, there's a strong chance ($>75\%$) we'll wrap up in 2 weeks. Thus, by adding the knowledge of the variance, the 75% confidence bracket has magically shrinked the duration estimate by 50%: from 4 weeks to just 2 weeks. So, why bother with the Markov Inequality when Chebyshev's Inequality has tighter bounds and will make our supervisors and customers happier?

It all hinges on our base assumptions. Our calculations, obviously, won't change the reality, but our assumptions could not be consistent with it. Does the variance truly exist?

While theoretically linked to integral convergence, how can one determine beforehand the existence of the variance? Like in the case of the average, one can always sample and calculate a variance for this sample, but if it does not exist, the calculated value will be meaningless.

---

having a well-defined average. Just like in the case of selection bias some of the unbounded cases are not even observed. Things like the time between extinctions, personal and professional projects dropped due to its difficulty, deaths during wars, personal damages (which can result in the death of the individual, family, tribe, or species), and so on are never observed, and therefore, it cannot be said that they have a well-defined average.

Consider a sample that spreads across a vast range, several orders of magnitude. If values are wildly different, variance may not be the right metric. If a task sometimes takes an hour, other times a day, occasionally a month, and sometimes never concludes, the variance might not be applicable[16]. Blindly using the variance and the Chebyshev's Inequality would, in essence, be sidelining the outliers of the true distribution, focusing only on typical cases. That is, using the variance will always makes our bosses happier, at least initially.

When should we use one method or another to estimate uncertain situations? Should we use the central limit theorem, the law of large numbers, Chebyshev's inequality, Markov's inequality, or something entirely different? The assumptions are the key. This chapter will try to clarify some of the basic concepts by applying the them to topics such as income inequality, service level agreements, and project estimation, hopefully contributing to a more profound understanding of the panoply of techniques, their strengths, and limitations.

Income Inequality

"Why is this person sleeping in the street?" Corso asked.

"You know, not everyone has a comfortable home. There are people so poor that they lack a place to eat and sleep," I explained to my son, Corso, feeling a sense of shame as I realized I was not intending to help her from the street, offer her money for a hotel or a meal, or even meet her gaze.

"Really?" he says, in disbelief, as if his father were pulling his leg.

I have this recurrent feeling of shame and guilt when I see such glaring inequality in Switzerland or Spain, the countries where I have lived. It is like an evil corrupting our souls. How is it possible that there are people sleeping in the streets in the richest countries of the world? What about people without shoes when we throw away around 5-10 kg of clothing per year and person worldwide[248–250]? What about the billion people starving

---

[16]If there is the possibility, even a remote one, that the random variable can take on an infinite value (e.g., a task is never finished, losses that wipe out a company, an event that kills a person, a family, or a civilization), then the average and the variance do not exist, even if you can calculate them using a sample.

while wasting almost a 200 kg of food per person each year worldwide [232]? The most surprising fact is that these numbers are worldwide averages and do not consider the factor of 5-10 increase in waste in the richest countries. The concept of inequality is not inherently wrong, but its scale, on a multi-billion scale, is.

We, the living, have already won the lottery; we are the winners of a multi-generational evolutionary race, direct descendants of winner after winner among tens of millions of sperm cells arriving first to an unfertilized egg and successfully navigating the uncertainties of development. How did some people lose the last millimeter of this evolutionary marathon? How is it possible that a person does not have shoes or a simple meal? A person without shoes or a daily meal in the US or Europe is like someone successfully crossing the Sahara desert barefoot and then dying of thirst in front of the privately owned shores of the Nile River. Although it's not the cleanest river, it provides fresh water.

It is great to live in a world where hardworking, intelligent, and creative people are rewarded almost infinitely. But why does getting the wrong life lottery ticket and being born in a certain country or family entail being poor, unhealthy, and uneducated? Why does the person who cleans and educates our children earn three, four, or five order of magnitudes less than the person who leads some companies?

One of the most used measures of a country's wealth and well-being is the Gross Domestic Product (GDP). For example, the Spanish GDP can be understood as the average income of all Spanish residents multiplied by the population. In other words, the GDP can be seen as the gross income from labor, capital, and real estate generated by all the citizens of a country in a given year. During 2016, the average income in Spain was around 28,000 euros [17]. Markov's inequality suggests that no more than 3% of the population can

---

[17]By the way, this is not the typical income in Spain. To understand the reason for this paradox, one should be aware of the difference between the mean (or average) and the median of a distribution. It is quite unfortunate that we still use average GDP as a measure of a typical person's wealth, just as it is unfortunate that some people believe that producing more-leading to a higher GDP-entails a higher quality of life. This belief contradicts both physics and common sense because increased production, consumption, and pollution often go hand in hand. It is equally puzzling that productive endeavors like cooking at home, taking care of children, planting your own tomatoes, or learning something new are undervalued in this framework.

have an income of more than 1 million euros, and no more than 3 out of every 100,000 inhabitants can have an income of more than 1 billion euros. Is this approximation correct?

On one side, it is an empirically valid approximation given that income and wealth across countries is distributed as a Pareto distribution with close to 1 exponents (around 1.5 for income and around 1.2 for wealth) [20,44,107,120,194]. That is, the income and wealth distribution are fat-tailed as expected from the rampant inequality we live in. This unequal distribution is possibly generated by a series of underlying stochastic mechanims that creates more and more inequality over time including multi-generational accumulation, capital accumulation through interest compounding, and increased proportions of saving with increased income and wealth.

On the other hand, the approximation above has limitations due to the method used to calculate the average income. This is because income distribution often resembles a Pareto (or 80/20) distribution, characterized by a heavy tail that decreases at a rate close to $1/x$. While this is consistent with Markov's inequality, the small exponent in the distribution's tail means the sample average may not converge reliably with existing sample sizes, even with Spain's population of nearly 50 million.

Unless we modify the method for estimating the average, Markov's inequality won't give the best possible approximation to the income tail distribution. The same could be said for other estimates such as project cost, the number of deaths in wars, stock prices, security risks, etc. If the distribution is fat-tailed, the estimate of the average and variance won't converge or will do so very slowly, making the use of inequalities problematic[18].

Markov's inequality can be used as long as the average exists. But, sometimes the average does not exist or it is extremely difficult to estimate.

In any case, regarding the initial discussion about inequality, it seems to be one of those cases where we are choosing the wrong questions—the ones that can be answered rather than the ones that should be.

---

[18]For example, estimating the average for an 80/20 Pareto distribution using the sample average requires over 10^9 times more samples than estimating the mean of a Gaussian distribution [225]. In such fat-tailed cases, a more robust alternative is to first estimate the distribution parameters by fitting them to the data and then calculate the underlying average.

Service Level Agreement

"Do you want to take a look at the new SLA web page?" She asked sheepishly, as if it were of minor importance. To be fair, in the grand scheme of things involving the planet, the solar system, or the galaxy, the SLA is indeed of minor importance, except when we break it.

"It says that we should resolve 90% of the cases in two weeks. That seems unlikely. How did you arrive at the numbers?" I asked, trying to hide my concern.

"Well, it's up to you to decide, but you know, management is unhappy. It takes too much time to solve the problems and there are too many." I was again unknowingly in a catch-22 situation, losing in any case.

Have you been there? Staring at a spreadsheet, trying to conjure a Service Level Agreement that will appease both management and reality. It's tempting to err on the side of optimism, but as anyone who's dealt with the unpredictable nature of reality, calculating an SLA is one thing, and setting a goal for it is another. Sometimes people use a different name for this slightly different concept: Service Level Objective. Some may even mix both for their benefit, and you won't be able to argue about statistical niceties and definitions with your unhappy boss or customer. What is the correct method to estimate an SLA? Should we assume a Gaussian, Log-normal, or a Pareto distribution, or should we instead rely on the Chebyshev or Markov inequalities?

If you have to calculate something as uncertain as an SLA, the underlying assumptions are critical. The more you assume (e.g., the variance exists, or the distribution is Gaussian), the more appealing the resulting SLA will be to your boss, but the actual likelihood of achieving the agreed level of service will likely decrease. An SLA implies a commitment even if it is an aspiration or goal for the team. This is why it is named a Service Level Agreement, not a Service Level Aspiration. Unfortunately, in most cases, the actual service level doesn't change a bit after the determination of the SLA, whatever the agreement may be.

As you can see in the table below, as you go to the left, you mostly get less tight but more robust bounds, especially in the tails. Gaussian distributions, and to a lesser extent the Log-normal distributions, accumulate most of the probability density close to the average. By contrast, the Chebyshev and Markov counterparts, similar to a Pareto fat-tailed distribution, concentrate most of the probability in the tails.

Probability $\mu = 2, \sigma = 4$	Normal	Log-normal	Chebyshev	Markov
$P(x - 2 \leq 4\text{days})$	84%	91%	$\geq 0\%$	$\geq 50\%$
$P(x - 2 \leq 8\text{days})$	98%	97%	$\geq 75\%$	$\geq 75\$$
$P(x - 2 \leq 12\text{days})$	99.9%	98%	$\geq 89\%$	$\geq 83\%$
$P(x - 2 \leq 16\text{days})$	99.997%	99%	$\geq 94\%$	$\geq 88\%$

Note the sensitivity of the resulting bounds as a function of the statistical assumptions. The direct calculation using the log-normal and especially the normal distributions will provide the manager with better SLAs, although likely incorrect. The Chebyshev and Markov inequalities are more pessimistic but for certain applications with high levels of uncertainty are perfectly fine.

The trick is to not sign SLAs on the tails of the distribution but rather just on the center part—let's say for 70%, 80%, or 90% of the cases, but never for the remaining 5%, 1%, or 0.1%, which are typically ill-behaved, representing the real, fat-tailed world.

This is not Rocket Science

"This is not rocket science! Why can't you give me a clear answer on how long it will take?" He was starting to get angry and frustrated. I had already provided a range of estimated effort based on historical data, but he wasn't satisfied with the range. He wanted a precise number—magically conjured from thin air, in just a few seconds—and more importantly, a number lower than the range I actually gave him.

The truth is, estimating the cost and timeline for any project is a complex task that goes beyond just software development. The difficulties of project estimation are prevalent across various industries.

Estimation and planning are often, tautologically, the root causes of project cost and timeline overruns. A project is considered to be overrun when the initial estimates of cost or timeline are significantly below the actual values.

This situation can either indicate that the project is late due to incompetence, or more charitably, that the estimates were incorrect. Why do we always consider the project from the failure perspective? Did the project fail or just the estimation?

The following table summarizes the industries with the most and least cost overruns [74]. IT projects are not just in the ignominious 5th place, but they are also in the first position when considering the cost overrun of the projects in the tail. In other words, if an IT project goes badly, then it can go extremely badly—more so than any other type of project. The probabilistic distributions of IT project cost and duration have fat tails—fatter even than those of nuclear storage facilities, Olympic games, nuclear power plants, or aerospace projects, to name just a few. IT projects are more unpredictable than rocket science.

The data shows, both interestingly and surprisingly, that estimation failures are very common, and the situation worsens with factors such as project type, project size, requirement changes, technology (especially new technologies), delivery team experience, and the modularity of the delivered solution (e.g., photovoltaic solar power projects are quite predictable).

While it's understandable to desire an accurate estimate for a project's benefit, cost, and timeline, the reality is that these predictions are not reliable—especially estimates of benefits. Project cost and duration estimation is far from an exact science. Estimation challenges are a widespread issue across project types, and accepting and understanding the limitations and reasons behind these difficulties can help organizations better prepare for the uncertainties they will inevitably face.

Table 4: Empirical base rates for overrun risk across different project types. Only the most and least risky project types are shown. The table shows project overrun risk as (a) mean cost overrun, (b) percentage of projects in the upper tail (defined as ≥ 50 %), and (c) mean overrun in the tail [74].

Project Type	Cost Overrun	% Projects in Tail	Tail Cost Overrun
Nuclear Storage	238 %	48 %	427 %
Olympic Games	157 %	76 %	200 %
Nuclear Power	120 %	55 %	204 %
Hydroelectric dams	75 %	37 %	186 %

Project Type	Cost Overrun	% Projects in Tail	Tail Cost Overrun
IT	73 %	18 %	447 %
...	...	...	...
Roads	16 %	14 %	109 %
Pipelines	16 %	9 %	110 %
Wind power	13 %	7 %	97 %
Energy Transmission	8 %	4 %	166 %
Solar power	1 %	2 %	50 %

Information, Signal, and Noise

"Do you know what happened today?" I asked her, my lips curling into a slightly mischievous smile.

"..., no?" Bego didn't seem particularly interested. Perhaps my expression suggested that I found something amusing, even if only to myself.

"It's the most amazing thing that's happened to me in recent years."

"..., alright. Tell me."

"Did you know that I have the hearing of a professional musician? Certified," I declared, hoping to pique her curiosity.

"What are you talking about?" She asked, not fully grasping the implications of my statement.

"Today, during my medical checkup, they tested my hearing. The nurse asked if I was a professional musician because of my exceptional hearing," I chuckled, adding with a hint of pride, "This should finally settle the debate about my supposed 'deafness.'"

But it didn't. In fact, it made matters worse. To her, it became clear that when she spoke, I often chose not to listen. I've since tried explaining that this is a common phenomenon among long-term couples. I attributed it to our inherent ability to optimize information intake, blaming it on Shannon's Source Coding Theorem. "It's Shannon's fault," I said. Somehow, I don't think my mumbling convinced her. To understand why I blamed information theory for my selective hearing, we need to look at Shannon's fundamental insight about how information works. His Source Coding Theorem sets a boundary on data compression. The theorem states that there's a limit to how much you can compress data transmitted over a channel. A message with symbols a_i, each with a probability p_i, can't be compressed more than its Shannon Entropy, denoted by $H(B)$ [19]:

$$H(B) = - \sum_i p_i \log_2(p_i) \text{bits/symbol}$$

For instance, fig. 3 illustrates the number of bits per second needed to send a symbol from a binary data source with two symbols, 0 and 1, having probabilities p and $q = 1 - p$, respectively. For example, to convey the results of the repeated throws of an unbiased coin toss (where $p = q = 0.5$). This requires at least one bit per symbol. As the odds of either symbol being emitted even out, the uncertainty and consequently the Shannon Entropy increases, raising the transmission cost of transmitting the results of the stream of throws to its maximum exactly at the point where the probability of tails equals the one of heads.

Instead, if the coin always shows heads, we wouldn't need to send any actual data, just the count of coin tosses. Likewise, if the content of a message is known, like my wife's penetrating gaze, then only a few bits suffice to convey that information.

This is why, when a message is reiterated continuously, its informational content diminishes, becoming redundant, and the brain ultimately ignores it. You see, darling, it's not negligence, I love you beyond words, but the immutable laws of nature sometimes keep me from hearing you.

Shannon's insights formalizing information theory extend far beyond the simple coin tosses or domestic conversations. They form the foundation for exploring a variety of fascinating topics, which this chapter will address, including, among other things, the application of the Source Coding Theorem to optimal coding, optimal testing, and criteria for determining when exploring makes sense, the logic behind the famous Ockham's Razor, the concepts of signal and noise and their relation to my exceptional hearing and my awful listening capabilities, and finally, guidelines for deciding when to shout at or not shout at our children.

---

[19]In any case, Shannon's entropy should not be confused with its thermodynamic or probabilistic counterparts, though they are related.

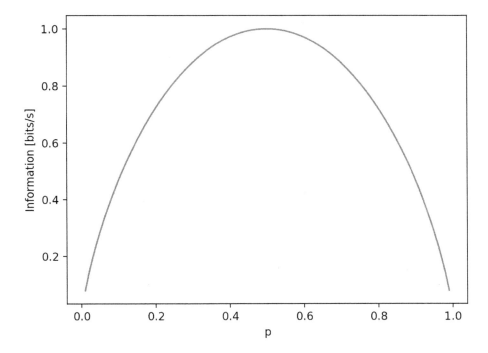

Figure 3: Information content generated by a test with two possible outcomes, success and failure, with associated probabilities p and $q = 1 - p$.

Head or Tails

Let's forget for a moment the story with my wife and my prodigious hearing; anyway, it's an unsolvable problem and has a doubtful empirical basis (as I have tried to find evidence for it). Instead, let's imagine that we want to transmit information regarding a biased coin-flipping experiment where the probability of heads is $p = 0.9$ and the probability of tails is $q = 0.1$. According to Shannon's source coding theorem, the minimum coding rate is a surprising 0.037 bits/symbol. That is, almost 30 times lower than the bit rate of the trivial case (i.e., sending a one for heads and a zero for tails, one bit per coin flip).

How can we achieve such a compression feat?

A simple way to build a more efficient communication protocol is to realize that different sequences of bits have different probabilities, and therefore we can encode the most likely sequences of throws with shorter codes and the unlikely sequences of throws with longer ones. For example, we could encode pairs of throws in the following way:

throws	probability	code
tail-tail	$0.9^2 = 0.81$	1
tail-head	$0.9 \cdot 0.1 = 0.09$	01
head-tail	$0.1 \cdot 0.9 = 0.09$	001
head-head	$0.1^2 = 0.01$	000

In the case of the trivial encoding, we require 2 bits per sequence of 2 throws (i.e., 1 bit per throw), while in the second case, we need $1 \cdot 0.81 + 2 \cdot 0.09 + 3 \cdot 0.09 + 3 \cdot 0.01 = 1.26$ bits per sequence (0.63 bits per throw). That is, we have compressed the information rate by around 30% by changing the coding scheme of the sequence.

As the information gets more predictable, the number of bits needed to send it is reduced. Sometimes words are not needed with your partner, friend, or colleagues. Sometimes a predictable look is worth a thousand words.

Optimal Testing

"Are you crazy?" She stared at me, trying to discern any semblance of sanity behind my reluctance to visit the Hagia Sophia in Istanbul.

Back in 2007, Bego, who was my girlfriend then, was planning to visit the mosque. I, however, thought that sitting down for a coffee in the hustle and bustle of Istanbul's Grand Bazaar was a better use of my time.

I love the idea of wandering aimlessly through the streets of unfamiliar cities, stumbling upon serendipitous discoveries: a curious bookstore, a hidden restaurant, a cozy place for a latte, or unique and inexpensive shopping finds. When faced with a choice, should I tread an unknown path or stick to a familiar one? The No Free Lunch Theorem for Search and Optimization implies there isn't a one-size-fits-all strategy. Different cities and neighborhoods call for different approaches.

However, one might draw from the insights of Shannon's information measure. The Source Coding Theorem suggests that the information within an event is proportional to the logarithm of its probability. Such an information measure could help assess events that generate information, like tests, decisions, and travel plans. The outcomes of these events can be likened to messages conveying details about our reality.

Consider a test that yields two possible outcomes: success or failure, with associated probabilities p and $q = 1 - p$. According to Shannon's perspective, the information content of this outcome is:

$$H = -p \log_2(p) - q \log_2(q) \text{ bits/test}$$

As depicted in the previous fig. 3, the information content peaks when $p = q = 0.5$, a state of maximal uncertainty. Surefire successes or inevitable failures do not give new insights, but the unexpected that lies in the unpredictable in-betweens.

So, whether I'm testing a hypothesis, crafting software or hardware tests, making a pivotal decision, or selecting a travel route, an information-centric perspective using the Shannon's formula might nudge us toward the path of greatest uncertainty. While the Hagia Sophia is undeniably an iconic destination, it's somewhat predictable.

As a tourist, venturing into the city center, I'd expect a profusion of shops, eateries, and bustling crowds. But such sights might be monotonous; many city centers bear a striking resemblance, down to the same chain stores. If instead I wander away from the urban heart, I might find uneventful expanses with some sporadic tree, shop, or trashbin—a rather dull view. Between these two extremes lies the vibrant middle ground of the Grand Bazaar, with its eclectic mix of furniture, hardware, and even lingerie vendors. It's here that exploration seems the most rewarding—exactly where I found myself that day in 2007, sipping what turned out to be the best coffee in Istanbul, while Bego explored the Hagia Sophia.

Minimum Description Length and the Ockham's Razor

"Corso, would you like to be shaken, stomped on, and bothered by your friends?" I was trying to convey the idea to my five-year-old son that winning his brother's friendship requires a more subtle approach. It wasn't the first time, and it wasn't going to be the last.

"But, what happens if I never have friends?" As usual, like my wife, Corso disarmed me with an unexpected question.

"Well, that's very unlikely. You already have friends. Right?"

"Yes, but what happens if they don't want to be friends anymore?"

"... but this is not the point!" I thought. I breathed deeply for a few seconds and let go of my frustration while leaving the kitchen with the mask of a patient parent.

Very unlikely but possible events are still possible. Like when my boss asks whether the project will be finished on time with absolute certainty. In these cases, I feel obliged to acknowledge the possibility of delays, and she certainly doesn't like it.

My son's concerns about friendship and my boss's desire for certainty point to a fundamental human challenge: how do we evaluate competing explanations of reality? When Corso jumps to unlikely scenarios, when my boss demands impossible guarantees, or when friends defend their beliefs in astrology or psychoanalysis[20], we're all struggling with the same problem—how to separate probable truths from improbable ones. This is where Ockham's Razor, one of humanity's most powerful thinking tools, comes into play.

The term Ockham's razor didn't appear until a few centuries after the death of William of Ockham (1287-1347). Ockham is not even the inventor of the principle, but the association of the "razor" with him may be due to the frequency and effectiveness with which he used it. There are several popular formulations of the principle, including:

> *Entities are not to be multiplied without necessity.*

> *Always prefer the shorter hypothesis.*

> *[...] with four parameters I can fit an elephant and with five I can make him wiggle his trunk.*

One interesting aspect of Shannon's work is that it allows for the formalization of Ockham's principle from first principles.

Let's assume we have some data D and several hypotheses $H_1, ..., H_m$ that could explain the data. Ockham's Razor can be interpreted as a method for choosing the hypothesis that requires a minimal description length of both the hypothesis and the data:

$$\min_i \text{Length}(H_i) + \text{Length}(D|H_i)$$

Where $\text{Length}(H_i)$ is an imaginary function that returns the minimal number of bits required to describe a given hypothesis, and $\text{Length}(D|H_i)$ is another imaginary function that returns the minimal number of bits required to encode the data given the hypothesis H_i.

And what is the minimal encoding length of a hypothesis or data? According to Shannon, the minimal encoding length of a message is equal to the logarithm of its probability. Thus, Ockham's principle can be reformulated in terms of Shannon's information measure:

---

[20]Although there has been a resurgence in the use of astrology, there is no support for astrology [8,49]. On the other hand, it seems there is some empirical support for the modern version of psychoanalysis [2,132,209].

$$\min_i - \log_2(p(H_i)) - \log_2(p(D|H_i))$$

Ockham's Razor, or the Minimum Description Length, not only aims to maximize the fit of the data to the hypothesis $p(D|H_i)$ (i.e., the probability of the data conditional to a given hypothesis is true), but also considers the likelihood of the hypothesis itself $p(H_i)$, as not all hypotheses are equally likely a priori (e.g., Is my daughter an alien or just autistic?).

Interestingly, the last expression is equivalent to selecting the hypothesis H_i with the maximum probability given the data $p(H_i|D)$, which represents the most likely a posteriori hypothesis. The two expressions are connected by the simple Bayes rules. We just need to apply the exponent to the expression and divide by a common factor $p(D)$, the a priori probability of the data, to get the a priori probability of the hypothesis given the data:

$$p(H_i|D) = \frac{p(H_i)}{p(D)} p(D|H_i)$$

It is remarkable that selecting the hypothesis H_i that minimizes the length of the explanation given some observations D is equivalent to selecting the hypothesis that maximizes its probability conditional to the existing observations. In other words, finding the most likely hypothesis for a given data is equivalent to our formulation of Ockham's Razor. As J. Jaynes noted, this effectively represents the procedure that a perfectly rational being would use to choose between different hypotheses.

How is it, then, that people sometimes still consider the most unlikely hypotheses as the most likely ones? Why equally intelligent people disagree with each other? The disagreement does not even require that the observations D are fundamentally different between individuals, it just requires that their a priori beliefs about the different hypothesis $p(H_i)$ are. That is, when there is a strong disagreement between people, it is not even necessary to believe that the others are stupid, of a lesser intelligence, or that they do not know all the facts, it is just necessary to understand that people do not share the same believes a priori (e.g., climate change, UFOs, god or gods, and so on.)

But is Ockham's razor an infallible method? Of course not. Otherwise, humans, as I have already explained, the result of more than 4 billion years of evolutionary trial and error, would be the ultimate Bayesian automata. We are inconsistent, random, emotionally unstable, and incredibly better. Perhaps our deviation from perfect Bayesian reasoning isn't a bug but a feature. Just as I eventually understood that my son's seemingly illogical leap to worst-case scenarios might serve some adaptive purpose, our cognitive shortcuts and emotional responses might represent an optimal balance between accuracy and speed in the face of survival. While Ockham's razor provides a powerful theoretical framework for finding truth, human intuition—with all its apparent irrationality—might offer its own kind of wisdom, honed by billions of years of evolution.

How can we explain that? We know from the No Free Lunch Theorem that not all optimization methods work equally well, and it seems that in the harsh wild environments where our ancestors evolved, methods that benefited speed over accuracy with little energy footprints prevailed. Those are heuristics—tricks, if you will. This topic deserves deeper exploration, which we will pursue in the following chapters.

Immigration Subsidies and Don't Shout at Me

"They have more rights than we do. The school cafeteria is free for them," Raquel argued again about immigrants having more rights than Spanish citizens.

"Don't you think that, first, I would know this, being a primary school teacher myself? Second, there's no law favoring immigrants. There are, however, subsidies for the cafeteria for those with lower incomes, which isn't specific to immigrants, though they typically qualify because of lower incomes. Third, if such legislation existed, there would likely be an uproar," Bego countered, presenting what she felt was a definitive argument.

"You don't know what is really going on. Immigrant children definitely receive all sorts of subsidies, and their parents too. Everyone knows it. You live in a bubble," Raquel insisted.

It might seem unbelievable that two people could disagree so strongly on basic facts, yet it happens frequently. This intuition is stated formally in Aumann's Agreement Theorem. If two Bayesian agents—though perhaps my wife Bego and Raquel, with all their qualities, don't fit perfectly into this category—have the same prior beliefs and share the facts, then they should arrive at the same conclusions. How do we explain these major disagreements between people then? We should ask ourselves: Is it that Raquel and Bego started with different preconceptions? Do our trusted news sources paint different realities, leading to unshared facts? Or, perhaps uncomfortably, are one or both of them letting emotion override logic, making us less than perfectly rational actors in this argument?

There are three possibilities according to Aumann's Theorem: the prior beliefs are different, the facts are not shared, or one or more of the agents are not rational.

My wife and I seldom engage in these debates because we, like most people, either avoid politically charged topics or because we often surround ourselves with like-minded individuals, consuming news from similar sources, residing in the same neighborhood, towns, or countries, and having similar incomes. By sharing our lives with people who have the same beliefs and information sources, most of the friction disappears, but we end up living in a bubble. As Raquel rightly said, Bego and most people, including her, live in their information bubbles.

Sometimes we wrongly believe that the disagreement comes from not having knowledge of the facts, even if we insist on sometimes repeating or shouting them. However, as Aumann's Theorem tells us, it is only necessary to have different beliefs, facts do not always matter. We try to believe that exposing the facts will update the beliefs of others, but in many cases, it doesn't work. For example, imagine that I see a flying sausage on a Friday night. Depending on my beliefs, I could interpret the UFO sighting as the new prototype of the USAF fighter, the start of the war of the worlds, the unexpected side effects of alcohol abuse, or the start of a schizophrenic episode.

Shouting louder or repeating the same points won't magically bridge the divide. Think about trying to have a conversation in a noisy room. The louder you get, the louder everyone else gets, and the harder it becomes to understand anything at all. The core message gets lost in the noise. That is, amplifying the signal does not necessarily help. In addition to facing diminishing returns as we saw previously, it's a known fact that amplifying input data amplifies both the signal of interest and the inherent noise. This phenomenon is well-known in electric engineering and telecommunications. Simple and sophisticated algorithms trying to filter unwanted noise can distort the signal in unwanted ways. For example, the simplest of the averaging techniques attenuate frequency components above the averaging period, rendering the high frequencies invisible when they might be needed. Or for example, there's the familiar and yet surprising issue of sound quality diminishing when old vinyl recordings are remastered and "cleaned" into digital formats. Amplifying and filtering the signal does not necessarily improve its quality. Who has ever heard of a discussion or argument ending well after shouting to each other?

Although amplification and filtering distort the signal and could increase the noise, it's worth noting the significant advancements in telecommunications and computing that have been made thanks to the systematic use of signal processing techniques. Without amplification and filtering, we wouldn't be able to transmit data across oceans or even beyond our planet. But, as we will see in the chapter for the case of feedback control, filtering also has its fundamental limitations that impact its effectiveness. Perfect noise filtering would essentially filter out the desired signal as well [139].

This is equivalent to the well-known data processing inequality theorem from information theory. The theorem states that the information content of a signal cannot increase—only decrease[140]. That is, regardless of how sophisticated the data processing algorithm is, the information at its output cannot exceed the information content of its input. As the saying goes: garbage in, garbage out.

Fundamentally true and obvious, yet people repeatedly fail to understand and believe it (e.g., Theranos' Edison device, which was claimed to extract vast amounts of medical data from just a tiny drop of blood using advanced algorithms; financial firms assuming that complex risk models could reliably predict mortgage-backed security performance despite having incomplete or poor-quality data; IBM claiming that its Watson AI could revolutionize cancer diagnosis and treatment by analyzing patient data and suggesting treatments more effectively than human doctors; Google believing that by processing massive amounts of search query data, it could accurately predict flu outbreaks; or some AI researchers assuming that with enough processing, facial recognition and image enhancement could reconstruct missing or low-quality details without hallucinations).

Even considering the different backgrounds and beliefs, it is still surprising to find ourselves in these irreconcilable debates. It is easy to understand that different people have equally different backgrounds and beliefs. Even so, these impossible debates still catch us off guard. How is it possible? Because sharing the facts is also not as trivial as it seems, and tremendous efforts are spent consciously and unconsciously on building ignorance in the general population. There have been and still are many well-known examples of active misinformation campaigns including trade secrets, confidential, secret, and top secret information, climate change, women's multi-orgasmic capabilities and their genitals, beryllium and tobacco toxicity, ancient indigenous knowledge about plants or fossils centuries before western science took credit for it, or the recent fake news, to name a few [181]. There are groups of people, companies, and governments actively building ignorance for specific purposes and interests.

Is it also possible that Raquel and Bego had different recollections or interpretations of the facts? What are our respective information sources that create this difference? What are our a priori beliefs? Are we rational beings subject to Aumann's Agreement Theorem?

Listen to the messenger, not just the message.

Signal and Noise

Unlike my wife, if there are enough people in a conversation, I struggle to follow anyone. I am unable to keep up with any of the simultaneous conversations, not even a single one. I can distinguish conversations when there are two or three people engaged in a dialogue. However, when additional people join, the sounds of the conversations start to mix and I feel isolated and unable to follow them, unlike many people who seem to do so effortlessly. The voices blend together into a cacophony of sounds, and I can't hear anyone. It feels as if I'm completely deaf. Isn't it curious, considering my supposedly perfect hearing? At parties, celebrations, and similar gatherings, it's not unusual to find myself cleaning dishes, cooking, or on the terrace talking with one person. An escape from the, to me, indistinguishable noises. It's a shame I don't smoke; it could be a great excuse.

This phenomenon can be related to a renowned result in Communication Theory called the Shannon-Hartley Theorem. Yes, another theorem from the great Claude Shannon. According to the theorem, given an information source and a communication channel, like myself and the air carrying voices, there exists a coding technique that allows a specific rate of information to be transmitted over the channel without errors. Yes, without errors, even in the presence of noise. There is a way to transmit and process the information that allows perfect retrieval, with the rate being higher or lower depending on the signal-to-noise ratio faced by the receiver and the medium itself (e.g., water is a better medium for the propagation of information using sound than air, and vacuum is a better medium than air or water for electromagnetic waves).

In other words, given that both my wife and I receive the same signal and noise levels, it seems that my wife possesses a more effective receptor or processor. In addition, considering that my hearing is quite sensitive (as determined by the physician who examined my hearing), it appears that my processing capabilities are substantially inferior compared to hers. Encountering this evidence of my apparent cognitive limitations is disheartening, but likely an accurate finding.

Strong and Weak Noise

"Jone, can you please come out of the water?" I called out, but my daughter completely ignored me, submerging repeatedly in the water as if she were a mermaid.

"Jone! Can you come out?" Instead of responding, she dived again in the opposite direction. She is autistic, but somehow, my voice seemed to prompt her to dive further. Autistic but evidently not deaf.

"JONE!" I shouted, louder this time. She looked at me, as did the other families picnicking at Mies Beach near Coppet. Paradoxically, in her gaze, I saw a silent understanding, as if she were the only one who saw me as a sane parent. Why did I shout like that? Shame on me, the irrational parent yelling at his daughter who was playfully swimming in the lake.

I lost my temper, something not uncommon with my daughter or my other children. Did I really need to shout, rather than just slightly raising my voice? Perhaps the Shannon-Hartley Theorem might give me a good excuse.

An interesting facet of the Shannon-Hartley Theorem is its description of the relationship between the maximum information rate and the signal-to-noise ratio; the relation is not linear but logarithmic, represented by $\log_2(1 + S/N)$). This logarithmic relationship, like many relations in the real world, is nonlinear. To make sense of this, let's break it down into two regimes:

A first regime with low signal-to-noise ratio ($S/N \ll 1$), where the signal is barely discernible from the noise. Like when we try to unsuccessfully talk in a disco, or in our daily influx of information, such as news feeds or gossip, where the majority of what we receive might be "noise" with minimal valuable information.

A second regime with high signal-to-noise ratio ($S/N \gg 1$), where the signal is clear with respect to the noise. Like when I shout to my children preventing them to cross the street, or when the advertised price for a product closely matches its actual cost (e.g., price for commodities like gold, computers, phones, paper, and so on). In this second regime there's hardly any noise distorting the signal.

We can summarize these scenarios in the following table showing the maximum capacity of the communication channel $C_{\max}$:

Shannon-Hartley Theorem	Strong Noise	Weak Noise
$C_{\max} = B \log_2(1 + S/N)$	$C_{\max} \propto S/N$	$C_{\max} \propto \log_2(S/N)$

Why does this matter?

In the first scenario, we face a situation with significant noise compared to the signal. If we double the signal-to-noise ratio, the channel capacity also doubles. This means that a quantitative increase in the level of the signal yields a corresponding increase in the volume of information that can be transmitted. The additional effort is rewarding: you achieve a direct increase in information due to the strengthened signal. For instance, when whispering, speaking below the ambient noise, amplifying our voice directly improves a listener's ability to comprehend. Similarly, when conducting an initial systematic search of scholarly papers and books about a subject that we ignore increases enormously the information at our disposal. Given our ignorance, engaging in a small subset of information offers a substantial upgrade in our understanding. Even in the case we don't find anything, the sheer absence of scientific references on a subject can be telling, especially since negative findings are often left unpublished. The lack of scientific information typically tells us that there could be no such relation.

Consider a contrasting scenario in the low signal-to-noise regime: a complex project involving numerous individuals. Here, even a minor decline in the signal-to-noise ratio—be it due to team conflicts, relocating a major portion of the team to another time zone, or misplacing critical documents—leads to a near-proportional drop in the project communication bandwidth. In such intricate settings, a minuscule decline in the signal-to-noise ratio results in a proportional decrease in transmitted information. Such scenarios are inherently fraught with risk due to their unpredictable nature.

What about the second signal-to-noise regime? In the second regime instead, we're in an environment with low noise compared to the signal. The signal is either very clear or the noise very low. Here, doubling the signal yields only a slight rise in the channel's capacity, leading us into the realm of diminishing returns. To genuinely double the capacity, the signal-to-noise ratio must be squared. Expending energy on amplifying the signal in such situations is largely futile—unless, of course, it's a matter of immediate danger, like a child in the path of an oncoming vehicle, or because the autistic daughter is obliviously ignoring her father while swimming. There shouting might be the most logical response because minimally increasing the signal won't help.

Similarly, how much more knowledge do I amass from reading an additional newspaper after already going through several? Or what about reading my fourth, fifth, or even tenth C++, Java, or Python manual?

Inverting again the argument for the low noise regime, the equation suggests that in environments with high signal-to-noise ratios, it's often more efficient to tone down the signal. This allows for the same volume of information to be conveyed with less energy expenditure. Personally, I might take this to heart. Rather than elevating my voice to draw my children's attention, I could have adopted a softer tone, conserving energy while achieving the same outcome, none. Beachgoers would likely appreciate it, casting me in the favorable light of an exemplary parent.

Group Discussion

"Did you hear what Alfredo said about his job? It was hilarious, wasn't it?" Bego asked me after a family gathering.

"Which of the conversations was that?" I replied, only half-joking because that day I didn't feel like lying about what I hadn't heard.

This recurring scenario made me wonder: just how far below optimal was my ability to process multiple conversations compared to my wife's seemingly superhuman capacity?

Let's consider a scenario where my wife Bego is at a family gathering with around 10 people simultaneously discussing a multitude of topics. My wife, like my mother-in-law, seems to be able to follow several of those conversations while I typically retreat to a quieter place away from the cacophony of voices. In such a situation, the signal-to-noise ratio (S/N) is around 0.1 - with the majority of the noise originating from the other conversations, becoming even less if the TV is on.

Given that the human auditory bandwidth B is around 20 kHz, the maximum amount of information that can be transmitted is calculated using the Shannon-Hartley expression:

$$C_{\text{max}} = B \log_2(1 + S/N) = 20000 \log_2(1 + 0.1) = 2750 \text{bits/sec}$$

Considering that the average length of an English word is approximately 5 letters and the alphabet consists of 26 letters, equating to around 5 bits per letter and 25 bits per word, the maximum capacity is roughly $C_{\text{max}} = 2750/25 \approx 100$ words per second. This implies that in a crowded conversation involving 10 people, each person would be limited to approximately 10 words per second.

This aligns with the typical speech rate of 1-3 words per second for a normal English speaker. Therefore, it seems that my wife possesses a human speech processing system that is close to optimal, less than an order of magnitude below the maximum possible, while mine appears to be significantly worse by an order of magnitude. Such is life.

Feedback

As society permits control engineers to operate more such danger-
ous systems, we who teach those engineers and fashion their tools
cannot hide from responsibility under a cloak of mathematics. We
dare not instill the notion that mathematical rigor is the only goal
to strive in control. We must also instill respect for the practical,
physical consequences of control, and we must make certain that
its underlying principles are taught clearly and well.

> *Gunter Stein, Respect the Unstable, 1989.*

On a sunny August morning in 1927, Harold Stephen Black, a twenty-nine-year-old systems engineer, took the Lackawanna ferry to work at Bell Telephone Laboratories. As he gazed at the Statue of Liberty, he experienced an epiphany that would initiate the modern era of feedback control.

I suddenly realized that if I fed the amplifier output back to the in-
put, in reverse phase, and kept the device from oscillating (singing,
as we called it then), I would have exactly what I wanted: a means
of canceling out the distortion in output

Although the explanation from Black may be somewhat obscure, the concept of negative feedback is straightforward. It is a mechanism to adjust subsequent actions based on past errors. We all know it, feedback is the capability of altering our behavior after a repeated series of errors; in theory a couple of errors, in practice a multitude.

The modern era of control theory and the systematic application of negative feedback to engineering began with Black's idea of utilizing negative feedback to trade off a portion of an electronic amplifier's gain (which is nonlinear and highly influenced by weather and landscape factors) in exchange for improved bandwidth and linearity [21]. The gain of the negative feedback amplifier is therefore linear and possesses a wider bandwidth due to the linearity and bandwidth characteristics of the components employed to construct the feedback path (e.g., resistors, capacitors, and inductors in the case of Black's electronic amplifier).

Negative feedback is a simple and nearly magical mechanism. It enables the control of time-varying, nonlinear, and unstable systems through the basic mechanism of adjusting future behaviors proportionally to the magnitude of the error—the difference between the real and the expected output. These controllers serve as a means to balance perceived output errors with appropriate inputs to keep the system under control.

However, a negative feedback system only functions when we compare expectations with actual reality—true reality, not some fabricated version. In the case of the linear amplifier, the components of the feedback path should provide a timely output measurement that is free from distortion and noise. A late or inaccurate measurement renders the mechanism useless. Black's insight, that reliable information is crucial for effective control, extends far beyond the realm of electronics. In society too, our ability to self-correct and progress hinges on our willingness to confront uncomfortable truths, not silence or distort them.

Much has been written on this last point, yet we often fail to follow it: resorting to blame, criticism, silencing, or killing the messenger; congratulating the emperor for their new clothes; guilt by association; smoke and mirrors; hocus-pocus; failing to recognize honesty as the best long-term policy; and, of course, the well-known BS.

Not only is the measurement system important, but also the controlled and control systems, and their interactions with the environment, are of fundamental importance. Feedback and self-referential mechanisms modeled using control theory offer an interesting perspective for understanding some of the basic building blocks of our society and technology. This chapter, the first of two exploring several aspects of control theory, will focus on its basic properties, while the next one will examine its robustness or lack thereof.

---

[21]Although H. S. Black started the modern era of negative feedback applied to engineering, the great physicist James Clerk Maxwell already published more than half a century before the stability analysis for a feedback system [147]. In fact, Maxwell preceded the works of Norbert Wiener, Harry Nyquist, and Hendrik Wade Bode by almost a century.

Among other topics, this chapter will include a discussion of the self-synchronization of Thailand's fireflies and why sometimes management is needed, the pervasive interaction between positive (explosive) and negative feedback, the ultimate soldier capabilities of my children, the criteria for choosing between decentralized and centralized control, and finally, a reflection on keystone species and why my mother is so important.

Fireflies and Conductors

Jone was trapped in one of her infinite echolalic loops saying, "Tomorrow, we won't be eating couscous at the lake." Corso was in the throes of a typical six-year-old tantrum, because I had turned off the TV after an hour of watching Pokémon. He was throwing teddy bears, horses, cars, and even an apple and an orange flew out of the kitchen. At that very moment, Galo was scared and wanted me to pick him up and comfort him. The situation seemed to overwhelm him, and he started crying. Amidst this chaos, Jone entered a second self-reinforced mental loop, crying louder and repeating, "Corso is not happy, and it's not my fault. Corso is not happy, and it's not my fault. Corso is not happy, and it's not my fault." I won't bother documenting how many times she repeated the phrase while crying, as it would make for a tedious half-hour read.

Do I live in a mental institution? No, it's just another day in my life. How is it possible that all three of them ended up in an unstable mental state at the same time? How did they achieve such a feat of coordination without someone leading the performance? Yet, here's the curious thing, modern organizations always have a hierarchical structure with several layers of management to coordinate all the people working in them[22], and a classic orchestra seems to

---

[22]While some organizations like professional orchestras clearly benefit from central coordination through conductors, the necessity of middle management in modern organizations remains a debated topic that resists simple conclusions. In one natural experiment, Google attempted a flat organizational structure with a minimal number of management layers. However, they soon found that some level of management was necessary for efficient operation. Around 2009, Google launched project Oxygen, one of the most influential projects regarding Google's management philosophy, where they used data to understand the effectiveness of managers. The outcome showed that good managers exist and indeed have a positive impact, and based on the data, Google developed a set of guidelines for them [77].

require a conductor[154,178]. By contrast, my kids—like a pop band—don't seem to need anyone to synchronize their behavior.

As already observed in 1917 by Philip Laurent in the journal Science, large-scale self-synchronization also occurs in nature:

> *Some twenty years ago I saw, or I thought I saw, a synchronal or simultaneous flashing of fireflies. I could hardly believe my eyes, for such a thing to occur among insects is certainly contrary to all natural laws.*

This natural phenomenon was scarcely believed. Is it possible to coordinate a large number of individuals without a central authority? Is the utopian anarchist dream possible? Can we achieve synchronous behavior without a conductor, general, brain, or boss? It wasn't until the mid-1960s that biologists John Buck and his wife traveled to Thailand to study the phenomenon firsthand. It was actually possible, and it was happening in nature.

In 1984, Ermentrout and Rinzel proposed a simple model of the firefly's flashing rhythm, which is thoroughly detailed in simplified form in Steven Strogatz's book *Sync: How Order Emerges From Chaos In the Universe, Nature, and Daily Life*[214].

Like fireflies, the immune system, brain neurons, my children, and a pop band, all get synchronized without a central authority. The key is feedback: listening to your surroundings and adjusting your behavior to match the average. In the case of fireflies, they sync with the average luminosity to attract females. In the case of my children, perhaps they sync their moods to attract my attention.

Curiously, as human organizations grow larger, they seem to diminish the relative importance of feedback mechanisms, especially signals from the bottom of the hierarchy. Why is it that we, unlike fireflies, struggle to maintain this elegant, decentralized harmony as we scale? Examples abound in authoritarian regimes, large public and private bureaucracies, top-down projects, political parties managing countries, mega-projects, or even couples that don't listen to each other. Nature has learned the hard way the ineluctable value of negative feedback, and we will have to as well if we want to survive.

If an engineering or human system claims to be robust without several layers of negative feedback, we should be skeptical. Most likely, it won't pass the test of time.

Positive and Negative Thinking

"Imagine the level of perfection I could reach with your constant reminders and polishing," I half-joked to Bego, after yet another nudge about my imperfect household chores. It's clear that negative reinforcement mechanisms sometimes fall short—especially in my case.

Negative feedback is not only the fundamental mechanism that makes control systems work—it's also central to human relationships. When our boss, friend, spouse, or colleague isn't satisfied with our conduct, performance, appearance, or anything else, they generously let us know. This feedback often has a negative emotional impact on us. Feelings of guilt, fear, worry, depression, stress, concern, or preoccupation may set in. Our colleagues, friends, and loved ones are effectively asking us to change; there is a gap between their expectations and their observations of our behavior. Sometimes we agree, and sometimes we don't.

At its core, this feedback mechanism could be seen as the same basic mechanism that drives a control system. The signal sent by one of our peers informs us that we are not meeting their expectations. Consequently, we adjust our behavior to address this disparity. Our peers are attempting to guide our behavior and align it with their point of view. How else could we adapt to the complex and unpredictable systems known as marriage or friendship?

Although psychologically discomforting and sometimes even painful, the only path to improvement and change is through faithfully recognizing discrepancies between the world and our expectations. It's not praise that catalyzes positive change. The lack of negative feedback, particularly in couples or teams that fail to communicate their disagreements, is detrimental. The negative aspect of feedback is essential unless you do not intend to change course.

The value of positive thinking is often overstated.

Multiple-loop Dynamics

Before 2008, I remember watching real estate prices climb incessantly. No one could predict the precise moment a bubble would burst, but everyone felt they were riding one, hoping to profit. I didn't anticipate the crash and bought an apartment at the bubble's peak in Girona, my hometown, while living in Geneva. Consequently, I found myself on the losing side when the exponential growth in prices came to an abrupt halt. It's somewhat ironic that, as a newly graduated economist, I hadn't been more cautious, trapped in a positive feedback trap: as prices rose, more investors entered the market, driving prices even higher in what seemed like an endless cycle.

An abrupt end to exponential growth is natural. It always happens. Exponential growth in any domain cannot persist indefinitely. This truth applies to economic growth, population surges, advances in computation and storage, nuclear chain reactions, Ponzi schemes, and even the spread of viral videos — all experience an end to their exponential growth. The challenge lies in determining when and why it will cease, and in identifying the negative feedback loop that will curtail the explosive growth of the positive loop.

Positive feedback loops are eventually tempered by negative feedback loops that inhibit the explosive behavior of the former. Consider arms races and debt, economic growth and inflation, population surges counteracted by famine and war, consumerism leading to environmental collapse, pandemics culminating in the death of their hosts, or even human emotional outbursts followed by physical exhaustion. Though it's widely recognized that explosive or exponential growth cannot persist indefinitely, there's a prevailing belief that perhaps we can ride the wave just one more time.

The 2008 real estate crash also found its equilibrium through a negative feedback loop. Fortunately for me, the decline eventually plateaued, and the prices today are nearly as high as they were before. The lesson remains: in any system, whether financial markets or natural phenomena, what goes up exponentially must eventually find its balance through opposing forces. The question is not if, but when.

John Boyd and the OODA loop

"Could you please stop? Don't take more food until everyone is at the table. Stop. Stooop. Stop! Don't you understand!?" I ask Jone again, raising my voice. I'm not sure if she doesn't hear or just doesn't listen. Is it her autism, her personality, or her pre-adolescence?

"Yes," she replies, which could mean "I do hear," "I do understand," or "I don't care."

"Don't you hear me? Stop!" I catch her again, reaching for the omelette. It's a losing battle as she lunges for the chips, omelette, or rice more quickly than I can juggle cooking, cleaning, changing diapers, and ensuring she doesn't eat the food on the table (a mild exaggeration, as I'm far from being a super-dad). Like a ninja, Jone appears and disappears from the kitchen and I'm unable to keep up with her pace.

Half a century before my daughter devised her omelette-stealing tactic, John Boyd, a U.S. Air Force Colonel, developed a theory about such situations. John Boyd was a fighter pilot and instructor, aircraft designer, military reformer, strategist, and, in some ways, a philosopher. He is best known for his contributions to maneuver warfare theory, fighter training, and the development of the F-16. One of John Boyd's key concepts was the OODA loop (Observe, Orient, Decide, Act).

My younger son learned these lessons even earlier than Jone, and at two and a half years old, his tempo is off the charts. At his young age, he has accomplished several feats, including inserting not one but two plastic beads into his nose while I was solving a programming puzzle, requiring a night in the hospital; receiving several hits from his brother while I was having coffee; and the not-so-unusual act of head-butting a table (his favorite) while I dared to start a conversation with my wife. I don't have children at home but rather battlefield prodigies. I wonder if they would be selected for Ender's Battle School.

I first encountered John Boyd while reading Donald G. Reinertsen's *The Principles of Product Development Flow*[186]. Military tactics, processes, and organizations, with their long hands-on tradition, should serve as inspiration for engineers and managers. These practices have evolved and passed the test of time, so the Lindy effect—which will be explained later—has filtered out unsuccessful military methods and organizations, leaving only those with proven results. Even if you are a pacifist, you should acknowledge that such institutions have endured for an extended period and should be studied accordingly. Biological systems, religions and churches, some companies, and cities share this property.

The OODA loop represents a combatant's recurring decision-making cycle. In Boyd's words, "In order to win, we should operate at a faster tempo or rhythm than our adversaries." This refers to the relative importance of speed over raw power, decentralization over centralized control, goals over plans, tactics over strategy, and prioritizing the main effort over the idea that all battles are equally important. My children have mastered the technique by operating at a tempo higher than mine. Even if I catch them occasionally, they always win, and I just end up frustrated and angry. In my domestic battlefield, my children unconsciously demonstrate Boyd's principles perfectly: they observe my distraction, orient themselves to the opportunity, decide to act, and execute their snack raids—all while I'm still processing what's happening. Battlefield geniuses.

In the context of sampling and control theory, the connection between John Boyd's words and the control benefits of a faster sampling period, increased computational capability of the controller, reduced measurement delay, and decentralized control should not be overlooked. The faster the loop, the more likely we can control an uncertain environment—with our adversaries being part of it. Decentralization allows for quicker loops at the edges of the control system (which doesn't mean a lack of centralized control), enabling faster adaptation to local conditions.

Dressing a negative feedback loop with a fancy acronym is quite common. Examples include Plan-Do-Check-Act, Plan-Do-Study-Act, Deming cycle/wheel, Shewhart cycle, Define-Measure-Analyze-Improve-Control, Kaizen, and more. Whether it's military strategy or parenting challenges, these cycles all describe the same fundamental truth: success depends on the timely observation and reaction to the unexpected environment changes. If you encounter a similar concept again in the future, don't necessarily dismiss the new acronym outright, but at the very least, remember that it represents a negative feedback loop.

Decentralized Control

I was employed at the European Organization for Nuclear Research (CERN) for more than a decade. CERN is the home of the Large Hadron Collider (LHC), the world's largest and highest-energy particle collider. CERN's main mission, beyond its own survival, is to provide particle accelerators and other infrastructure for high-energy physics research. What is the secret behind a large and enduring organization like CERN being able to construct some of the largest scientific experiments at the cutting edge of technology for nearly 70 years? How is it possible to structure a long-lasting organization without succumbing to bureaucracy while simultaneously pushing the boundaries of science and technology? How can one strike a balance between an efficient and well-structured organization and the chaos and freedom required by a research program?

CERN is not a flawless organization, nor is it composed of flawless engineers and scientists. Yet, CERN's longevity is commendable. So, how is such a balance achieved?

Theories about decentralization, such as John Boyd's maneuver warfare, appear sound on paper. However, human history is riddled with large organizations, including governments, armies, multinational corporations, churches, and cities. They all use different variations of centralized decision-making. How is it possible?

On one hand, these organizations must have reasons behind their success; otherwise, we would be living in a libertarian society composed of loosely connected individuals and families.

On the other hand, the theoretical foundations for the existence of these organizations are relatively weak. Traditional mathematical models have mostly been inadequate when faced with the complexities of chaotic systems, complex adaptive systems, social systems, ecological systems, human brains, etc. There is not a fundamental explanation about how to control large and complex organizations efficiently, just some bits and pieces. Control theory primarily addresses simplistic problems. More complex issues are tackled using approximation and divide-and-conquer strategies, which result in various levels of decentralization.

What are the key factors that establish a trade-off between these opposing tendencies of centralized and decentralized systems? The theory of large-scale decentralized control has identified six factors that favor decentralized solutions over centralized ones: scale and computing capability, latency and communication bandwidth, coupling, robustness and reliability, uncertainty, and resource distribution.

Let's dive into each of the topics of this esoteric list.

Scale and computation. Scale changes everything. The complexity of decision-making and regulatory structures increases rapidly with scale. The same strategy cannot be used when managing a family, a community, a village, a city, or a country. Similarly, in the context of linear systems—the simplest possible mathematically—finding the solution to the optimal control problem takes a time proportional to the cube of the number of subsystems (i.e. $O(n^3)$, where n is the number of subsystems or the dimension of the state space). For nonlinear systems using the Bellman Dynamic Programming equation, the computational complexity gets worse and the time required to solve the problem is exponential with respect to the number of subsystems or states[26]. This scaling law is reflected in organizational structures: it is rare to find effective teams of more than ten people, public schools maintain significant independence from district policies, and dioceses operate with considerable autonomy from central church authorities. Similarly in software, it is quite typical to split teams and systems as the system grows. Each subsystem is developed independently while at most keeping certain interfaces stable and maintaining service levels agreements.

Latency and communication. If expediency is needed, organizations cannot rely on centralized decision-making processes, especially when information must flow up and down through a multi-level hierarchy (for example, information might travel from soldier to lieutenant to captain to major to colonel to general to marshal, and then, orders might travel back). The decision-making delay grows with the number of hierarchical levels (i.e., total delay scales like $O(\tau \log n)$, where n is the number of subsystems or components structured hierarchically). When time is of the essence, decentralization becomes mandatory.

The delay not only affects the system's response time but also affects its computational complexity and implicit uncertainty. Even in the linear case, equations affected by delayed states, perturbations, or noise add a number of extra states proportional to the delay and the number of state dimensions.

This is particularly evident in warfare, where fourth-generation warfare, represented by guerrilla forces or terrorist groups, has proved effective against large conventional armies. The United States and Soviet Union experienced this in Vietnam and Afghanistan, respectively, as did the United Kingdom and Spain in their conflicts with the IRA and ETA. Like the mythical hydra, if one head is cut off, two more take its place. The response time of decentralized forces is far superior, and conventional armies have adapted by deploying autonomous units like Green Berets, Navy SEALs, and other special forces. These teams operate as independent agents, making real-time decisions based on local conditions and terrain while maintaining strategic goals rather than adhering to prescribed tactical methods and plans.

This principle extends to everyday situations: a coach cannot play for their players, teenagers must learn to make their own decisions, and in today's fast-paced environment, people must act without waiting for a signal from the mighty lord nor the company CEO.

The truth is that is not always possible to communicate the state of the system or to appropriately handle it. For example, even if they wanted to, my wife, my mother, my boss, my neighborhood baker, and mechanic would not benefit from me deciding for them. I do not have the information to decide, they wouldn't be able to communicate it to me, they do not even want to, it will arrive late, and I do not have the capability to decide, especially for my wife and the mechanic. I typically do for my kids, and I already fear the results. Encoding tacit knowledge is extremely difficult, it is not just a matter of bandwidth and computing power. How do I teach my kids what is right and wrong? How do I explain my business colleagues that the "a simple button" will cost two months of development? This is also one of the lessons of maneuver warfare. As the commander is not in the field, in a rapidly changing environment, he will not be able to receive all the required information nor make appropriate decisions in time. Setting the goal and allowing the soldiers to proceed independently is the only realistic alternative.

Note that computing power, communication latency, and bandwidth have improved by several orders of magnitude during the last century. As Yuval Noah Harari, the author of *Sapiens*, pointed out, this is an important new characteristic of our socio-political environment. These huge amounts of computing power and information exchange could change the status quo in favor of more centralized organizations. Big time for tech tyrants and micro-managers.

Coupling. Most things are connected, but some of the connections have a very weak coupling. While this concept might seem abstract, it's easily observable in daily life. My mother and I are part of the same extended family, but to a great extent, her daily decisions do not affect me, and vice versa. We typically chat every couple of days, sometimes a week, I admit. But our daily decisions are unaffected by these conversations. Sometimes we think that we have the right to give an opinion about each other's thoughts or actions, but we have very little real influence or control over each other. If two subsystems are not strongly coupled, they can be optimized and controlled separately. Coupling the decision-making of otherwise uncoupled systems should not be done, it won't pay off. If I make decisions about my life with my mother, it should be useful, not just for my mother, but for both. Even if she would like, why should I dress my daughter in flowery dresses when she does not like them? I do not like a house with a spa, but should I prevent my mother from building one in her home? The situation completely changes with my wife since, as the name indicates, she is my couple. If I buy the most expensive laptop or I return a bit later home, it has a direct effect on my wife and children's well-being. Our connection makes a joint decision far superior, albeit more difficult.

Robustness and reliability. From a naïve engineering point of view, it might seem that decentralization entails higher levels of robustness and reliability. However, the 2008 financial crisis and the COVID pandemic do not seem consistent with this hypothesis. If the subsystems are not coupled, decentralization increases the system's robustness. However, if they are coupled, as financial institutions actually are, decentralization could either increase or decrease their robustness—depending on the sign of the coupling constant. The same applies to families, tribes, cities, countries, and climate. For example, let's imagine I'm being chased by a predator. Should I run and escape without considering any other factors? It depends. What is the robust behavior if my wife and children are also being chased? Should I keep going to the office even when some of my colleagues are sick? But what should be the robust behavior in a pandemic? Should an IT system remain available in the face of partial failures? But what should be the robust behavior in the face of a possible security breach?

Uncertainty. In the face of uncertainty (which is always present), reduced delays generally improve the stability and performance of the control system. Hence, decentralization is advantageous under conditions of higher uncertainty. Conversely, a more predictable and stable environment provides a relative advantage to more centralized approaches. Recon teams, proofs of concept, start-ups, and young people often do better when exploring options independently, which are later exploited by more structured teams and organizations once the original uncertainty has been reduced.

Resource Distribution. In my work we plan at different time horizons: weekly, quarterly, and biannually. The plans are continuously in flux, but as the software development team can only handle a limited number of projects, planning is still necessary. We have to decide which subset of all possible projects to tackle and the decision should be taken collectively involving the different stakeholders including developers, managers, customer service, and operations team [172]. That is, shared and scarce resources require a more centralized decision-making approach.

Instead, modular and distributed resources, require a more decentralized approach allowing for a better adaptation to the local conditions. A fantastic example is the incredible specialization of finches' beaks discovered by Charles Darwin in his voyage to the Galápagos Islands in 1835. In his 1859 *Origin of Species*, Darwin speculated that these birds, resembling starlings, came to the Galapagos Islands by wind, and then Evolution took over shaping the species as a function of the local diet available[47].

An analogous situation happens with parents. If you have two children, you can often see each parent specializing in one of the children. However, the arrangement breaks down when your partner is not present or you cheerfully decide to have a third child (or more). It is then that centralized decision making and coordination is necessary. As I say to my children: "I only have two hands." The phrase encapsulates a fundamental principle of resource allocation: when resources are limited and demands are high, some form of centralized coordination becomes not just beneficial but necessary. The challenge lies in finding the right balance between centralized resource management and maintaining the flexibility provided by decentralized systems.

In summary, a centralized approach should be prioritized for control systems with a relatively small number of subsystems, especially if they are coupled, where the control system measurements and response latency are relatively fast, particularly when dealing with a well-understood system that has a low level of uncertainty. Conversely, a decentralized approach should be chosen for systems composed of a relatively large number of independent subsystems operating under a higher level of uncertainty or with a relatively low measurement latency with respect to the subsystem dynamics. .

Everything is Connected

Everything you see exists together in a delicate balance. As king, you need to understand that balance and respect all the creatures, from the crawling ant to the leaping antelope.

[...]

Yes, Simba, but let me explain. When we die, our bodies become the grass, and the antelope eat the grass. And so we are all connected in the great Circle of Life.

Mufasa, The Lion King, 1994

"Unbelievable! Don't you hear your kid asking the same question for the tenth time?" I had just finished working and had gone downstairs to make some coffee. I don't remember anything else; my mind was in the limbo between my work and my personal life while preparing and drinking the coffee, completely ignoring my kid.

"Sorry, I didn't hear it." I'm sorry because we don't have time, because every time I'm not available for my kids, my wife has to take over, because my kids react immediately to any attempt by my wife or me to talk to each other, make a phone call, or even read. Every action has a reaction, even an unintended passive one, like in this case.

The principle of "no free lunch" is analogous to the idea prevalent in biology about the interconnectedness of all life. All actions entail a reaction, sometimes complex and surprising. In other words, an action has a consequence, a price tag, and although not all connections are equally important, all life is certainly connected. We are all intertwined.

For example, in biology (and in my family), the removal of keystone species (or in this case, a keystone person like my mother) can have dramatic effects. What happens when we remove the lion, the bees, or the wolf from an ecosystem [23]? How paradoxical it is to see ecosystems recovering after re-introducing the missing apex predator? It is illuminating to understand the chain reaction formed by the removal and re-introduction of the feared predator.

Similarly, what will happen to my family once my mother is gone? Who will be the nexus? Will I lose contact with my siblings Ilde and Astrid, as well as my cousins and aunts? If there is some terrible misfortune, who will offer the necessary comfort (and possibly a bed and a bowl of soup)?

Keystone species are those plants or animals whose absence is critical to the survival of other species in the ecosystem. They are connected to a large proportion of the ecosystem. Counter-intuitively, keystone species are often apex predators like jaguars, grizzly bears, elephants, lions, or sharks. They help maintain balance in the ecosystem.

However, not all keystone species are apex predators. One interesting example—not to mention my mother, despite her attraction to leopard-patterned pants and jackets—is the ochre starfish, which helps keep populations of mussels in check. In one experiment the ochre starfish was completely removed from a typical piece of shoreline, causing the mussel population to explode, as it had no other natural predators besides these sea stars, and overran the ecosystem, resulting in a 50% reduction in the number of other species [18].

Every action we take in the environment has a reaction, and some of these reactions can be quite dramatic.

---

[23]Peter Wohlleben in the *The Secret Network of Nature* provides great examples of how nature connects all living things in sometimes unexpected ways. He shows, for example, how the removal of the wild salmon from rivers affected tree growth and soil quality, or how the re-introduction of the wolf in Yellowstone increased the soil humidity and vegetation growth, too [244].

Perfection is the Enemy of Good

In preparing for battle I have always found that plans are useless, but planning is indispensable.

Dwight D. Eisenhower, 1950s.

Yesterday, two days after the Russian invasion of Ukraine, I was perplexed by the divergent opinions expressed in some typically enlightened forums. Everyone seemed to have a different perspective on the nature and purpose of the invasion. While I understand that the true nature and purpose are not yet fully known, and perhaps they never will, it is unsettling to see people so certain about something as complex and uncertain as war. Does this clueless assertiveness mirror the ignorance not just of the general population but also of the Russian Commander-in-Chief? It is indeed a frightening thought.

As we can see when we approach the issue from a control systems perspective, the presumption of certainty is a recipe for disaster. Whether it is a linear or a nonlinear system, there are two fundamental limitations of negative feedback systems that affect their performance and robustness in the face of uncertainty [139]: namely, the trade-off between performance and noise sensitivity, and the trade-off between noise sensitivity and disturbance rejection.

First, the input-output tracking performance of these systems is inherently linked to the system's sensitivity to noise. Surprisingly, the control system performance is degraded with each additional reduction of its sensitivity to the random fluctuations of the measurements. As we make these feedback systems more insensitive to noise, their performance is fundamentally degraded; it is mathematically impossible to escape from this trade-off. This, like the re-introduction of apex predators in ecosystems, seems to be counterintuitive. A system that is able to totally ignore the noise will equally ignore its inputs. In other words, if the feedback control system does not observe the environment, then it does not work. Obviously, spawning orders without detailed attention to the observations leads to disaster. One would think that making a system more robust to the measurement noise would automatically improve its performance, but it is exactly the opposite. As the system is made more insensitive to noise, it is equally made insensitive to the effects of the system's inputs, and therefore, its performance degrades.

Conversely, a highly performant system, one that follows exactly the inputs, is equivalent to a system that overreacts to noisy measurements.

Consider the analogy of being the perfect partner or subordinate, diligently fulfilling the desires of a boss or loved one. This arrangement works flawlessly until the desires of the latter are not correctly communicated or understood, or God forbid, the desires are just wrong. Blindly following orders is a curse (although our loved ones may not always grasp this concept). It is like blindly following a GPS-enabled application to reach your destination only to realize that you are on a one-way street.

Now, let's apply this concept to our Commander-in-Chief. Picture all the subordinates dutifully carrying out precise orders. However, if the Commander-in-Chief is misled or uncertain about the reality of the battlefield—for example, if subordinates are unwilling to give him bad news—, then even a perfect master plan will result in disaster.

What happens instead if we consider a different kind of Commander-in-Chief who reflects carefully, considers multiple opinions and sources of information, and does his or her best to filter out measurement noise? In this case, the ability to react swiftly to rapid environmental changes will be compromised. A rapid response to information implies sensitivity to noise, whereas a reduced sensitivity to noise leads to a slower response and poorer performance. There exists a trade-off. Perfection is the enemy of good. Flawless performance or robustness is utterly useless.

However, there is not only one but two fundamental limits to any control system using negative feedback. If the first limit implies a trade-off between performance and noise sensitivity, the second implies a trade-off between noise sensitivity and uncertainty. The controller, the manager, the Commander-in-Chief, must decide whether to reduce their sensitivity to measurement uncertainty or to improve their response against unexpected changes (i.e., disturbance rejection in the control systems jargon). If we take time for the information to clarify, then we will likely miss some unexpected risks and opportunities. A Commander-in-Chief would like to avoid reacting to false information (e.g., Ukrainian troops are in Moscow), but would want to react immediately to changes in the environment (e.g., Ukrainian forces will massively deploy drones to counteract Russian air and naval forces). It turns out that rejecting noise equally rejects the real unexpected changes in the environment. Therefore, we have to decide how much we trust our inputs. Do we want to be more or less sensitive to subtle changes in the information flow? You cannot have both.

For instance, does Vladimir Putin know exactly how China, Europe, the US, or NATO will react to the war? Does he have a good understanding of Ukrainian forces and capabilities? More fundamentally, can anyone truly predict the outcomes of such complex geopolitical interactions? Does he have a good understanding of Russia's ones? What happens if there is unprecedented bad weather? What if the Russian soldiers are not willing to harm their former compatriots? What if the projected increase in gas and petrol prices does not cover the expenses of war? What if the war lasts longer than expected? These uncertainties do not arise from uncertain measurements of the environment but from an uncertain modeling of the system. If Mr. Putin wants to react to these unexpected events in a timely fashion, he will necessarily also mistake potential situations for real ones.

Our Commander-in-Chief must choose whether to protect his decision-making from noisy measurements or from unexpected developments. If we choose to filter the ever-changing flow of news, an unmodeled error will be detected at a similarly slow pace.

Let's examine another example in the context of project management. Let's assume that we only observe the project status once a month, this will help us to filter out the daily noise (e.g., someone getting sick, a computer breaking down, etc.). However, by design, we will also lose the ability to observe if every Monday there is a power cut that interrupts all the work.

As Nassim Taleb observed, a system that is completely immune to noise is exceedingly fragile. Counter-intuitively, sensitivity to random events makes the control system more robust. Worse is better.

This interplay between robustness, sensitivity, and performance highlights a fundamental trade-off at the heart of control systems. In this chapter, we will delve into its wide-ranging implications, exploring topics such as the hidden truth behind the "Boy Who Cried Wolf" tale, the distinction between feedback and feedforward mechanisms, the surprising fragility of systems that are both highly optimized and robust, the irrational inability of organizations to accept errors and reject uncertainty, and, finally, the concept of antifragile systems as an alternative paradigm to robustness and optimization.

The Boy Who Cried Wolf and 50 Hz Rejection

"Jooone, can you please stop playing with the water?" I have already told her a zillion times. She has a weird fascination watching the water drip out of her hands. The fascination wouldn't be a problem, except for our bathroom looking like the aftermath of an Atlantean war after one of her sensorial pursuits.

"Jone! Can you stop?" And she stops for a minute or two until I leave her presence to restart again.

"JONE!! Don't you listen to me?"

"Yes." And once I leave, she keeps playing with the water.

As a father, I sometimes feel like the 50 Hz signal from our power network. It is always there with its noise and light flickering, but unless it fails to provide its power, it's not noticed by almost anyone.

The 50 Hz (60 Hz depending on the country) electrical signal powering our appliances is a blessing in our homes and a curse for high precision machinery. This 50 Hz signal is the prime example of a disturbance. It is not only present in electrical signals but also in the light intensity fluctuations of our buildings, the vibrations of power cables, and the humming of power supplies and appliances. At night, you just need to be really quiet to hear it. Most likely you are so used to it that you have forgotten the capability to hear it until the noise disappears (e.g., when you go into the mountains, in the middle of nowhere, there you realize that an insidious buzzing has finally stopped).

In the particle accelerator I worked at, electromagnets required a part-per-million precision in the magnetic fields used to guide and accelerate particles, and therefore in the current supplied to generate them. A typical solution to remove the annoying disturbance is to have a 50 Hz notch filter applied to the output measurement. This filter removes all the 50 Hz signals from the measurement. However, given the fundamental relation between disturbance rejection and noise rejection explained in the previous section, the filtering of the noise causes the control system to ignore real 50Hz disturbances from other systems, and also prevents the control of input signals in that frequency range.

The 50 Hz rejection mechanism works in a similar way to "The Boy Who Cried Wolf". In the story, the tricked villagers no longer listen to the shepherd boy, and therefore, they don't realize when the actual wolf is coming. In their attempt to filter out false alarms, the villagers decided to filter out what the boy said at the cost of missing a real wolf, and they did.

Jone, my daughter, often ignores me. It is not just her. My other children often, and hopefully unintentionally, do not seem to hear me. My voice has become ambient noise to be filtered, and consequently, sometimes useful information is lost.

Feedback versus Feedforward

I always thought that I was shy and introverted. However, it turns out that when I reflect on my behavior in relation to my colleagues, it is quite the opposite. At work, I tend to be the first person to openly express my opinions and take action. As my wife has reminded me several times after one of my adventures into the unknown: "There have always been fools ready to take the spear and volunteer for the mammoth hunt. By some evolutionary miracle, the world is not full of cowards and your genes are still here."

Although being proactive, the first to act, is often seen positively in current management trends, it also has some drawbacks. I have experienced the negative effects on several occasions, and I want to believe that if I make three or four more mistakes, I will learn from them.

The first person to act has not yet received feedback from the environment; the reaction signal from the environment arrives after the first action. Proactive behavior is therefore an act of self-confidence, often requiring a leap of faith into uncharted territory. Acting before having prior information is akin to exploration, and exploration often comes at a price paid by the explorer (e.g., as seen with the corpses piling up on the paths of Mount Everest or in the ranks of bankrupted and depressed entrepreneurs), with the eventual benefit extending to the rest of society observing the "fool."

Being proactive or not, in addition to being analogous to the exploration-exploitation trade-off, is analogous to the distinction between feedforward and feedback control systems.

In a feedforward system, the adjustment of the control variable is not based on error feedback. Instead, it relies on accurate knowledge about the behavior of the world in response to certain actions. The error does not influence its behavior. In a feedforward control system, if the system under control or plant is stable (i.e., it does not explode after setting it on fire), then the feedforward system is also stable. You push a bit, and it moves a bit. However, if the plant is inaccurately modeled, the response of the feedforward system will deviate significantly from expectations. In a feedforward system, errors are not self-corrected through the feedback loop, and we rely on perfectly modeling the environment's responses. Any estimation error of the environment's behavior results in a proportional error in the system output. A feedforward system is like a dictator who does not listen to anyone, taking rapid decisions at will. While this approach can be remarkably efficient when based on perfect understanding of the system, it becomes disastrous when faced with unexpected variables or changes in the environment. It's like walking blindfolded—you will likely end up in the wrong place quickly unless by pure luck you walk straight in the right direction.

This behavior is in contrast to a feedback control system, where an estimation error about the environment's input-output behavior has a reduced effect.

Since the measurement noise does not affect the output, a feedforward system is like a system perfectly robust to measurement noise (as it does not listen to it), and therefore, totally exposed to modeling uncertainties (e.g., our beloved Commander-in-Chief). It is largely useless except for perfectly understood and perfectly deterministic systems.

Once you grasp the basic capabilities of feedback and feedforward systems and their analogies, it is easy to extend and foresee the consequences in other cases where a feedback mechanism is not in place. This includes fixed-price contracts, waterfall project management, dictators, top-down management, representative democracies, etc.

Robust Yet Fragile

Fear is the mind killer.

Frank Herbet, *Dune*, 1965.

Fear is the path to the dark side... fear leads to anger... anger leads to hate... hate leads to suffering.

Yoda, *Star Wars I: The Phantom Menace*, 1999.

"Where is my underwear!?" I unfairly shouted in anger at my wife. She wasn't and isn't responsible for them, if such a role actually exists for my precious ones. I was just mad. Now, we laugh about it, but it was not funny when it happened. It sounds ridiculous because it is. I was angry, but obviously not about the missing underwear. My greatest friend and ally, my wife, suffered the consequences. She was simply close to me, and I was tired, not sleeping well, lost, and frustrated about my daughter's unsolvable condition. On top of that, I had just been informed that my contract wouldn't be renewed.

My weakest point, both personally and professionally, is that as I work harder, I become more tired, and it becomes easier for me to get upset over increasingly trivial matters. This personal sensitivity to stress and fatigue mirrors a fundamental principle in control systems theory—as systems become more optimized for performance, they often become more fragile and sensitive to perturbations. Under such circumstances, even something as minor as my filthy laundry can trigger an emotional outburst. Anybody can get upset, but not everyone gets upset for the same reasons. Many of my friends become more sensitive when they are hungry, while others do when they haven't slept well. As we demand more from ourselves, even slight disturbances can upset us. We all have our triggers; everyone has one.

Getting angry in a personal or professional situation is my worst fear. In hindsight, every time I have been even mildly angry, I could have improved the situation by simply walking away and taking a few minutes or days to calm down. Arriving late or even not attending a meeting is a lesser offense compared to uttering the wrong words to the wrong people, even when they'r justified. Adopting a slow and passive attitude in overwhelming and explosive situations could have been more beneficial. It's important to remember that while fear and anger are valuable evolutionary responses, work is not a life-and-death situation, and most likely they aren't appropriate responses. The Dune's Bene Gesserit witches and Master Yoda's teachings are right spot on.

It is paradoxical and shameful that a person like me is so close to the edge after a few setbacks. I was living in a perfectly safe and beautiful country, with a healthy child and a wonderful wife, enough money in my pocket to live several years without a job, a home, plenty of food, and a likely bright professional future. Still, my defenses were easily shattered after losing a job and realizing that my child was autistic. It is not an easy situation, but it is clearly neither a life-and-death situation.

A similar situation arises in highly optimized control systems. This can be explained from first principles through the relationship between the control system sensitivity and its complementary sensitivity functions.

The sensitivity of a feedback control system is defined as the relative change in the input-output function with respect to modeling errors of the system under control [12]. In other words, the sensitivity of a control system measures the robustness of the system to environmental or modeling uncertainties. The sensitivity is a fundamental concept. Given the uncertainty of reality and our limited capabilities, this measure allows us to anticipate the control system performance drop under changes in assumptions and conditions.

Sensitivity does not answer questions like "How will my boss react to a one-day project delay?", "How much hotter is climate change going to make things over the course of the next hundred years?", or the more daunting "How much emphasis should I place on preventing the echolalic episodes of my autistic daughter?". For all these questions, science has some approximate answers. They are not perfect, but we can work with them. Sensitivity instead asks what will happen if we ignore more than we thought; it is a second-level thought. That is, "What will happen if my boss doesn't react as I expect?", "What happens if poorly understood interactions between carbon sinks, the terrestrial biosphere, ocean chemistry, and permafrost create a reinforcing loop, accelerating climate change?", and finally, "What happens if my daughter's echolalia serves as an anxiety reduction mechanism or even some form of speech training?".

Ideally, decisions, plans, and feedback control systems should have a very small sensitivity to modeling errors; they should always be robust to incorrectly modeled environments, robust to our ignorance. However, there is once again a fundamental trade-off involving different aspects of the control systems' robustness.

It is an ineluctable mathematical fact that low sensitivity to environmental and modeling uncertainty implies a lack of noise rejection and poor performance, both shaped by the same transfer function: the complementary sensitivity function. Paradoxically, achieving high levels of robustness in performance often means sacrificing some degree of performance. Conversely, a control system that does nothing—an unresponsive control system with a null response—is the only perfectly robust control system. We can be either robust to modeling uncertainties or robust to noise and performance, but not both simultaneously.

Perfectly robust performance is problematic, to say the least, if not highly inadvisable.

Does anyone know of a truly robust elite athlete or racehorse? Does anyone know of an industrious workaholic with a fantastic family life?

For example, my experience as a professional athlete showed me how our Apollonian bodies were easily subject to severe injuries, sickness, or general deficiencies shown in blood samples. We were strong and weak. There is also ample evidence that many complex and highly optimized systems exhibit fragile behaviors in the face of relatively small perturbations. This is observed in ecological systems (e.g., keystone species, plagues, etc.), neuronal networks (e.g., unstable behaviors and seizures under certain synaptic changes), coral resilience to ocean acidity, power grids, traffic congestion, etc.

Striving for excellence in any endeavor comes with a fragility price tag. As you aim to perform better and more robustly, you also become more fragile. So, there should be benefits to mediocrity as well.

This section has been a rather lengthy and convoluted apology. Time has proven that we are a relatively robust couple even though we likely lack the excellence of a perfect family, with perfect pictures of themselves, a perfect house, perfect children, and perfectly clean underwear. It is a work in progress.

I am sorry and ashamed that my underwear received such unwarranted attention.

Catch-22

Like the previously discussed trade-off between feedforward and feedback approaches, I have always faced a persistent catch-22 situation during the delivery of software projects. On one hand, the organizations I have worked for have strict budget-driven project management standards that come with tight annual or bi-annual budgets, scopes, and deadlines. On the other hand, when the project budget is approved, neither my colleagues nor I have a clear picture of the necessary steps to achieve these goals. Such goals are described very broadly after a couple of meetings, perhaps three. In fact, we typically start the implementation without complete planning, design, or understanding of the problem. Project requirements are usually summarized in short descriptions (a paragraph at most) of the business goals, even though the work could span 6 to 12 months. How can we accurately estimate the required project cost, time, or benefits? How can we know if the development team has delivered the promised functionality?

This contradictory situation often leads to numerous misunderstandings and sometimes even quarrels. Fortunately, we mitigate this by building, testing, and deploying small chunks of work to obtain feedback as quickly as possible. The requirements for these small chunks are mostly unknown in advance, and developers gather them as the work progresses by collaborating with whomever is needed.

Despite the push towards Agile methodologies, the budget cycle of most organizations imposes strong constraints on the delivery teams. It is the well-known trade-off between feedforward and feedback approaches, or between exploration and exploitation. Although the work performed often requires a degree of random and exploratory behavior, organizations want deterministic exploitation-like budgets and timelines. They are expected to spend a specific amount of money, time, and resources, neither more nor less, within a designated budget cycle (typically one year).

To address this contradiction, project management has typically introduced tolerances for budgets and deadlines. However, this approach does not fully address the genuine need for exploratory behavior which, as demonstrated by start-ups and explorers, leads to either failure and ruin, or glory and wealth[24].

This unfortunate state of affairs also applies to the personal profiles valued by companies. Nobody appreciates mistakes, schedule and cost overruns, bugs and regressions, spelling errors, poorly formatted slides, or heated discussions. However, these are precisely the sources from which learning, exploration, and feedback can emerge. The pursuit of perfection—whether in projects, employees, or processes—represents a dangerous illusion: systems that are optimized for flawless performance inevitably sacrifice their capacity to learn, adapt, and evolve. In other words, what purpose does a perfect son or daughter serve? What about a perfect project, boss, employee, or colleague? Although it sounds fantastic in theory, in practice perfect performance entails an inability to adapt, leading to fragility.

Antifragile is not Robust

Life has a way of teaching us about fragility in the most personal terms. I learned this lesson in my thirties when my close to perfect life was easily disrupted. I had a beautiful and intelligent wife, a wonderful and well-paid job, and I was living in one of the safest and most advanced countries in the world. We didn't expect our child to be perfect, but we certainly didn't expect her to be autistic. The initial near-optimal situation was easily disrupted by the realities we faced. How was it possible? Why did it happen to us? These two common yet futile questions plagued our minds.

As we discussed earlier, in the realm of control theory, systems are designed to be as robust as possible given the desired performance. However, as we saw before, it is not possible to have a perfectly robust system that remains unaffected by modeling errors while also achieving perfect performance. Remember, perfect performance inherently makes a system fragile.

Does this concept of fragility relate to Nassim Taleb's notion of anti-fragility? According to Taleb, anti-fragility refers to things or phenomena that actually benefit from disorder, stressors, adventure, risk, and uncertainty. In a sense, a control system can be considered to be an anti-fragile system because its

---

[24]A long-standing and highly successful organization that has found a solution to this Gordian Knot is the Defense Advanced Research Projects Agency (DARPA). See a great introduction at [187].

behavior improves when it is sensitive to noise and disturbances. Without some sensitivity to noise or disturbances, the system would not function at all. Other examples of anti-fragile phenomena include evolution, entrepreneurship, and the act of learning from difficult circumstances.

However, it is essential to recognize that anti-fragility and robustness are distinct concepts. They are not the same.

A fragile system, like a coffee cup or a television, can withstand certain shocks and bumps, but as we increase their force, they eventually break. These objects exhibit a harm function that is convex (i.e., the harm increases more than proportionally with the energy of the impact). If you drop the cup 10 times from 10 cm, it may remain intact and still function as a cup. However, if you drop it from 1 meter, it will likely break into pieces. Even a cup made of steel would be equally fragile, though we would have to drop it perhaps from the top of a building. In any case, the steel cup will never improve with each drop. Buildings, bridges, nuclear plants, airplanes, and bank balance sheets are robust up to a certain level of variability and stress, but they may fail or collapse if that level is exceeded. They are robust yet fragile.

Conversely, an anti-fragile system exhibits a concave response to stress. More stress actually improves the system; it is not catastrophic but useful. Natural selection is a prime example of anti-fragility. A more volatile environment increases the survival rate of species by eliminating individuals that are not fit. Predators and illnesses eliminate the weakest individuals and benefit the collective as a whole. Some people argue that economic crises improve the overall health of the economy, especially if their income is not at stake.

While it is true that everything eventually breaks under enough stress, there are systems that improve under some stress. This understanding of anti-fragility offers both a theoretical framework and a source of hope: families, like other living systems, don't just resist stress—they can grow stronger through it. Though admittedly, I could have lived happily without experiencing the proof firsthand.

Haste Makes Waste

During a birthday party in my early thirties, I had an enlightening experience that helped me appreciate the intelligence of Eduardo and, consequently, learn to value divergent yet silent opinions. It happened during a game called *Survival on the Moon*, where group members were instructed to individually rank the usefulness of certain objects in the hypothetical situation of being stranded in the Moon (e.g., matches, food concentrate, two pistols, stellar map, etc.), then reach a consensus as a group about the relative usefulness of the objects. What struck me the most was realizing that Eduardo, with his quiet and non-confrontational attitude, got at the top of the ranking as an individual, while our group, including Eduardo and myself, marginally improved the ranking of one of the poorest performers (myself). It was a heavy blow to my self-esteem. I not just reached the bottom of the ranking, but I wrongly drove my team to incorrect decisions about the importance of the objects. I felt like a noisy duck in a swamp, making loud noises and creating lots of splashes, but lacking substance.

The additional time the group dedicated to discussions did not necessarily result in better decision-making. While some individuals in the group improved their rankings, not everyone did, especially the people that were not able to listen.

Although in nature and engineering, there often appears to be a trade-off between speed and accuracy, this trade-off did not seem to apply in the *Survival on the Moon* game. It is intriguing to observe how people like myself can interfere with such a fundamental principle.

Examples of the speed accuracy trade-off abound. Should I wait a little longer to determine whether an approaching animal is a predator or prey? Should I stop contemplating a problem and start actively working on it? Should I immediately respond to an agressive email or wait? When is procrastination a useful trait?

Unlike the well-known decrease in decision making performance during high-physical exertion, thirst, or hunger [42,86,87,91,112], many decisions improve over time as the information and computation accumulates. For such decisions, one faces a dilemma known as the speed-accuracy trade-off. This trade-off was first observed in animal and human behavior and can be modeled using control theory and statistical decision-making [97].

Interestingly, as we have shown, there are situations that do not follow the principle, and spending more time on a decision sometimes leads to degraded performance, especially when a pitiful human is involved. Following this insight, this chapter will explore the effects of decision speed on performance and robustness. We will explore the unavoidable pervasiveness of overshoot and undershoot and how they worsen with speed, the perspective of statistical decision-making on the speed-accuracy trade-off, the analogous topics of exploration-exploitation and bias-variance trade-offs, the incredibly useful and simple Lindy's Law, and finally, a recollection of one of my earlier software developer failures trying to re-write software instead of profiting from the accumulated knowledge of the existing system.

Overshoot or Overreaction

Those who are good at expressing anger will not be formidable.

Laozi, Tao Te Ching, 4th century BC.

The superior man is careful of his wrath.

I Ching, 1000-750 BC.

"Marc, I had a great idea! Let me explain it to you," my boss exclaimed, his excitement reminiscent of a child discovering a shiny pebble in a stream. For the next fifteen minutes, he delved into the intricacies of a corner case in a real-time control problem. Oblivious to the irony, he seemed to forget that just a month ago, he had essentially terminated my employment—albeit in a more palatable manner—by informing me that my contract wouldn't be renewed come September.

"Look, it's very interesting," I interrupted, slightly annoyed. "Do you realize that a month ago you informed me that my contract wouldn't be extended due to some staffing quotas? Why are you explaining this to me? It's basically irrelevant to my future since it will be designed and implemented one year from now when I won't be here."

"Sorry, I thought you might find it interesting," he genuinely replied, surprised by my reaction.

"In fact, what you're doing is quite impolite. I have quite a lot of work before my contract finishes, and if I happen to have some free time, I'll use it for my family or for something that truly interests me," I said, now visibly angry, as he kept widening his eyes as if a transcendental revelation had fallen on him.

A couple of hours later, after reflecting on the situation, I realized I could have simply relaxed and sat through his explanations. I could have let time pass and arrived home early. However, I overreacted. Instead, I could have been wondering how the man didn't seem to care or have a clue about the situation. Adopting a more curious and wonder-filled mindset would have been a better approach. What did I get out of my words? What did he get?

The emotional reaction of anger in animals, including hominids, originates from a positive feedback loop leading to an explosive chain reaction. Throughout our evolution, this kind of explosive reaction has been extremely useful. Imagine the tragic consequences of getting angry or afraid slowly after encountering a dangerous threat. Unfortunately, in my day-to-day desk job, overreaction has never been useful to me.

In the context of control theory, controlling an unstable system, one with potentially explosive reactions to small changes like our emotions, nuclear fission plants, or stock markets, faces a fundamental trade-off between overshoot and rise time[139]. As we attempt to move the system faster, we also experience a larger overshoot or overreaction, as the system moves beyond our expected setpoint before settling there later. Conversely, if we try to reduce the speed of the movement in an unstable system, the size of the overshoot decreases proportionally. A fast reaction of an unstable system always entails an overreaction. This could partially explain how our perspective over unfair or scary situations levels out over time.

These findings have important policy implications. Dealing with unstable systems requires a delicate approach; otherwise, we are likely to overreact.

Unstable systems should be controlled gently. If you find yourself getting angry at work, it's best to take it slowly or even go for a walk, as the underlying emotional cascade is explosive, and you will likely overreact if you hastily act.

Do not send emails while angry, as you are more likely to misfire and regret it later.

Undershoot and Why Things Get Worse Before Getting Better

Upon joining a new team, it took several weeks to discuss and agree on the idea of implementing a peer review process for all source code changes. This simple practice has proven to be remarkably cost-effective, transforming our workflow more than any other improvement. It has been the best improvement ever, and the evidence seems to equally indicates it[83]. Nowadays, no one in the team can imagine working without a peer review process. However, initially, it was challenging to establish this practice as everyone perceived it as intrusive, ineffective, and potentially harmful. Interestingly, when we later shared the success of the practice with other teams, they also reacted in a similar cautious way.

Although everything is great and wonderful now, implementing and convincing people about the practice was quite difficult. Is this normal?

This kind of reaction to change is typical in the control of non-minimum phase systems. These systems are characterized by initially moving in the opposite direction after a change. They oppose change. In other words, they exhibit the prototypical behavior of "things getting worse before getting better." Typical examples include adding coal to a furnace, which initially reduces the temperature before increasing it, or certain medical procedures such as removing a diseased appendix by performing surgery.

Analogous to the control of unstable systems with a trade-off between overshoot and rise time, controlling a non-minimum phase system involves a fundamental trade-off between undershoot and settling time. If we want the system to reach its new stable set point faster, then the undershoot or reaction in the opposite direction will be larger [139]. A fast reaction in a non-minimum phase system always entails an undershoot.

In other words, reducing the speed of change will reduce the reaction against the change. When dealing with a system that reacts negatively to changes, like those involving people, it is advisable to proceed slowly to avoid oscillations and strong opposition after the change. The faster you go, the more back and forth you'll experience, it can backfire.

Therefore, changes on non-minimum phase systems should be introduced at a pace slower than the system's natural response time. Non-minimum phase systems exhibit a kickback effect after a sudden surprise. This fast-paced world we are living in is therefore doomed to have instabilities and kickbacks, constant over-reactions and counter-reactions to change are, and will be, the norm.

This reminds me of the wise words spoken by my brother-in-law during a conversation about the legislative changes made in Spain regarding homosexual marriage. "I believe it is better to proceed with more caution. We are going too fast, slowly would be better. Even though I agree with them, I wonder if we are moving too quickly for the conservative portion of the population." Although we all want changes in our societies, the change should not be faster than the capability of people, our culture, and our laws to adapt.

Statistical Decision-Making

"Marc! Maarc!! MARC MAGRANS!! Do you hear me?" My Catalan teacher wore an indignant expression, as if something dear to her had been snatched away by a fourteen-year-old.

"Ah..." I glanced around, finding an angry teacher right in front of me. Beside me, my best friend Anna couldn't help but laugh. I was still struggling to comprehend the situation, while the rest of the class joined in the laughter.

"This is unbelievable! Are you even paying attention?" The teacher's voice grew louder.

"Yes?" It suddenly clicked for me. I had been lost in my thoughts for an extended period. In this case, my slow reaction didn't entail a better response. These days, my wife occasionally gets angry with me as well when I zone out, but I never daydream for that long. Such a shame.

This past classroom incident got me thinking about the relationship between response time and decision quality. While my delayed response was purely due to inattention, there are situations where taking more time to respond actually leads to better outcomes.

Unlike me, in the context of statistical decision-making theory, when defining optimal decisions, slower responses are typically more accurate[184]. I guess I'm far from these optimal algorithms.

For instance, in project management, determining the optimal threshold to detect schedule or cost overruns encounters a similar trade-off. If the cost or schedule surpasses a certain threshold, it prompts a project review and appropriate actions. Setting the threshold requires mindfulness, as a low threshold detects problems earlier but tends to yield false positives, resulting in additional costs associated with the unnecessary review process. Conversely, a higher threshold minimizes false positives, but if a genuine problem arises, it incurs costs proportional to the increased detection time. This fundamental trade-off applies to all monitoring and alarm systems because the statistical significance of the reconstructed signal increases with time; being too early renders it insignificant.

An optimal threshold strikes a balance between the costs of delay and unnecessary alarms. However, it's not uncommon for these costs and benefits to differ among individuals and groups within the same organization, and so does the threshold. A manager prefers to minimize the project risk, and an early alarm could prevent a project overrun. In contrast, the person actually doing the job likely prefers to do the job rather than discussing and documenting the status of the project.

In my case, when I zoned out in front of my teacher, the additional delay clearly violated the optimal speed-accuracy trade-off: the extended processing time didn't yield any improvement in response quality." Instead, I had been daydreaming about an entirely unrelated subject, perhaps a better use of my time given the boring class. It's a trait that evolution has inexplicably preserved in some humans, despite its obvious disadvantages in terms of survival. How is it that my ancestors managed to avoid being eaten by lions while lost in their thoughts? Well, perhaps I'm one of Nature's failed experiments, operating well below the Pareto Frontier of the speed-accuracy trade-off that natural selection usually optimizes.

Explore or Exploit

As I grow older, I find myself unexpectedly revisiting certain textbooks and papers—a behavior I never anticipated, given my past preference for learning new things rather than reviewing old material. This shift has led me to question whether it stems from an increased awareness of age-related knowledge loss, or if it reflects a growing difficulty in acquiring new information.

Similar to my experience, individuals and groups constantly face a recurring challenge of choosing between exploring new alternatives and exploiting known ones. It's like an adjustable parameter in our own life optimization algorithm. How much randomness should we incorporate into a hill-climbing algorithm? When should we decide to settle on a particular real estate agent to buy a house? When should we continue searching for alternatives? Should a predator keep hunting in the same patch of land or explore elsewhere? Should a company focus on incremental product development or launch entirely new products? Should I dedicate time to learning something new or hone my existing skills?

The sweet spot in the exploration-exploitation trade-off depends on various factors, including the environment (e.g., more information about the available options favors exploitation, while more uncertainty favors exploration), the capabilities of the individual or group (e.g., prior experience or cognitive capacity favors exploitation, while the possibility of learning new skills or capabilities favors exploration), and the spatial or temporal dimension of the challenge (e.g., local resources favor exploitation, whereas the patchy location of resources favors exploration).

The exploration-exploitation trade-off can be considered equivalent to or analogous to the speed-accuracy trade-off. Investing more time and effort in searching for alternatives generally leads to better information and improved decision-making. However, the drawback of spending more time and effort on exploration is that it diminishes the speed of decision-making and reduces the resources available for exploiting existing solutions.

This exploration-exploitation trade-off manifests concretely in natural foraging behaviors, where evolution has shaped optimal search strategies through millions of years of natural selection. Interestingly, in nature, the random walk is not the optimal foraging and search strategy, but rather the Lévy flight.

This means that a random walk with steps following a fat-tailed distribution that combines local exploitation of nearby resources with exploration of distant resource patches is optimal. This applies to how marine predators search for prey like sharks, tuna, and sea turtles, birds searching for nests or food, or honeybees during nectar collection. These situations have in common sparsely distributed resources with a search area that is relatively large with respect to the searcher's detection range[236].

Sniper Rifles or Machine Guns

A sniper, especially a skilled one, typically aims to take down a target with a single bullet. While the objective may be grim, the precision rifle of a sniper proves to be highly efficient in specific battle scenarios. However, this tactic is not always the most effective. In dynamic combat situations, where targets move unpredictably and conditions rapidly change, extreme precision becomes less valuable than adaptability and rapid response. This can be observed in movies and in real battles (although I cannot speak with authority on the second), where a wide array of weapons are employed.

A similar principle applies to diverse project management practices. In some organizations, even a minor adjustment to the baseline end date can trigger a political drama with extensive documentation, presentations, and meetings. While these ceremonies do not alter the underlying reality (i.e., the lateness, which is essentially an update in the end-date estimate), they serve as social instruments for assigning blame, shame, and as some believe, as a learning mechanism for past mistakes. They also implicitly communicate the message that estimates should account for higher percentiles of uncertainty. In such environments, estimates should be conservative, never relying on the average estimate. Conversely, I can imagine an ideal organization acknowledging that uncertainty and change are inherent to complex projects. In these environments, stakeholders should focus less on assigning blame and more on adapting to emerging challenges, treating estimate adjustments as valuable feedback rather than failures. In such case, senior management should recognize and absorb estimate uncertainty, recognizing that projects involving uncertain requirements, new technologies, or new teams often require the necessary exploratory work.

When optimizing in an uncertain environment, we can choose to employ tight yet biased a priori estimates, or embrace the unknown uncertainties. Like the trade-off between sniper rifles and machine guns, some decisions entail a bias-variance trade-off. In fact, the bias-variance trade-off can be viewed as a generalization of the exploration-exploitation trade-off. During exploitation, we rely on our a priori information, which introduces a bias rooted in the known past. On the other hand, exploration embraces an uncertain future, welcoming variance and serendipity, likely helping us to identify the real goal and the best approach at the expense of time and results uncertainty.

It's worth noting that the term "variance" can be misleading, as it may not even exist or may not be accurately measurable in many real-world problems beyond the realms of physics and statistics textbooks. Some problems exhibit fat-tailed distributions, and in others, the set of future possibilities isn't even known. These situations are common in domains such as stock markets, project management, and warfare. Nevertheless, the term "bias-variance trade-off" continues to capture our imagination.

Lindy's Law

Friendship is like wine: it can mature into something exquisite over time, turn bitter with neglect, or spoil beyond salvaging. Why do we keep and nurture some friends while others fade? What is the secret to curate these relationships?

Lindy's Law, or the Lindy effect, is a conjecture about the life expectancy of non-perishable goods such as ideas, books, technologies, buildings, and perhaps, friends. This conjecture, popularized by Benoit Mandelbrot in 1982[142] and later by Nassim Taleb[223], suggests that the life expectancy of certain things can be estimated based on their actual lifespan. According to the Lindy effect, the longer some goods have existed, the longer they are expected to continue existing.

Time itself serves as a filtering mechanism that reduces uncertainty. Nothing else is needed to evaluate the value of some things. Yet paradoxically, in the technology sector, this principle is often overlooked in favor of pursuing novelty. People frequently choose untested new technologies over proven ones, either driven by the allure of potential breakthrough gains or perhaps due to an inherent bias toward innovation over stability. Is it because new technologies offer significant potential gains for early adopters, compensating for the likelihood of failure? Or is it that we are just too optimist or stupid?

Given the Lindy effect, why don't we make wiser choices when it comes to adopting technologies or acquiring new skills? Old technologies have passed numerous survival tests and are likely to withstand the test of time. Will we still have wheels, windows, smartphones, and Wi-Fi a hundred years from now? Of those, which things do you guess will remain? Are those the ones with the longest actual lifespan? Friendship, too, appears to follow the Lindy effect, like a tree that starts off fragile but gains strength over time.

Lindy's Law does not explain why certain things possess lasting value, but whether they are likely to last. The Law recognizes that things gain value simply because they have endured the test of time, even if we don't fully understand the reasons behind it.

Re-writing Software From Scratch

Around 2004, I found myself juggling multiple roles in Valencia: working part-time for my ingenious and stubborn father-in-law and girlfriend in Valencia (yes, it was an explosive combination), completing my degree in Economics, pursuing a career as a professional decathlete, building new software from scratch, and, of course, trying to keep my girlfriend happy. I was completely unprepared for these challenges. Looking back, it was an impossible balancing act. Although I obtained my degree, I failed in the other three aspects, with the most devastating being the personal one. Fortunately, the end of my failed relationship led me to Switzerland and eventually to my current family and job.

Professionally, it was my first attempt to rewrite an inadequate but working software system. I was a naive, overconfident young engineer with a know-it-all attitude. Several individuals within the small company relied on this software, and as it turned out, my failure to replace the old system was fortunate. What began as a failed attempt to rewrite internal software unexpectedly evolved into something more significant: after several years of development, it became the foundation for a new product line—a Laboratory Information Management System. The credit for the success belongs to the determination and boldness of my father-in-law and his daughter, who believed in the idea for several years, and, of course, to the development team that transformed the idea from a prototype into a functional product. Nonetheless, I take pride in my initial, partially-failed contribution to the project.

This happy ending should not overshadow the fact that the rewrite of the company's internal software failed. Rewriting long-standing yet imperfect software goes against Lindy's Law. Starting from scratch erases the accumulated knowledge embedded in the source code and infrastructure. It only makes sense if it is rewritten by true experts in the existing system, and even then, success is not guaranteed.

Waste

A theory is the more impressive the greater the simplicity of its premises is, the more different kinds of things it relates, and the more extended is its area of applicability. Therefore the deep impression which classical thermodynamics made upon me. It is the only physical theory of universal content concerning which I am convinced that within the framework of the applicability of its basic concepts, it will never be overthrown.

Albert Einstein, Autobiographical Notes, 1979.

During my daily battle against entropy—tidying up scattered toys, organizing papers, washing endless dishes, and managing overflowing emails—I am constantly reminded of the profound wisdom contained in the Laws of Thermodynamics. I find Einstein's quote fascinating, although I realize that comprehending his admiration for this fundamental milestone in physics may be beyond my reach.

Why does thermodynamics appear both deep and simple from Albert Einstein's perspective? Speculating on the thoughts of a physicist of Einstein's stature is pretentious and naive. Still, I am fascinated by the intriguing simplicity and common sense conveyed by the first and second laws of thermodynamics [25].

The First Law of Thermodynamics (also known as the Law of Conservation of Energy) states that energy cannot be created or destroyed in an isolated

---

[25] In addition to the first and second laws of Thermodynamics, there are the zeroth and the third laws. The zeroth law establishes the existence of the temperature measurement while the third law sets a minimum absolute value for the temperature at 0 Kelvin when the entropy also reaches its minimum or ground state.

system. It can be transformed from one form to another-work into light, light into electricity, electricity into heat, and so on—but it is impossible to create energy from nothing or to destroy it altogether. Thus, the creation of a machine that produces work without energy input is not feasible. In other words, there is no free lunch in nature; if something happens, it is because some energy has been spent.

The Second Law of Thermodynamics (also known as the Law of Increasing Entropy) states that the availability of useful energy (also referred to as exergy or free energy) always diminishes. It is impossible to create a machine that continually extracts energy from the environment. Therefore, perfect efficiency is unattainable, and all processes generate irreversible waste. It is not just that any lunch has a cost, but it always costs more to produce than its actual energy content. This means you should never come across a "meal" for sale priced lower than its production cost. Google, Facebook, or Twitter do not provide free services, cheap McDonald's burgers or Zara clothes are not truly cheap, and likewise, clean air and water are not free—someone or something is paying the price. The price of consumer goods, specially when they are free, does not reflect its true cost.

Learning the rudimentary principles of thermodynamics is like learning from our parents that we need to pay for things such as water, light, clothes, and rent through our jobs and daily chores. It is obviously true, but as a child, I never liked the idea and somehow magically managed to not believe my parents. From my point of view, my parents were effortlessly waking up, going to work, and keeping up with the daily chores without effort. Now, as a parent myself, reality has hit home: every morning I witness firsthand the energy cost of maintaining order against chaos—from preparing breakfast to managing homework, from cleaning spills to resolving sibling disputes. My father, from his grave, and my mother, during her visits, stand vindicated as they watch my perpetual struggle against disorder. I still wait for the day when waking up in the morning will become as easy as it appears in those YouTube videos where influencers showcase their mindful morning routines.

These two laws establish physical limits to our capacity for action. It is impossible to act without energy (including materials, work, heat, fuel, etc.), and every action generates irreversible waste, especially when kids play, fight, cry, or shout at each other.

This chapter will be a deep dive into some interesting applications of the

Laws of Thermodynamics, including the waste associated with sorting my children's toys, the best climate change mitigation strategy, a non-edulcorated view of recycling, and finally, a comment on the famous Philip B. Crosby's "Quality is free" motto.

Toys, Wine, Water, and Oil

"Stop right there, princesses! No TV until this mess disappears," I called out desperately, watching them freeze mid-sprint toward the remote control, their eyes already glazing over in anticipation of screen-induced bliss.

"Galo did it! I'm not going to do it!"

"No, Corso did it!" At that moment, I found myself contemplating two absurd solutions: either install surveillance cameras worthy of a maximum-security prison to solve these daily mysteries, or track down Doc Brown and his DeLorean to prevent a couple of romantic evenings with Bego—an obviously irrational thought, yet one that stubbornly remains in my mental catalogue of impossible fixes.

I should not explain that to my kids, but in the grand scheme of things, both the act of sorting and the one of disordering toys contribute to an increase in entropy. There is not much difference to the universe. Any of the two acts finally waste the precious solar radiation thrown to us from the Sun's fusion reaction after traveling 150 million kilometers. What a waste. However, as most people, I'm concerned about the former, the toys, the dust, the furniture, and so on. Ultimately, both actions add to the overall entropy of the universe, both approaching us to the universe death. It's a common misconception to conflate macroscopic disorder, such as the mess created by my children, with the concept of entropy increase. Sorting out toys also involves irreversible energy waste. This waste includes the expenditure of fat, glucose, and ATP when muscles move and the brain coordinates the sorting task. The energy is eventually dissipated as environmental heat, at a rate similar to that of a light bulb being returned to the stars as infrared radiation. This increase in heat, in the movement of molecules, represents the ultimate destination of the free energy. This heat close to the ambient temperature cannot be further recycled.

A classic example that is widely understood is the irreversible mixing of water and wine, or in my youth, the mixture of wine and coke to create calimotxo, an obnoxious cheap beverage to get drank in parties. The resulting mixture is clearly more disordered, with no easy way to separate the water and wine. However, an equal increase in entropy occurs when we mix water and oil. From a macroscopic viewpoint, the final state appears more ordered, with the oil floating on top and the water settling at the bottom. However, the truth is that the macroscopic ordering is outweighed by the equalization of molecular movement and the generation of heat by the new mixture. Entropy always win.

In fact, all processes, even those that appear more ordered, contribute to an increase in entropy. A notable example being the metabolism of living organisms. Although they exhibit intricate arrangements of matter, each step of their metabolic processes, at all levels, generates more entropy and waste. In a sense, life acts as a mechanism to accelerate thermodynamic reactions, and humans, along with their technology, represent the latest advancements aiding thermodynamics to accelerate its course [203], our contribution to the universe end. It is like biological and cultural evolution have been designed by the God (or Devil) of Thermodynamics, accelerating the death of the universe[53,64].

Solar Panels and Carbon Footprint

> *Even the most ardent environmentalist doesn't really want to stop pollution. If he thinks about it, he wants the right amount of pollution. We can't really afford to eliminate it—not without abandoning all the benefits of technology that we not only enjoy but on which we depend.*

> *Milton Friedman, There's No Such Thing as a Free Lunch, 1977.*

"Electric cars are the future. They are environmentally friendly," someone exclaims from time to time. It seems that some people think they can save the planet simply by using their credit cards. However, the true meaning of saving the planet is still an open question, as the planet will persist regardless. The fate of humanity remains uncertain though.

Generally speaking, for those grounded in reality, spending more money likely implies that greater energy, work, and resources went to its production, and therefore, by the inexorable Laws of Thermodynamics, more waste is generated, too. The quintessential ecological advocate resembles a resourceful beggar utilizing scraps, not someone driving an electric car dressed in eco-responsible attire, feasting on vegan pesticide-free food, and living in a minimalistic carbon neutral homestead.

The green energy sector presents a comparable conundrum. At first glance, solar panels are championed as a "renewable" and "green" energy source. Yet, the construction and operation of these panels, among other technologies, cannot escape the Laws of Thermodynamics and Engineering. What kind of waste results from the creation of wind turbines or solar panels? Can we even manufacture these panels without using fossil fuels? More specifically, is it feasible to construct trucks, shipping containers, airplanes, or cement factories powered exclusively by electricity given the significant difference in energy storage density? Even if we massively invest in solar and wind power, how will we store these intermittent energy sources to provide a continuous and on-demand flow like the one provided by fossil fuels and nuclear sources? [210]

Today, with the mounting concerns surrounding the greenhouse effect, the carbon footprint stands out as a pivotal waste metric (though water and energy consumption are also gaining traction). In the realm of electricity generation, this metric captures the direct and indirect carbon dioxide (CO_2) emissions linked to the operation, construction, and eventual decommissioning of a power plant.

For example, a 2011 report by the UK Parliamentary Office of Science and Technology gauged the carbon footprints of various electricity generation techniques [204]. As the Laws of Thermodynamics would suggest, all technologies incur waste—even renewable ones. That said, electricity sourced from fossil fuels has 2 to 40 times the CO_2 emissions of photovoltaic, geothermal, wind, nuclear, or hydroelectric alternatives. Renewable energies aren't flawless; they're just less wasteful. A magnificent illustration of the above is given by Vaclav Smil in *How the World Really Works*[211]:

> *No structures are more obvious symbols of "green" electricity generation than large wind turbines—but these enormous accumulations of steel, cement, and plastics are also embodiments of fossil fuels. Their foundations are reinforced concrete, their towers,*

nacelles, and rotors are steel (altogether nearly 200 tons of it for every megawatt of installed generating capacity), and their massive blades are energy-intensive—and difficult to recycle—plastic resins (about 15 tons of them for a midsize turbine). All of these giant parts must be brought to the installation sites by outsized trucks and erected by large steel cranes, and turbine gearboxes must be repeatedly lubricated with oil. Multiplying these requirements by the millions of turbines that would be needed to eliminate electricity generated from fossil fuels shows how misleading any talks are about the coming dematerialization of green economies.

Throughout our lives, we both consume and generate waste. A better, second-best ecological policy, following the one advocated by Thanos, the Marvel supervillain, champions the lifestyles of vagabonds, loafers, and other less industrious workers—a perspective seldom discussed.

In developed economies, it's time we reconsidered traveling, commuting, the amount and types of gifts we give to our children, the food we eat, the houses we build and renew, and so on. That means curbing our consumption—even if items are stamped as bio, renewable, organic, local, or eco-friendly. The most ecological consumption is the one that does not happen. Unfortunately, such a policy is as unpopular as the most effective diet: reducing food intake. They are simple, understandable, and uncontroversial methods that neither experts nor laypersons particularly fancy.

Recycling

Since we moved to Commugny, a small village between Geneva and Lausanne, my children have developed a love for recycling. Regrettably, this isn't due to exceptional parenting skills or their teacher's persuasive superpowers; it's more about finding toys in recycling bins and discovering that someone else's garbage can be another person's treasure, like a beloved teddy bear or roller blades. This enthusiasm wasn't always present. In the past, I, like my mother and friends, struggled sorting garbage into the different containers. It shouldn't be so difficult, right? Yet, I confess, I have mixed plastics with paper, paper with metals, metals with glass, and organic with everything else. Visiting the impollute recycling center, known as the "Déchetterie," and receiving the patient and polite advice from the people working there has substantially increased my recycling skills.

I recall the time I brought my mother to the Déchetterie during Christmas. There happened to be a Christmas buffet there with wine and other Swiss delicacies. Have you ever encountered a free buffet at a waste disposal facility? I wonder if Roy, the Blade Runner Nexus-6 replicant, experienced such a thing in his eventful life across the solar system. You can find it here in Commugny, close to my home in Switzerland. I still remember Pili's expression as she enjoyed a glass of wine while throwing the trash in each specific container.

It was all that, but I'm sure the taxed garbage bags also helped on steer our family towards recycling [26].

Recycling is not just important in human affairs, but it has also been one of Nature's keys for several billions of years. Even if God exists, she must have faced challenges in designing the nearly perfect recycling machine known as Earth's biosphere. Who could be against recycling? It clearly works in nature. If you are against recycling, chances are you might be a bad person, too. Jokes aside, if you are against recycling, it's best to keep it to yourself, especially when it comes to your kids and their teachers.

The reality is that recycling has been a common practice throughout human history. There is evidence of its existence even during pre-industrial times, and it has become particularly relevant during times of war due to financial constraints and material shortages. However, not all societies have deemed recycling to be useful as there is an economic and technological trade-off involved.

As mentioned earlier, any physical process requires energy and is inherently imperfect. So, how does recycling compare to other garbage disposal methods like incineration and landfilling? What is its impact?

Extensive research has been conducted on this topic [25] and producing materials from recycled resources often (though not always) consumes less

---

[26]Despite its tidy and spotless déchèterie, and admirable recycling culture, Switzerland still ranks among the world's most wasteful countries. While not reaching the levels of the US or Kuwait, its per capita waste places it alongside other surprising "green" giants like New Zealand, Norway, and Canada. Interestingly, Spain produces considerably less waste per person than Switzerland, showcasing a less "green" but less wasteful approach. Yet, even Spain's waste output significantly surpasses that of other less developed countries, underscoring the link between economic development, consumerism, and waste generation.

energy and has a lower global warming impact compared to using virgin resources. Nevertheless, our current society does not prioritize recycling. For non-renewable materials like glass, metals, and plastics, the savings achieved through recycling are significant, which makes their more widespread use essential. In the case of paper products, despite being widely recognized for recycling, the energy savings are comparatively smaller; both recycling and incineration of paper are similarly energy-efficient and less energy-intensive, and therefore have a lower global warming impact, than landfilling, one of the worst environmental options.

Recycling creates waste, too. It just turns out that the quantity of waste is smaller than that of the remaining alternatives.

Fix the Chair

"Even if you think you're only going to stay for a couple of months in a house, don't keep a broken chair. Now, it is your home and you never know how long you'll end up staying. Over time, you'll keep seeing the broken chair, thinking it's just a temporary situation. Some years later you will see the chair again and you will wonder why you have not fixed it yet." A solid and life-tested piece of advice from my wife's school principal before she took a long-term leave to become a Swiss immigrant with me. Although the advice relates to physical possessions, I believe it has a wide application, including feelings and relationships.

It is a thermodynamic fact that things decay over time. Whether it's a sofa exposed to three children and a dog, dishes that fall or break, t-shirts with holes, my own face and body, or the relationships with my wife or friends, everything undergoes wear and tear. Even my F-91 broke and I had to replace it. But why should you hurry to fix them? Why is a just-in-time approach to fixing your stuff better than a lazy and cheap one (e.g., batching the fixes once a month or a year or at some point in the future, a distant future sometimes)?

This tendency for the cost of disorder to grow more than proportionally is what I call the combinatorial power of a mess. Although from a mechanistic perspective time is reversible, from a thermodynamic perspective it is not. Time has a direction like an arrow pointing forward, never backward, and it doesn't allow broken cups to be miraculously recomposed after breaking into pieces. The arrow of time could be understood as a consequence of there being more bad combinations than good ones. "More" here means combinatorially more and more (i.e., there is a factorial component in the ratio between the two possible types of combinations).

For example, in a two-element system like a pen and its cap, there are only two correct positions within the whole continuum of possible positions in 3D space. The pen and the cap can be localized anywhere in space (i.e., $\mathbb{R}^3 \times \mathbb{R}^3$); in addition, each one can be rotated arbitrarily (i.e., an additional $\mathbb{R}^3 \times \mathbb{R}^3$ space). The space of possibilities for closing the pen has twelve degrees of freedom on an infinite space: six for the position of the cap relative to the pen and six for its rotational orientation. However, there are only two successful configurations: the cap placed on one end or on the other end. So, from the vast number of positions and orientations, only two lead to a correctly arranged pen. A three-element system, like a screw, a bolt, and a screwdriver has an additional $\mathbb{R}^3 \times \mathbb{R}^3$ continuum of possibilities, six more degrees of freedom. These infinities grow so fast that it is just unimaginable, especially given the ease with which we manipulate these objects. During some event involving a pen or a screw, there is a high probability that the components fall out of their unique correct positions. Otherwise, ask my children about the mysterious disappearance of all the colored pen caps. Where are they? How much time does it takes to find them and put them back? Once they fall out of their correct position, these objects lose their expected function, and someone has to spend time and energy putting them back in the correct position.

Have you ever had to sort and fold a sofa full of socks? Is it even possible to have a cubic meter of socks in a sofa? Anyway, how many socks does a person need, and what are the reasons behind having a sofa full of socks? Thanks to my brother, I have firsthand empirical evidence on the matter, unfortunately without a clear answer to these transcendental questions. I patiently folded them with my mother, requiring time that was more than proportional to the number of socks. It took more like a couple of days instead of an hour or two. The cost of fixing something accumulates explosively with the number of things to be fixed.

This is why we should fix things at home and at work as they appear; why stopping our exercise routines is an almost sure one-way street; why technical debt is so disastrous, entangling the source code in impossible ways; and why children as well as adults hate the effort of sorting out a mess. The cost of fixing an accumulation of broken things is not equal to the addition of their individual costs; the complexity of a mess grows explosively with its scale.

Quality is Free

Quality is similar to a pendulum swinging: when projects fall behind schedule, the pressure mounts to cut corners. Then, if a serious problem suddenly arises, the focus shifts to assigning responsibility, generating incident reports, and demanding quality improvements. Ideally, we should have an independent and robust quality criteria in place. In practice, we lack such criteria and simply follow the mood of our managers.

Philip B. Crosby, one of the pioneers of quality management in the 1970s, believed that organizations implementing sound quality management principles would realize cost savings that outweighed the expenses of the quality system. Thus, he famously claimed that "quality is free."

However, the laws of thermodynamics offer a counterpoint: true quality cannot be free. Its implementation requires resources (such as manpower, supplies, office space, new procedures, and new tools), and it cannot be perfect (as people may not fully comprehend the concepts, the implementation may not be well-suited to the problem at hand, and so on).

A more nuanced perspective is that quality assurance and control can potentially enhance the efficiency of our processes, leading to long-term savings. Nevertheless, just because something is possible does not guarantee that the benefits will materialize. The laws of thermodynamics show us that implementing Quality will undeniably consume resources and energy, and it will always be imperfect. This principle extends to the implementation of any new processes or tools.

As we will explore further, this issue remains controversial and is likely dependent on the specific details. Quality is not always free [99,100].

Reliability and Redundancy

I live in Switzerland with my wife, children, and dog, far away from our families in Spain. In secret, both my wife and I fear the day when we might both fall ill, especially if it becomes serious. We worry about what would happen to our carefully optimized life in this wonderful country, far from our families. Nevertheless, we consider ourselves fortunate, as we are not a single-parent family and we have some savings. I still remember with a bit of fear the few weeks when my wife had to be in Barcelona and I had to work and take care of the kids and the home alone. Through that experience, I realized that not enough credit and support are given to those, mostly women, who single-handedly care for their children. Our current lifes in the city, far away from nature, with nuclear and many times single-parent families are one of the biggest mistakes of our times. Surrounded by crowds of people, we are alone.

In our case, we are, happily, two parents rather than just one, following one of the principles of reliability—the duplication of critical components. When a system has duplicate components performing the same function, the components—my wife and I—are said to be redundant. Increasing the number of redundant motors in an airplane, the number of servers or computers in a computing cluster, or the number of people in a team, enhances the reliability of these systems.

Redundancy is not only a characteristic of many engineered systems but also a primary attribute of living organisms that have evolved over time. We have two lungs, two eyes, two hands and feet with five fingers each, and so on. Moreover, biological systems possess a significant amount of extra capacity. Put simply, in addition to redundancy, biological systems have been designed with a safety margin like that of well-engineered bridges and buildings. We can survive for extended periods without certain basic nutrients, and adapt to a wide range of air qualities and temperatures. Moreover, biological systems exhibit a distinctive property of functional degeneracy, where the same function can be achieved through different means. For instance, a blind person relies on their hearing, sense of touch, and can sometimes use echolocation to partially compensate for the lack of sight. Our bodies can metabolize carbohydrates, fats, and proteins, and our fingers can adapt when one of them is lost, or even use those on our feet [27].

The mathematics of redundancy is well-known and straightforward. If one component can fail with a probability p, then a system composed of two redundant components will fail with a smaller probability of p^2. Both components would need to fail simultaneously for the system to fail. Adding additional redundancy exponentially reduces the probability of failure of all the components at the same time. For example, if I have two phones, each with an individual failure probability of 1% over a year, their joint failure probability would be 0.01%.

Interestingly, as a consequence of increasing redundancy, the probability of partial failures increases linearly with the number of components ($1 - (1 - p)^N \approx Np$). This means that as the level of redundancy increases, the system is always in a state of partial failure. This concept reminds me of the ongoing logistical effort involved in managing my three kids and dog. There is always something to be done—arranging new passports or identity cards, visiting doctors, dentists, or the veterinarian, buying clothes and food, meeting the teachers, bringing the kids to some birthday party, paying bills, and so on. I can't help but wonder how my life would be with five or ten kids.

Fortunately, my wife rarely falls ill, and even without relying on our respective mothers, who live far away from us, we survive. Nonetheless, we still miss having them close.

In this chapter, we will explore some interesting aspects of reliability and redundancy, including the concept of chain-link logic, representing availability as downtime per year, the theoretical availability we are providing to our children and some limitations of any such estimation, why Boeing chose to

---

[27] Curiously enough, although redundancy and safety margins are well-known and used in engineering, degeneracy is not. It is a most surprising fact given its proven usefulness across evolutionary times.

have two engines instead of one, three, or four in commercial airplanes, the limitations of Linus' Law and N-version design, and some of the limitations of redundancy.

Chain-Link Logic and Trash Bins

One morning while walking to the school with my kids, I was astonished while watching an elderly lady diligently cleaning the traffic sign in front of her house in Commugny. She was cleaning the sign as if it were just another routine chore for her. Equally amazing is the pristine cleanliness of the streets, parks, and forests in Switzerland, despite the scarcity of trash bins on the streets.

In a similar vein, it is surprising to see that all the public furniture is well-maintained, unlike when I was living in Igualada. There I witnessed a 20 cm thick granite bench broken after being installed a few weeks before. How does one manage to break a bench made of 20 cm thick granite? It would require considerable effort and possibly tools. Why would someone expend all that energy on such a mischievous feat?

More generally, what factors contribute to some countries appearing cleaner, more organized, and more productive than others? Are higher salaries the key? Is there less inequality? Are the citizens better educated? Are the politicians more trustworthy? Do higher or lower taxes play a role? Are the elderly actively involved in cleaning and maintenance tasks? Do they have other responsibilities? What is the secret ingredient for a well-organized country?

Everyone has different theories about the origins of these differences between countries. But what if there isn't a single reason? What if this perceived well-being follows a chain-link logic?

What happens with systems composed of several necessary but non-redundant components? Such systems follow a chain-link logic, the opposite of a redundant system. Similar to a chain, if any of the links break, the chain loses its function. The failure probability for a system composed of N non-redundant components, like a chain, is $(1 - (1 - p)^N \approx Np)$. The failure probability increases proportionally to the number of components because nothing should fail for the system to work. In other words, for the same level of reliability, a system with ten times more components requires ten times higher reliability per component. This is analogous to when we have to go out together, and all the kids need to be clean and dressed before leaving-it can be a small nightmare. You cannot go out with one of the kids naked and filthy, even if sometimes you can threaten them to do so.

It takes only one vandal or litterer to degrade a neighborhood; conversely, for a neighborhood, a city, or a country to thrive, the entire population must be well-educated, polite, and respectful of others and the law. A small number of individuals can break the chain.

Reliability and Downtime

"Why did we just achieve 99.78% uptime of the services? Last month was close to 99.92% instead" One senior manager inquired after showing the graph from the last two years.

"Well, we deployed new versions of the software a couple more times and we had a regression, too. The difference between last month and this month is around one additional hour of uptime".

"One hour? I thought it was more!?"

"It is quite a lot, but our deployment process requires us to stop all services during deployment. Perhaps we can spend a bit of time improving our deployment process."

"What? No, don't waste your time just for one hour. Nobody notices."

What is the true significance of a specified level of reliability? If we define reliability as the probability that a system operates correctly, an effective way to grasp this probability is to consider the amount of time that the system must function without issues. Looking at reliability numbers from this perspective is a simple and eye-opening experience.

Table 7: Downtime in percentage and its approximate correspondence in time. The table sacrifices precision for clarity and easy memorization. The times in *italic*, 10 min and below, indicate the impossibility of human intervention within the given time to recover. Therefore. the intervention should be automatic in these cases.

Downtime [%]	per year	per month	per day
90%	40 days	3 days	2 h
99%	4 days	10 h	*10 min*
99.9%	10 h	1 h	*1 min*
99.99%	1 h	*6 min*	*6 s*
99.999%	*6 min*	*30 s*	*<1 s*
99.9999%	*30 s*	*3 s*	*<0.1 s*

As an individual, I'm sick less than 4 days a year (99%). However, combined with my wife and acting like a redundant system, we should be at the 99.99% reliability level, or even higher because my wife hardly gets sick. So far, it has been true; we have never gotten seriously sick both at the same time. My kids and dog, Patxi, should be satisfied customers, on average, they lose their adult services only 1 hour per year. Unfortunately, I cannot count on my mom as she is in Spain. Otherwise, we could be providing a 99.9999% service to them, an incredible 30 seconds a year, an engineering feat. At least in theory.

Nuclear Families and Fault Tolerance

"Why don't we buy a farm to live all together?" Vane half-jokingly proposed. At first sight, it seemed like one of her lovely impractical and crazy ideas. However, these large properties offer a low cost per square meter, and besides, what is better: a familiar friend or an unknown neighbor? We were good friends in a similar phase of life: spaniards living in Geneva for the last ten or more years, her husband was also and IT geek starting a new job, and we both had kids of a similar age. Most importantly, we all felt relatively isolated in Switzerland, far from our extended families, with friends scattered across the globe.

I believe this is not only a phenomenon experienced by immigrants (some of them called expatriates to give them a more romantic and higher-status allure) but also a recognized demographic shift that started during the early industrialization era of the seventeenth and eighteenth centuries and has recently intensified throughout the 20th and 21st centuries. Even though we reside in big cities surrounded by other humans, we often don't truly know them. The number of extended family members living together in the same house, village, or neighborhood has steadily decreased. This phenomenon, coupled with the reduced number of children per family and the increased longevity of people, is catapulting us to the 4-2-1 families (i.e., 4 grandparents, 2 parents, and 1 child). Our children will face extreme loneliness, without either siblings or cousins; they will be isolated, working in another city or country, far away from their only remaining family, who are growing old. All these relatives will leave behind a substantial inheritance—one our children will enjoy alone.

This move towards solitude also entails an additional challenge.

As is well known in the theory of fault tolerant systems, a fault-tolerant system requires at least four members, not just two or even three for redundancy, because one of the members could be unwell or even manipulative. The implications are clear. We need at least four family members who can communicate with each other and compare their versions of events to uncover the truth. If we only had two or three family members, it would be difficult to determine who is manipulating the situation [28]. Have you ever tried to find out who is telling the truth between two kids? You need at least four observers. Three children are not enough.

Analogously, it is a wise and natural practice to establish connections with multiple individuals within a group. This protects us against harmful individuals and situations. Have you ever had a boss who prevented you from communicating with senior management or colleagues from other departments? Or a subordinate who withheld information from both their peers and subordinates? Don't let them have that control over you; open side channels to resolve the uncertainty as a fault-tolerant system. You need at least three connections to each of the groups you belong to. After all, it's also more fun.

---

[28]In general, a group containing f manipulating sociopaths cannot have less than $3f + 1$ members. Otherwise, it is not possible to find out who the toxic elements are. For a more detailed explanation in the context of distributed systems, the reading of *Reaching agreement in the presence of faults* is highly recommended [171].

Durability of Cloud Storage

You can read the following sales pitch in the documentation of a famous cloud storage provider:

> *Our cloud storage solution [...] are all designed to provide 99.999999999% durability of objects over a given year, is. This durability level corresponds to an average annual expected loss of 0.000000001% of objects. For example, if you store 10,000,000 objects, you can on average expect to incur a loss of a single object once every 10,000 years.*

The durability figures presented by the cloud-based storage provider are indeed impressive. However, it is equally important to understand how they were calculated and what they really mean.

In another section of the same webpage, it is mentioned that the objects stored are automatically distributed across multiple devices spanning at least three data centers. From this, it can be inferred that the cloud provider considers each of their data centers an independent failure domain, assuming there is no common cause that can affect the three data centers at the same time. This implies that the total failure probability can be estimated simply by multiplying the failure probabilities as p^N, where p is the failure probability of an individual device and N is the number of redundant copies of the storage.

Based on this assumption, if we further assume an annual failure rate of approximately 0.1% for the population of storage devices (i.e., one of every 1000 devices fails in a given year), then theoretically, having just three redundant copies of the storage would result in a 99.999999999% durability. It might seem a solid and conclusive argument, but is it?

The claim of 99.999999999% durability means that, on average, over the course of one year the storage provider will lose only one of every billion objects, or from an inverted perspective, one specific object will be lost after an average of 100 billion years. This time frame is equivalent to more than 20 times the age of the solar system. Such an extraordinary duration casts doubt on the feasibility of the claim, although to their credit, they never express it this way.This absurd statistical statement is similar to the claim made by Goldman Sachs CFO David Viniar in August 2008, when Goldman's flagship GEO hedge fund lost 27% of its value since the start of the year due to what he described as "25-standard-deviation moves, several days in a row." This either indicates a lack of probability theory knowledge or some doubtful moral intentions behind the claim. I'm not sure which scenario is worse.

Similar skepticism should be applied to the previous section discussing our theoretical 99.99% parental reliability. In our lifetimes, it is almost certain that my wife and I will be unavailable for our children for a relatively extensive period of time (e.g., more than a day). Hence, achieving 99.99% parental availability is highly unlikely, and certainly not desirable. We could get sick together, have a car accident, travel together without them thanks to my mother's and sister's goodwill, be working at the same time, or we can simply be taking a coffee in Tanay without phone coverage.

To gain a broader perspective on these high reliability figures, we can also consider the probability of natural existential threats like meteorites, supervolcanos, or extreme solar flares. The likelihood of such natural events occurring, which could affect the humans maintaining the cloud infrastructure, electrical network, production facilities, etc., is estimated to be around one event every 100 million years [28]. The occurrence of a major extinction event approximately 65 million years ago caused by a meteorite slightly larger than the Lac Léman, serves as a reference point. It is interesting to note that these natural existential threats are far less frequent than the implied durability estimates from the above cloud provider.

If we take into account the past nuclear war close calls, the expected time between these catastrophes is reduced by several orders of magnitude to approximately one event every 100 or 1,000 years, and this is quite optimistic given the large historical record of nuclear close calls [29]. This does not even consider the more unknown threats of artificial superintelligence, pandemics caused by globalization and bioengineering research, or unchecked nanotechnology research, to name the most cited ones.

Furthermore, we can also consider a less catastrophic scenario of a coordinated cyber or physical attack on all data centers. How unlikely is such an event? Or assuming that the cloud provider technology is beyond any doubt, how long will the cloud provider continue to exist as a company? It is unlikely that it will outlast institutions like the Catholic Church, but will it last longer

---

[29]See for example the list on wikipedia, the pessimistic account in [196], or the more optimistic review in [227].

than Coca-cola or Nestle (we could apply Lindy's Law here)?

Given these considerations, how should we interpret the durability figures from the cloud provider? While it is important to acknowledge the excellent service they provide, it is also reasonable to question the numbers they present.

Failure of the Weakest Link

"Can you pass me the salt?" I asked my father-in-law while starting to cook the paella.

"We didn't bring it. All rented houses have it," he confidently assumed.

"And the oil? It is difficult to find groceries on Sunday..." I said, a bit annoyed and mischievously humorous about my father-in-law's oversight.

"Let me look for it," he replied, and immediately started swearing while opening cabinets and drawers with an increasing infrasonic roar. "It should be around here!! All kitchens have oil." Unless they don't. Nobody thought about the salt or the oil, but all the other ingredients.

A paella day without salt and oil (or without a pan or fire) is not a paella day anymore. This illustrates a fundamental principle of system reliability: Like cloud-based datacenters being hit by a planet-killer asteroid, all complex systems always have common failure modes or some kind of weak link. They look extremely robust and reliable, but they aren't. Most dishes can be made in different ways (degeneracy) except if some key ingredient is missing. We could have organized ourselves and arranged for several people to bring the salt and oil, but we didn't. However, in this fictitious universe of families of perfect planners, where I don't belong, something else could have happened, including bad weather, a heart attack, a car accident, or a nasty argument between family members.

For example, during the design phase of an airplane, the engineers could decide to build a redundant control system to compute the movements of the flight control surfaces (e.g. ailerons, flaps, air brakes, etc.). The redundant control system could send and receive the information to a voting system which selects the most common ones to the actuators and computing elements. Once the engineers finish the design of the redundant control system, they look at their work and rest satisfied. They might think that they can reduce at will the probability of control system failure.

But then the plane starts flying. What is the real probability of failure? Unfortunately, even with a perfectly reliable control system, the overall reliability will never be better than that of the one of the voting system, and especially, the power distribution. Redundancy has diminishing returns imposed by the least reliable of the components.

In order to improve the reliability of a system, the weakest element of the chain should be identified and used as the basis for our design choices and calculations. In a sense, redundancy is more a means to fix reliability problems for a non-reliable component than a way to infinitely improve the reliability of the system as a whole. Redundancy does not increase the overall reliability beyond the limits of common failure modes. So, don't over-engineer a solution—sometimes it does not help.

Linus's Law

"Marc! Watch out!" Bego shouted.

"Ow, ow, owwww." Galo started to cry after falling on his head. Why should he use his hands when he could cushion the fall with the big ball between his ears?

"I thought you were watching," I said as she pierced me with her wife's gamma-ray-like vision.

A similar, yet more predictable, situation unfolded when I optimistically tasked my autistic daughter with keeping an eye on her 2-year-old brother while we were shopping. Moments later, my younger kid had already vanished among the racks of women's skirts and sweaters.

This pattern of ineffective oversight relates to Eric Steven Raymond essay *The Cathedral and the Bazaar*[185], where he paid tribute to Linus Torvalds, the creator and principal developer of the Linux kernel, and the open source software movement by stating that "given enough eyeballs, all bugs are shallow." In other words, with a large number of people watching closely for software bugs, nearly every software problem will be identified quickly, and the solution will become apparent to someone. Thus, according to the theory, open source software development is meant to dominate.

Unfortunately, as Robert Glass points out in *Facts and Fallacies of Software Engineering*[83], "there is no empirical data to validate Linus's Law. Research on software inspections suggests that as the number of inspectors increases, the rate of bug discovery diminishes rapidly, with the curve flattening at around 2 to 4 peers."

Although inspections and peer reviews are cost-effective, the process of finding issues in source code has diminishing returns as the number of people reviewing the code increases. Most likely, as the number of people increases, there is also a dilution of responsibility and an actual reduction in the issues found. This has been extensively studied in the case of the Bystander Effect, the tendency of people to be less likely to offer help or assistance to a person in need when they are in the presence of a group compared to when they are alone [72]. Additional eye balls could worsen the situation as everybody thinks that someone else will take care of the problem.

Similarly, in the context of software development teams, the dilution of responsibility can be observed between software development and IT operations. This problem has been tackled by creating what are called DevOps teams. These teams are composed of both software development and IT operations members. The problem is solved by creating teams with one unique goal: deliver high quality software to the customers. This new structure prevents the creation of gaps between these two different teams and, in principle, some problems disappear (e.g. persistent performance issue in production not reproducible in the development environment, lack of performance and stress testing, changes working in development environment but not in production, etc.) [115,116]. This idea has been further extended to DevSecOps, including Information Security representatives, and then even further to product delivery teams, including a product owner or one or more customer representative.

N-Version Software and Common Faults

"An eOrganization task force has been launched to address this complex and critical matter." The history of this and similar initiatives likely began and ended at this point. Senior management was satisfied because they had shifted the actual decision-making and its associated risks to an external group of experts, much like the n-version engineering design approach relies on multiple independent designs. The experts were left to dive into the intricacies of the problem without wasting senior management's precious and limited time and attention. Finally, the problem itself was happily left alone in the limbo between the two, bothering some other people. However, just as evidence suggests that different design teams often share common failure modes, it's likely this task force, despite its diverse expertise, might fall prey to similar groupthink pitfalls and not achieve true independence in their solutions.

Sometimes, a task force or committee seems like a promising idea. Isn't it obvious that N minds working together should reach better solutions than a single one? You gather a group of highly motivated and intelligent experts, assign them a specific goal, and expect them to think and eventually produce a recommendation, solution, strategy, architecture, or something similar. It seems obvious, but is it true?

A committee of experts resembles the n-version or multi-version design methodology, which advocates for employing a voting system with several independent designs. The idea behind this approach is that different designs will have independent failure modes, allowing for aggregating the results to create a more reliable system (at a proportionally higher cost).

However, evidence on multi-design methodologies shows that failure modes across different design teams are not truly independent [34,62,126]. It should come as no surprise that the n-version design methodology has its limitations. The presence of common and persistent errors and misconceptions among politicians, historians, scientists, engineers, or any type of experts is not an exception but rather the path along which progress is made. In other words, exploration inherently carries an unavoidable difficulty and requires unique insights, many times coming from individually gifted people, not from groups. But when is it a good idea to entrust a fundamental problem to a group of people?

Similar to the limitations of Linus's Law and the n-version design methodology, the empirical evidence on group decision-making has also shown its strengths and weaknesses. Groups perform better on well-structured, closed problems, within a shared domain of expertise. However, group brainstorming and information sharing tend to be less effective than the same processes used by individuals or nominal groups (i.e., groups of individuals who work alone and then share the solutions)[114,168,246]. Perhaps the most interesting part of the research is the realization that human collective intelligence is most effective when the task at hand can be done in parallel, when people do not block each other, when it is modular. That is, although psycho-social factors like free-riding, social loafing, or bias sharing are important, the most important factor is related to the task structure. This helps to explain why designing a system, brainstorming, writing a book, moral reasoning, or inventing a new mathematical theory work best for individuals, while quiz games and puzzles, problem and solution analysis, or formal procedures and checklists are better performed by groups.

The Problem of Redundancy Problem and the Dangers of Child Care

Redundancy like any other technique is not a silver bullet. As Scott D. Sagan highlights in *The Problem of Redundancy Problem*[195], there are several ways in which redundancy can go wrong and even backfire.

Firstly, adding redundancy to a system can increase its complexity. Efforts to enhance safety and security through redundant safety devices may unintentionally lead to more frequent system failures. This is known as the "normal accident" theory.

It is akin to trying to improve your children's education by providing them with a tablet, a phone, toys, judo and violin lessons, additional homework, and enrolling them in an international school with Chinese and English immersion programs. While all these things may seem interesting and educational, how often have you observed your kids being more fascinated with the toy boxes rather than the toys themselves? Have you ever noticed how your kids become less troublesome after moving from indoors to outdoors? Sometimes, it feels like we make things unnecessarily complex. More is eventually too much.

Secondly, as we have already explained in the case of the nuclear close call and the cloud provider durability figures, there are common mode failures to consider. For example, Boeing's analysis of modern jet engine reliability revealed that each additional aircraft engine increased the likelihood of the redundant engine keeping the plane in the air. However, it also raised the probability that a single engine failure could lead to an accident, such as starting a fire that destroys all the other engines. As the number of redundant components increased, the probability of partial failure increased too, eventually leading to a catastrophic one. As a result, Boeing determined that placing two engines on the Boeing 777, rather than three or more engines like other long-range aircraft, would result in a lower risk of serious accidents.

Similarly, if I fall sick, it's not improbable that my kids or my wife will fall sick, too. We are close to each other and the virus or bacteria can be passed along. If I ask my mother for help, a similar thing can happen and she may catch it, too. This is a common mode failure of family operations.

Thirdly, as we also explained before with the diminishing returns that affect source code inspections, peer reviews, and group decision-making, the diffusion of responsibility or lack of ownership can result in "social-shrinking". This occurs when individuals or groups reduce their reliability, assuming that others will take care of the task at hand. This aspect is rarely examined in the technical literature on safety and reliability, as it primarily focuses on purely mechanical systems and does not adequately translate to complex organizations. In mechanical engineering, redundant units are typically inanimate objects unaware of each other's existence. In organizations, on the other hand, redundant units consist of individuals, groups, or agencies that are aware of each other. This awareness can significantly influence the reliability of each unit. Why should we work if another person will eventually do the job?

The practice of creating DevOps, DevSecOps, and product delivery teams, tries to reduce this dilution of responsibility phenomenon by creating teams with one common goal. Unfortunately, the approach fails when the groups do not act as a single team, each trying to set and optimize their own goals. Developers want to write code as fast as possible. Quality assurance experts and testers do not want to let any bug go undetected. Information security professionals want to prevent security breaches. IT Operations want to ensure maximum availability and minimum support and maintenance overhead. And product owners want to ship new features constantly. These goals make sense individually, but they are partially contradictory and if they are not properly integrated they will generate friction between the different groups. At the end of the day someone should help the customer. Right? In principle, once these different groups are unified they should deliver high quality services to the customers, by any means necessary.

In a different context, if I'm taking care of the kids with my mother, sister, and wife around, it might be tempting to briefly look away assuming that there are enough adults present. Someone else should be taking care of them. The increased number of adults would not necessarily improve the safety of the kids.

Lastly, redundancy can be counterproductive not only due to the dilution of responsibility, but also because the extra components encourage individuals or organizations to engage in riskier behaviors. Systems and organizations can be designed to be safer and more secure, but people may develop a false sense of security, too. Research has shown, for instance, that laws requiring "baby-proof" safety caps on aspirin bottles did not led to a decrease in child poisoning because parents, feeling safer with the new caps, left the bottles outside of the medicine cabinet[235]; flight deck automation seems to have caused some new human errors due to the complacency or decreased vigilance [169,241]; and similarly, mandatory seat belt laws seem to have not saved lives, they just shifted causalities from vehicle occupants to pedestrians and cyclists[3].

In summary, it is important to keep an eye on your kids even if they are wearing a helmet while biking or using armbands while swimming. This does not necessarily make them safer.

How much Reliability?

We were chattering with our neighbors during a summer barbecue day. "Bego never gets sick; she's unbreakable," I said proudly and half-jokingly.

"Dear, it's not that I never get sick. The truth is, I can't be sick." Nothing good ever comes from a phrase following the word "Dear."

These days, even in affluent nations, women still tend to handle most of the childcare and housework while also working on paid jobs outside their homes. Unlike a spouse and mother, a salaried employee has access to paid sick leave.

Can one truly never be sick? What does "never" really means?

This situation is similar to defining the necessary dependability level for a specific service. Regardless of whether we consider my wife, someone answering the phone, a web application, or professionals working at an office, aiming for flawless reliability is impractical for various reasons: power outages, natural disasters, fire hazards, health concerns, unexpected absences, or even extraterrestrial invasions that might compromise the service. There are external risks that affect the total reliability of systems.

Take, for example, a hypothetical internet provider that guarantees availability 100% of the time. Individual consumers could still encounter problems due to personal illnesses, power interruptions, or system updates. These external failures can easily account for 0.1 to 1 % of the annual user time (i.e., between four days and ten hours each year). Under those conditions, a failure or a set of failures that reduce the reliability of the service by 0.01% would be hardly noticed by most customers (i.e. one hour annually, especially if the downtime is evenly distributed throughout the year).

Similarly, when considering the level of reliability we should aspire to as diligent individuals, we can reflect on how often others fail to respond to our requests. Is it one out of ten? More? Less? People fall ill, take leaves, attend meetings, run late, forget appointments, misunderstand dates or times, get distracted by other matters, and so on. Any reliability level far above what we observe in these interactions would likely go unnoticed in the grand scheme of things, it would not significantly add value to our career prospects, or be noticeable to others. Therefore, there's no need to strive for excessive reliability. Instead, it might beneficial to relax and take note of Bertrand Russell's advice in his essay *In Praise of Idleness*[192].

How many times can Bego afford to fall ill without causing inconvenience? Fewer than once a year seems implausible given the numerous minor and major issues that are capable of derailing our daily routines, ranging from our death (with approximately a 1/300 probability per year) to the death of a close relative (around a 1/30 chance per year), or merely taking a vehicle for maintenance (an annual necessity). So then, what constitutes reasonable sick leave allowance for my wife?

Consistency versus Availability

I'll never forget the day Manolo, still single and without kids, said during lunch, "Anybody can have 3 hours a day for himself!" He was convinced, although he didn't have, like all of us, kids yet. We all laughed, except Manolo in disbelief: "What? Don't you think so, Marc?"

Many things change with a family. One of them is that decisions and time are no longer solely yours. Can we have a barbecue with this or that friend on Saturday? If you make the decision right away, then your friends are happy, but your wife or children could prefer to do something else. If you tell your friends to wait, then the spontaneity of the interaction is lost, and they could finally decide on a different plan.

The above is analogous to the limitations exposed by the CAP Theorem, one of the most famous results in distributed systems theory. The theorem was first presented as a conjecture by Eric Brewer in 1998 and later proved by Seth Gilbert and Nancy Lynch in 2002. The Theorem states that a distributed data store cannot simultaneously provide consistency across replicas (C), availability (A), and partition tolerance (P). There is a trade-off between these attributes[33,80]. In other words, a distributed storage system can potentially suffer from network partitions (i.e., temporarily broken communication between two or more subsystems), and the designer has to choose between availability (i.e., access to the data) or consistency of the data between replicas (i.e., making sure that all the replicas contain the same data). Similarly, when making plans with our extended family and friends, my wife and I have to choose whether to wait for each other's presence and then agree on a date, or plan activities independently of each other, potentially leading to inconsistent decisions. This is not unusual for us. So far, we always choose consistency over availability in our relationship. In this light, a divorce or teenagers' independence can also be considered as a movement towards availability over consistency and redundancy.

One of the fundamental points of the CAP Theorem is that a distributed system is never entirely safe from network failures, and network partitioning has to be tolerated. Likewise, we cannot always be with our beloved ones. In the presence of a partition, there are two options: consistency or availability. When choosing consistency over availability, the system will return an error or wait until the communication is recovered. When there is a network partition and nodes cannot communicate, it is not possible to guarantee that a particular piece of information is up-to-date and perfectly shared between the nodes. On the other hand, when choosing availability over consistency, the system will always process the query and return, for example, the data available from one arbitrary node of the distributed system, which may not necessarily be the most up to date one, especially if this node is "me".

However, as Eric Brewer notes, the CAP Theorem does not imply that designers should always choose two out of the three options. First, because in the case of distributed computer systems, partitions are rare, and if the system is not partitioned, there is little reason to forfeit consistency or availability (e.g., you can call your partner and check your respective agendas while your friend is waiting for an answer). Second, the choice between consistency and availability can occur many times within the same system at different granularity levels. That is, subsystems can make different choices depending on the operation, specific data, or the user involved. Finally, all three properties are more continuous than binary. Availability is obviously continuous from 0 to 100 percent, but there are also many levels of consistency, and even partitions have nuances, including disagreement within the nodes about whether a partition exists (e.g., when I do not remember that I have to pick up my kids, even after acknowledging the message from my wife, creating an asymmetric partition).

Partitions also happen amongst people and teams, but just like in the CAP Theorem, you can fine-tune the availability-consistency trade-off based on the decisions (e.g., deciding on the barbecue dessert, such as choosing between pineapple or cake, might not be so critical, so it can be decided without a family consensus).

This chapter goes hand in hand with some of the implications and extensions of the CAP Theorem we just presented, including the Bitcoin consistency versus availability approach, the consistency versus speed trade-off and its implications for decision-making and politics, the Boeing 777 design rules and the use of simple rules to improve our decision-making, monotonicity and its use in the design of distributed systems, the equivalence of monotonicity with idempotency and commutativity, and finally, an introduction to the idea of non-monotonic logic.

Does Bitcoin Sacrifices Consistency or Availability?

Do you know anyone who has lost money in cryptocurrencies? I know a couple of people, and I believe there are many more silent personal miseries. Nobody likes to be a loser, so they are not easily spotted. Disasters of our personal finances are not typically explained. So, I wonder if we are approaching a singularity point when desperate mothers from around the globe will unite to destroy data centers and rebel against the insane escalation of their children's financial risk. Where does the earned money go after being consumed through a sudden change in cryptocurrency prices?

Bitcoin, perhaps the most famous of all cryptocurrencies, unlike fiat currencies like the dollar or the euro, doesn't require a central authority or bank. During 2008 and 2009, Satoshi Nakamoto published the seminal Bitcoin paper [159], released the first open-source implementation of the protocol, and created the first Bitcoins. Little is known about Satoshi except that the name is a pseudonym, and that he is not necessarily Japanese. The Bitcoin cryptocurrency relies on an algorithm with the same name to create a decentralized ledger of payments, a digital record of paired credits and debits without duplicated payments. Unlike the value of other currencies, Bitcoin does not get its value from the trust in an underlying government or country to pay its debts, but from the trust people place in its algorithm and implementation, a completely new paradigm, since it does not depend on trusting some fiduciary money (like cheques, banknotes, or drafts).

The Bitcoin algorithm is based on two fundamental building blocks: Proof of Work (PoW) and the Blockchain.

PoW was developed as a means to fight email spam around 1992 [160]. The idea was simple. The email sender should add a nonce to the email message such that the hash value of the message plus the nonce is below some threshold value called difficulty. In other words, a nonce is a set of meaningless bytes used to make the message hash value fall below a certain difficulty. This computation, finding an appropriate nonce, proves that the sender has spent some time and energy before sending the message, indicating it is not spam. For example, if we use a 256-bit hash function and a difficulty of 10 bits, then we will need to try an average of 512 nounces before getting a hash value below 246 bits. Instead, if the difficulty is around 255 bits, then we will need more computation than there are atoms in the universe, a practical impossibility.

The second building block of the Bitcoin cryptocurrency is the blockchain. It is a growing list of records, called blocks, which are linked to one another using a chain of PoW nonces in a data structure named Merkle Tree. Each new block contains a nonce computed using the PoW hash of the current block and the previous nonce. By design, this link between two records is computationally expensive and, as the number of elements in the blockchain grows, the computational cost required to create the data structure grows proportionally to the number of blocks. This property makes the blockchain resistant to modification. The created ledger is effectively immutable as the number of blocks grows. Once a new block is added to the chain, the data in any given block cannot be altered without altering all previous blocks and their nonces. Altering any block requires recomputing all the PoW chain, making the feat impractical once several blocks have been added to the chain.

A Bitcoin client can achieve a continuum of availability-consensus trade-offs by configuring the number of blocks that must come after a transaction to be considered valid (i.e. children blocks connected to the block holding the transaction data). The more blocks that occur after the transaction, the more likely it is to have a system-wide consensus. That is, more blocks attached after the actual transaction block imply that multiple PoW have been accepted, and therefore a higher cost to invalidate the transaction. If the number of blocks to validate a transaction is reduced, the time to validate the request is correspondingly reduced and the system availability increased.

In a way, the PoW mechanism is analogous to the implicit signal that a person gives to the recruiter when sending a well-formatted CV, a university degree, a GitHub profile with several toy projects, and perhaps a written book. It does not necessarily prove skills, but certainly shows work and the motivation of the candidate to get a job. This is not, of course, exactly the same thing.

Consistent Design versus Development Speed

I have been in several teams, and every time they grow, I observe how the overall design starts to diverge. As the team expands, achieving a perfectly homogeneous design becomes increasingly challenging, and inconsistencies are more likely to arise. However, with effort, time, peer reviews, discussions, refactorings, consolidations, upgrades, and, occasionally, some drama, the system maintains a certain degree of consistency. The alternative is to slow down the development process and allow only a minimal number of people to build the entire system, maintaining control over all decisions. In this case, the system's design would be consistent but progress would be slower. On the other hand, if we aim for faster development, we must accept some level of design inconsistencies.

This situation is analogous to the PACELC conjecture, which extends the CAP Theorem to consider the cost of consistency in a distributed computer system. It suggests that, in the presence of network partitioning (P), we must choose between availability (A) and consistency (C) (as described by the CAP Theorem). Moreover, even when the system runs normally in the absence of partitions, else (E) we must choose between latency (L) and consistency (C). That is, consistency slows down the decision making process [1]. Does it always happen? Like other unsuccessful conjectures, the PACELEC conjecture is not always true. While it provides a good initial framework, we will show in one of the next sections that it is only valid for non-monotonic systems.

According to the conjecture, regardless of how replication is performed, there will always be a trade-off between consistency and latency. In situations where replication is carefully controlled over short distances, there are reasonable options because latency is small in local area networks. However, as replication is extended to wide area networks, there is no avoiding a significant consistency-latency trade-off. To illustrate, imagine the difference between choosing wedding arrangements across continents between your wife in Spain, your mother-in-law in the United States, and you in Australia. Either you leave your wife or your mother-in-law to take all the decisions, or you spend your love credit discussing the flower arrangements across time zones.

This is analogous to the changes that democracies undergo in critical situations where the typical parliamentary lengthy votes and discussions are replaced by an executive command under a state of emergency regime. You remove the need for consensus (or majority) and you gain speed to address a crisis, such as natural disasters, civil unrest, public health emergencies, or national security threats. A dictatorship could be interpreted similarly, although it's not exactly the same.

Consensus' Tyranny

"Galo! Could you please finish your breakfast? We are going to be late for school," I implore him as I open the door to let my other children get the bikes.

However, today Galo is moody and he looks at me in anger. There was no chocolate for breakfast and he thought that we, for some despicable reason, were lying to him about its location.

"Galo!! We're all going to be late! Hurry up!"

This frequent show will last for a few more minutes, and we will be late. Sometimes it's the chocolate, but there are many good reasons to be late: they don't want to wake up, we had an unsavoury discussion about Christmas presents, the chosen outfit does not pass the bar, or one of them can still be angry from yesterday, to name a few. Five minutes late to school, not the end of the world, though. One child is able to delay the entire family. An unfair situation that will eventually be resolved once they are old enough to go by themselves. Please.

A similar and more extraordinary phenomenon happens every weekend or holiday between six and seven in the morning. With that exact periodicity and narrow time band, at least one of my sons decides that a beautiful day is ripe with opportunities. It's mysterious why this only happens on weekends. Well, to be fair, it is not always the case. During holidays and weekends, if we have to wake up early to take the car and travel for long hours, then one of my sons becomes unusually tired to the point that he needs one or two hours more than usual to wake up. Only one child suffices to either wake up us all early or delay the rest of the family when we are in a hurry.

These everyday family experiences, where one child's actions can delay or disrupt the entire group, serve as a microcosm for larger systems in society and technology. Just as a single child can hold up a family's morning routine, a similar 'bottleneck' phenomena occur in various fields, from computer science to economics to politics.

For example, in the field of communication protocols and road traffic, there is the phenomenon known as "Head of Line Blocking." It occurs when a single slow packet or car at the front of the line prevents the ones behind them from moving. A single packet or car blocks the whole path. In decision theory, this phenomenon exists and is known as "Tyranny of Consensus", and in politics a similar phenomenon is named the minority rule, although in this case the intransigent minority achieves something instead of blocking the process (e.g., Kosher soft-drinks, extremely politically correct language guidelines, the veto vote in the UN, minority shareholders with large stakes exerting disproportionate control, etc.).

Is it not curious how often the same or very similar concepts across fields of expertise are named so differently? It's not the most efficient way to store our culture's capital and collective knowledge.

These situations represent one extreme of the PACELC conjecture or CAP theorem in a real-life scenario. Ensuring consensus means striving for perfect consistency among all parties involved, which can result in potentially infinite delay.

This idea is also similar to the idea of "Chain-Link Logic," explained previously, or to the concept of the bottleneck that will be explained later in the book. Again, not the most efficient way to store and share knowledge seamlessly across fields of expertise.

Boeing 777 Design Rules and Authority Limits

"If an improvement takes less than a day of work, just do it. You don't need management approval, although it is good if you discuss it with one of your colleagues." This is an implicit rule in our team. There is a balance between too much and too little formal approval processes, also known as change management.

As explained by Donald G. Reinertsen in *The Principles of Product Development Flow*[186], during the design of the Boeing 777, the company established a decision rule for trading off weight and unit cost. Any designer was authorized to increase unit cost by up to $300 by making design changes or material substitutions to save a pound of weight. As a result, Boeing enabled 5,000 engineers to make system-level trade-offs without needing to seek permission from their superiors. In this case, the consensus among senior management was reached beforehand to create and communicate the decision rule. The cost and delay caused by this initial consensus were then amortized during the design process across a multitude of decentralized decisions.

Similar decision rules are likely adopted in my family and possibly in yours as well. While not explicitly stated, there are still rules that are better adhered to. For example, minor expenses aren't even discussed by my wife or me, whereas buying a house will involve long discussions and time-consuming efforts to reach an agreement. Through trial and error, we figure out which decisions can be made individually, which require both my wife and me, and which involve the entire household—including the children, mother-in-law, or even the dog.

An analogous argument is presented by Donald Sull and Kathleen M. Eisenhardt in *Simple Rules: How to Thrive in a Complex World*[216]. Simple rules allow for the fine-tuning of the trade-off between consistency and latency in the real world.

Simple rules are short, straightforward guidelines that help navigate complex situations. They strike a balance between rigid structure and complete flexibility, allowing for quick decision-making while maintaining some consistency. In the Boeing example, the $300 per pound rule simplified countless design decisions. In families, unspoken rules about spending thresholds serve a similar purpose. These simple rules are effective because they capture the essence of accumulated wisdom, are memorable and practical, and adapt to changing contexts. By implementing such rules, organizations and families can streamline their decision-making processes, reducing the need for constant consensus-building while still maintaining overall alignment.

Consistency and Non-monotonicity

Sometimes parents go crazy. Sometimes, we lose our minds as well, and we can find ourselves working together as a F1 pit crew diligently helping one of our kids to dress up for school. While my wife puts the left shoe, I put the jacket, then magically the breakfast goes flying to the backpack, the winter hat flies into place, the trousers are adjusted, and a goodbye kiss is given while the kid steps out of the house. It's not especially efficient or elegant; in fact, it can be a bit ridiculous, and I wonder if it may have a negative psychological impact on our children. However, it's still impressive to witness this feat of human coordination and cooperation enabling dressing a child in pairs. How do parents achieve this coordination marvel without stepping on each other?

The scenario of parents dressing their child, while seemingly far removed from computer science, actually serves as an excellent analogy for understanding complex distributed systems. Just as parents must coordinate their actions to dress their child efficiently, distributed systems must coordinate their operations to maintain consistency. That is, parents dressing their kids, like a distributed computation, must coordinate their actions to ensure the child doesn't end up wearing underwear over their trousers—an inconsistency. The CALM Theorem provides a framework for understanding when this coordination is necessary and when it can be avoided, much like how parents might develop implicit rules for dividing tasks when dressing their child.

In computing terms, it's surprising that this dressing process is mostly wait-free, with parents diligently working non-stop. The trick lies in the fact that dressing a child is almost monotonic (and monotonous, too, after doing it a thousand times or more), allowing for a distributed wait-free implementation. Not entirely monotonic, though, because you can't put the shoes before the socks.

The CALM Theorem, proposed by Joseph M. Hellerstein and Peter Alvaro [98], stands for Consistency as Logical Monotonicity. Unlike the CAP Theorem or the PACELC conjecture, it offers a constructive perspective in the field of distributed systems. The theorem states, essentially, that a program has a consistent and coordination-free distributed implementation—meaning it can be fully parallelized without race conditions or synchronized operations—if and only if it is monotonic.

And what is a monotonic program? A program is considered monotonic if adding data to the input can only increase the program state. This is not the case for the parents dressing the children because you cannot add shoes before socks, trousers before underwear, or the jacket before the t-shirt. In other words, if you put the shoes without the socks, you will have to later remove them, breaking the monotonic property.

A futuristic, wait-free approach to child dressing could involve a series of fabric patches that can be added indiscriminately to any part of the child's body, performing the functions of clothing, shoes, and underwear. Once the kid is entirely covered in fabric, they would be considered dressed and ready for school—a wet dream for efficient parents focused on quality time with their children.

In other words, a monotonic program must never be retracted when new data arrives. Operations such as adding, piling, or counting numbers in a set, accumulating truthful evidence for an inference, or appending logs in a database are all examples of monotonic operations[30]. On the other hand, removing edges from a graph, deleting or updating information in a database, and accumulating information of contradictory validity for resolving an inference are all non-monotonic operations.

It's essential to note that both implication directions of the CALM Theorem are true ("if and only if"). Consequently, a non-monotonic function does not have a consistent and coordination-free distributed implementation. Things like dressing your kids, renovating an old house, or building software are non-monotonic. However, if we could discover a way to do these things monotonically, we could pour people on them and increase their speed indefinitely.

So, how does this affect the design of distributed systems? Traditionally, the approach to this question has been predominantly negative. Successful scalability has relied on reducing the consistency mechanisms to a minimum, moving them off the critical path, hiding them in a rarely visited corner of the system, and making it as difficult as possible for application developers

---

[30] Conflict-Free Replicated Data Types (CRDTs), and to a lesser extent Mergeable Replicated Data Types (MRDTs), are sets of data structures specifically designed to allow commutative, associative, and idempotent operations—although in the case of MRDTs, these properties are application-specific[110,208].

to obtain permission to use them [31]. However, the CALM theorem offers a positive answer to the same question about the design of distributed systems. It suggests that the data structures used to store information must be monotonic, making distribution without coordination possible.

Idempotency and Commutativity

I first met Bego when I was 16 years old in the swimming pool of an hotel in Castello de la Plana. A common friend with whom I was training, Irene, presented us. I would have never dreamed that such a hot and intelligent girl in a bikini would even notice me, shy and introverted as I was. I would have thought even less that the future woman she would become would willingly marry and have children with me. Like a stew that cooks slowly, we shared experiences and met several times over a long period: meeting at athletic competitions across Spain and Europe, training together for a couple of years under the orders of Miquel Concegal, and almost having an affair on a crazy night after an exhausting competition in Valladolid.

Friendship, like the one I have with Bego, Edu, my mother and sister, or Carlos and Vanessa, seems to get better or deeper over time. Layer after layer of shared experiences and feelings somehow resist the ups and downs of our interactions. Neither the good nor the bad is lost; everything just accumulates and integrates in our minds.

Our minds seem to effortlessly accumulate information without losing anything. Even though events happen in an unknown order and number of times, our minds appear to be monotonic. For a software engineer like me, this is surprising because the applications I work with do not always show this property. Deleting a record completely eliminates the information, unlike getting angry with a friend, which somehow changes my current understanding of the person without erasing my past understanding.

This surprising capacity of our minds to accumulate information irrespective of the order of events and their repetition can also be explained as a consequences

---

[31]Distributed consensus algorithms are the gold standard for implementing central points of coordination in distributed systems. Unfortunately, these algorithms are challenging to understand and implement. For example, the difficulties involved in implementing the Paxos distributed consensus algorithm are well-known[39].

of a system being idempotent and commutative. It turns out that these two properties are equivalent to monotonicity.

However, before this issue was settled by Joseph M. Hellerstein and Peter Alvaro in *Keeping CALM: When Distributed Consistency Is Easy*[98], it was thought that idempotency was the key to solving the consistency problem for distributed systems. Unfortunately, idempotency is not enough.

An idempotent service allows clients to perform the same call more than once and produce the same result. For example, I can remind my wife twice about an appointment with the doctor, and it won't cause any harm. In case—God forbid—she didn't listen to me the first time, repeating the message could actually do some good. On the other hand, if she already remembers, she will just be mildly annoyed, at most giving me a long stare, but it won't cause any harm.

If a message or its acknowledgment is lost, it is a great property of a distributed system to be able to safely send the message again without any unwanted side-effect. This is not a natural property of all systems. It does not make sense to drink the same cup of coffee twice because the second time it will be empty, let your kid hit his brother a second or third time, and you definitely shouldn't pay the same bill twice.

However, as the CALM Theorem tells us, idempotency is not enough. It is easy to understand why. Imagine I'm reminding my wife repeatedly that tomorrow's appointment has been cancelled and later that it has not. Depending on the order of the reminders, my wife will reach a different conclusion regarding the appointment. She could also reasonably conclude that I'm an idiot, too. Even if each individual message is idempotent, the sending order matters between different messages.

An avid reader could see that if the operations, in addition to being idempotent, are also commutative (i.e., the order of execution does not affect the result), then they are equivalent to being monotonic, and therefore, there exists a consistent wait-free implementation. This surprising equivalence between idempotency and commutativity on one side, and monotonicity on the other, is caused by the properties of idempotency and commutativity preventing retraction or inconsistency in the system state as new inputs are introduced.

In other words, idempotency guarantees that adding more data to the system does not undo or alter previous results. Adding commutativity ensures consistency even when the order of inputs changes; the commutative system incorporates new data without needing to revisit or reorder previous operations. Together, idempotency and commutativity ensure that the system state only grows or remains stable with additional inputs. There is no need to "revert" or "correct" the state based on the sequence or repetition of updates.

Somehow, our mind's data structures allow the accumulation of information irrespective of the order of arrival of events and their repetition. Nothing is lost, only accumulated as in a monotonic system, enabling the concurrent, non-blocking interaction with our surroundings, enemies, and friends.

Non-monotonic Logic

"Corso, Why are you crying?" I asked after he had just arrived from school.

"Because my friend Nil has not yet returned from school, and we have to go to the supermarket, and you won't let me play with him, and then it will be too late to play!" He continued crying but now with an angrier tone directed at his unfair parent.

"But nobody told you that you can't play. Nil is not home yet anyway, and going to the supermarket will only take a moment." I tried to clarify to no avail.

"You never let me play!!!"

Human reasoning often toggles between monotonic and non-monotonic systems depending on the context. While our minds can behave in a monotonic fashion by accumulating information, as noted in distributed systems that rely on idempotency and commutativity, they also exhibit non-monotonic traits when processing new, contradictory information.

Classical logic, even when it is misused, is definitive, and it is monotonic. Given a set of truthful axioms, once you reach a conclusion, it cannot be changed. However, reality does not seem to have absolute true statements nor strictly logical relations (e.g., if I go to the supermarket, it will be too late to play). Monotonic logic seems to be ill-suited for our day-to-day duties.

A non-monotonic logic is a formal logic whose consequence relation is not monotonic (e.g., "I initially thought that it was a stupid idea, but now I see its virtues"). In other words, reasoners using non-monotonic logic reach tentative conclusions, which can be retracted based on further evidence. In contrast, reasoners using monotonic logic never retract their conclusions. Facts accumulate without contradiction.

A classic example of non-monotonic reasoning is the "birds can fly" scenario. Initially, we might conclude that Tweety, being a bird, can fly. However, upon learning that Tweety is a penguin or a kiwi, we retract our initial conclusion. New information can invalidate previous conclusions in non-monotonic logic.

In non-monotonic logic, the conclusions do not "grow" step by step linearly, but in sudden jumps, first in one direction and then in the opposite one. This behavior is, in fact, typical of human reasoning, where our inferences change, sometimes drastically, as we gain more, better, or worse information. Classical logic, on the other hand, has a monotonic consequence relation, where adding a formula to a theory never produces a reduction in the possible set of consequences. Monotonicity indicates that learning new information cannot reduce the set of what is known. This is not how real-world knowledge evolves though.

For example, when my wife is late, after waiting for a while, I might suddenly start worrying about her safety and decide to call her. If she answers and tells me she has been chatting with a friend, I may become annoyed but I will retract my initially plausible conclusion about her safety. As the example shows, it is hard to imagine a person just using monotonic logic. Classical logic can sometimes misguide us. How can we survive in this world without changing our opinions constantly based on new information?

Fortunately, there is a way to combine monotonic and non-monotonic logic. In a sense, Bayesian reasoning is both monotonic and non-monotonic; evidence accumulates in the conditional probabilities of our hypotheses. This accumulation of data is monotonic as the probability distributions of the different hypotheses are continuously updated and evolve with the addition of new data. However, the decision-making process based on these probability distributions is non-monotonic, and the probability distributions are collapsed or reduced into a single decision using the expected value, the average, of the distribution or its maximum a posteriori estimate, to name the most famous mechanisms.

Time and Space

"I don't have time," said a young colleague without kids, justifying why he didn't spend time learning some necessary skills for his job. Now, with three kids, a wife, and a dog, my B.S. detector has become finely attuned to these kinds of arguments, including "Sorry, I've been so busy," "I have tons of work," "I worked all day long," "I had so many meetings this week, you can't imagine," and so on. It was during my engineering master's thesis that I understood that time is a flow equally limited and available for all of us. My thesis advisor was always too busy to review some results, so I sought advice from a different professor. This wiser and older person told me something basic yet profound, "You know, everybody has the same amount of time, including me. But it's a matter of priorities; he just expresses it that way." I'm grateful for his advice, even though he was considered one of the most disliked teachers at the university. An unwanted teacher with an unwanted student, what an unlikely team.

Time is a pivotal concept in the sciences. In relativity theory, space and time are intimately related and can be measured using the same units; in thermodynamics, time is tied to disorder; in economics, time and money; in evolution, time and variability; in decision theory, time and uncertainty; in queuing theory, time and throughput; and in control theory, time and accuracy. Time is also pivotal in our lives—its duration, the hours spent working, the growth and changes in our families, the aging and wear and tear of our belongings, and the evolution of our thoughts. We often undervalue it, treating it as infinite, when in truth, it is not only finite, but first of all a flow, not a resource. Time cannot be saved or accumulated, it just passes and we should do as best as we can with it at this precise moment. Time is the currency needed for other things to happen.

195

Yet time does not exist in isolation—it happens in space, within the environments we occupy, the relationships we nurture, and the systems we create to measure and manage it. In this chapter, we will sample some of these aspects, particularly in relation to history, computational complexity, language, communication protocols, and finally, household chores.

History, Chaos, and NP Problems

"We need to buy a house!" I exclaimed to my wife, making it sound urgent. It was late in the evening, after we'd finally convinced the kids to go to bed. My wife looked at me as if I had a screw loose.

"I've been looking for a house for three years. You never paid attention. What's gotten into you? Why the sudden rush?" she retorted, visibly annoyed. To her credit, she had correctly predicted that 2018-2020 was a good time to buy a house. But, blinded by my fears, I ignored her.

"It's the state of the world. It reminds me of the times leading up to both World Wars—although I was not there. Don't you think we should invest in tangible assets to shield our savings from potential depreciation? The ongoing war in Ukraine, the rise and aging of populism, the massive debt in many wealthy countries, and the looming inflation." I said while she looked at me in disbelief.

"I told you!"

But can I genuinely forecast the economic future based on a superficial understanding of past significant events? Will societies and institutions respond the same way they did in the past? Do I even know how they responded in the past? Do I even know how economics works in the present? Put differently, can we predict forthcoming events by studying a series of documented occurrences while ignoring undocumented ones? Can we delineate the entirety of world history through a handful of noteworthy events and gain clarity about what actually happened?

Although accurate forecasting seems challenging when applied to global events, it is incredibly effective in mathematics, science, and engineering. For mathematical functions, the input-output behavior is deterministic and almost perfect prediction is possible from just a few samples. By observing a sequence of input-output pairs, we can deduce both the past and potential future of a given mathematical function. As we explained before, this is one of the derivations from the Shannon-Nyquist sampling Theorem. But are there limits to our ability to reconstruct and predict mathematical functions?

It turns out that even for mathematical objects, due to the Butterfly Effect, accurately forecasting the future is not always possible. As eloquently explained in Steven H. Strogatz's book, *Nonlinear Dynamics and Chaos*[215], some mathematical equations are highly sensitive to initial conditions, causing trajectories to diverge exponentially with just infinitesimal changes in those conditions or the equation's parameters. This behavior isn't just found in mathematics; it's a fundamental principle of our scientific understanding of the world and influences fields like meteorology, ecology, economics, aerodynamics, epidemiology, chemistry, and more. Even in astronomy, when more than three bodies are involved in the dynamics, the system becomes chaotic and unpredictable.

This chaotic behavior establishes a fundamental limitation, similar to the nondeterministic polynomial (NP) time problems in computing, on our ability to predict and control the world [152]. Choosing the best transportation route (aka the Traveling Salesman problem), determining if two graphs are similar (e.g., using the graph edit distance), optimizing packing (also known as the Knapsack problem), or even the simple task of coloring a large map with just three colors becomes an almost impossible computational feat. These problems are said to be NP-complete. Like sorting my brother's socks on the sofa, the computational cost of NP problems grows disproportionately faster as the size of the problem's input space grows.

These computing problems cannot be solved in a time proportional to the size of the input. The computational time grows either exponentially or combinatorially with the input size; sometimes it grows even faster. Adding more microprocessors or clever algorithms only solves marginally larger problems. Sometimes, we informally say that these problems don't scale well.

Consider the table below for the Traveling Salesman problem, where we try to find the optimal route that visits a given number of cities. As the number of cities increases, the possible routes grow combinatorially, and already for 64 cities, the number of possible routes exceeds the number of atoms in the universe.

Number of Cities	Number of Routes
1	$1! = 1$
2	$2! = 2$
4	$4! = 24$
8	$8! = 40{,}320$
16	$16! \approx 2 \cdot 10^{13}$
32	$32! \approx 3 \cdot 10^{35}$
64	$64! \approx 10^{89}$

If the characteristics of chaotic systems limit our predictability and control horizon, the computational characteristics of NP problems restrict our ability to make optimal decisions no matter how much time we have. Many real systems are fundamentally unpredictable and uncontrollable. Spending more time on these problems does not make a dent on its resolution.

One thing's for sure: I should pay closer attention to what my wife says.

Compressed Data Storage

She stares at me without a word. Not angry, but not exactly happy either. What had I done or said? Should I have done or said something differently, or should I have just kept quiet? It suddenly dawns on me like a lightning bolt —I wasn't really listening to her. Luckily, my wife's words return to my mind after a few seconds of delay. A single look can be a marvel of information compression. Through her gaze, and by saving a bit on communication bandwidth (i.e., a few words), she sent me a compressed message that I had to painstakingly decipher after several brain cycles.

Uncompressed stored data occupies more space, but access to the data is faster. Compressing the data reduces the storage requirements and the communication bandwidth required to transmit the information, but it takes time to run the decompression algorithm. A compressed message requires more computational time, and the end-to-end latency increases, too. Depending on the specific instance of the problem, either approach can be practical. Interestingly, there are rare cases where it is possible to directly work with compressed data—as seen with compressed bitmap indexes—where working with compression is faster than without it.

Would it have been faster if Bego had explained to me that I was not listening? Would I have listened? Silence, rather than a continuous stream of words, interrupted my train of thought. Surprisingly, this could be an instance where a compressed message, reduced to the nothingness of the silence, had a smaller end-to-end latency.

Nada

In the last year or so, the following has become a daily conversational loop between my daughter, Jone, and me:

"How do you say 'orange cheese' in Spanish?" Jone asks.

"You know it. . . "

"Queso naranja," she replies to herself, and then, "How do you say 'queso naranja' in French?"

"You already know that too. . . "

"Fromage orange. How do you. . . "

"Wait," I interrupt, trying to get a bit more from the conversation. "And how do you say 'I want orange cheese' in Spanish?"

"Quiero queso naranja." But she rapidly adds: "Nada." Clearly and succinctly indicating that she does not want to start a language lesson with her dad. Like my wife's gaze, Jone shows another information compression feat close to the Shannon limit.

"What do you mean by 'Nada'?" Although I knew she was annoyed by my attempt to hijack her carefully planned script, I tried again to engage her in my game.

"Nada." She didn't like her game anymore and left me to check on the fascinating bumblebees flying around the garden.

Perhaps it is not clear from the conversation and context, but my autistic child was telling me that she didn't want to keep talking following my rules; she neither wanted to learn new language constructs, nor she wanted to be bothered by other translations than the ones she cared about, and she was slightly annoyed by my insistence, too.

"Nada" means all these things. I can understand that, and she knows I know. Curiously, in this case, the succinctness of my autistic daughter's language is clearly far ahead of mine. But, is it positive? Unlike in programming languages, succinctness here entails the dissolution of meaning. Like compression, it saves some time on one side by spending more time on another. A succinct language is either larger and more complex or more vague.

The worst part of "Nada" is that my other neurotypical children have learned the concept, and they have started to use it, profusely.

Protocol Expressiveness and Security

During politically charged email interchanges, I notice that the higher the rank of the sender in the company org chart, the more ambiguous the message is. Senior managers tend to send shorter and, curiously, more ambiguous emails, leaving interpretation and actions to their subordinates. It's as if senior management has an information exchange protocol to avoid being hacked by their opponents. Younger people, on the other hand, do precisely the opposite, sending long emails packed with factual data that can easily be bent to serve an opponent's goals.

An analogous but more concrete phenomenon is explained in *The Halting Problems of Network Stack Insecurity*. Len Sassaman, Meredith L. Patterson, Sergey Bratus, and Anna Shubina outline guidelines for designing secure input language protocols, and therefore, secure programs[199]. In doing so, they link the theory of formal languages with practical experiences and intuitions of both program exploitation and secure programming.

Essentially, for complex input protocols (also known as Turing-complete [32]), the software responsible for parsing and interpreting the input may encounter issues analogous to the "halting problem"—and thus, be undecidable. Therefore, when the exchange protocol is close to Turing completeness, there is no generic algorithm to establish the safety of the inputs. Could it be that senior

---

[32]A Turing-complete language or system is one that can simulate a universal Turing machine, meaning it can compute anything that is computable. This concept comes from Alan Turing's work on computability theory. While powerful, Turing-complete systems are also unpredictable: it's impossible to determine in advance whether a program will halt or run forever (the "halting problem") [152].

management intuitively grasped this long ago and simplified their emails to reduce the risk of being "hacked"?

Complex protocols seem to resist efforts to implement them securely. By their nature, they force programmers into the unwinnable position of trying to solve—or approximate solutions to—undecidable problems, an impossible task. Likewise, when you add complexity to an email or essay, it becomes increasingly easy to hack, distort, and misuse its contents.

Good protocol designers avoid letting their protocols become Turing-complete. Instead, they limit the expressiveness of their designs to meet only the essential requirements.

This is analogous to the apocryphal quote often attributed to Albert Einstein: "Everything should be made as simple as possible, but not simpler." In fact, Einstein said something similar but less succinct: "It can scarcely be denied that the supreme goal of all theory is to make the irreducible basic elements as simple and as few as possible without having to surrender the adequate representation of a single datum of experience."[63] While the apocryphal version may win for brevity and social media publication, the original quote reflects an essential balance: the pursuit of simplicity must never come at the cost of misrepresenting reality.

In practice, this balance is just as crucial in communication and design as it is in theoretical work. Whether crafting an email or a secure protocol, stripping away unnecessary complexity can prevent confusion, errors, or misuse—yet oversimplifying risks losing critical details that preserve functionality and meaning.

Contact

In Carl Sagan's "Contact," the aliens send a message containing instructions for a machine that creates wormholes, enabling travel across the galaxy. Instead of sending the actual machine or coming to Earth themselves, they transmit the instructions. I suppose the aliens' purpose is not just to save work, energy, and materials, but also to seek proof of intelligence and cooperation before establishing communication. The aliens, with this convoluted form of examination, test the 'barbarian monkeys' before making friends with them and handing over technology that could potentially destroy star systems.

Sending instructions represents a special form of compression. The message saves the aliens the hard work of building and transporting an obsolete machine, potentially saving a zillion extraterrestrial dollars.

A similar technique is found, for example, in the field of computer graphics. An image can be stored as either a Scalable Vector Graphic (SVG) file or as the actual rendered bitmap. For certain types of images (e.g., geometrical line drawings) the rendered bitmap is likely to occupy more space and have lower quality than the SVG file. Choosing to send the SVG or the bitmap shifts the balance of computation cost, storage requirements, and communication speed. Curiously, as noted in the previous section, the message becomes Turing complete and opens the door to an infinite number of security attacks.

This is also similar to the difference between doing a job yourself and asking someone else to do it. If you specify the job correctly and the person knows their craft, providing instructions saves you time, and you pay instead for their expertise.

Don't Repeat Yourself

"Why can't you follow the recipe?" Bego said, half-annoyed and half-jokingly. She was absolutely right; I don't like to follow cooking recipes to the letter.

"Today, I didn't have any chicken or coconut milk... and I didn't want to go to the supermarket..." I'm the man with an excuse for every situation. They leap out of my mouth before I even start thinking. Still you might think, what can possibly justify cooking Chicken Curry without chicken and without coconut milk?

A variation of this also occurs during the actual writing of a program. For example, we might approximately repeat certain code snippets in separate parts of the source code base, or alternatively, we can also create a shared library with common functionality. We might exactly repeat the code when sharing the code through a library, or we might use a slight variation by re-writing it. Naively, the shared library approach seems better. Why should we repeat the same lines over and over with small variations here and there? Shouldn't we just follow the perfect recipe all the time?

It turns out that the choice depends on various drawbacks that go hand-in-hand with the use of a shared library, including the loss of source code locality, over-generalization of the solution, coordination issues when making changes, and possible dilution of responsibility, to name a few. A shared library is less flexible and adaptable.

Following cooking recipes exactly is equally troublesome. Imagine that everybody followed the same Chicken Curry recipe from God's recipe cookbook. What would happen if we did not have the exact same ingredients? What if someone were allergic to coconut milk? How would we update God's cookbook of recipes if we discovered a way to improve it (e.g., fry the chicken for 25 minutes instead of 26 minutes)? Who is the editor of the perfect Chicken Curry recipe anyway? And perhaps more importantly, who actually enjoys following the exact recipe besides my wife and a few other weirdos?

Note that a duplicate solution is not necessarily redundant or degenerate. At first sight, duplication without redundancy does not seem like a functional attribute. We might see repetition as a waste. But is it really wasteful to cook rice in ten or a hundred different ways? Most people might disagree on aesthetic grounds, but what if we consider just the function? The variety of recipes likely stems from the availability of certain foods during specific seasons and in different regions. Shouldn't we see the different implementations of very similar software functions as finely tuned adaptations to the environment? And what about our children? Those imperfect copies of ourselves. Was evolution wrong? No, it was not. It should be obvious from the works of Charles Darwin and the fatal ending of the Cleon clone dynasty in Asimov's *Foundation* series.

A similar issue arises with the well-known relational database's golden standard of normalization, and more recently, with some attempts to reduce the number of documents or steps necessary in bureaucratic processes. Achieving these improvements often entails the development and maintenance of complex IT systems. Do these solutions always pay off? Are these integrated systems more robust?

And what about people and books (my preferred subject)? It seems that, in this case, some level of repetition helps. Very successful people tend to repeat the same message over and over in different talks and media. The same happens with some best-selling books, where the basic idea can be summarized on a page, even though the book itself spans several hundred pages.

Sometimes, repetition can be boring though.

Tidying Up

In addition to my textbook fetishism, I have a secret habit of watching videos about minimalist living, minimalist backpacking tips, and survival gear. I especially love backpacks. Although it is almost impossible to implement the minimalist advice in my own life. My wife, having observed my secret obsession for several years, argues that my behavior may have originated from a repressed consumerism. It is interesting because minimalism seems to implicitly indicate a reduced consumption lifestyle, even when minimalists seem to often obsess about what chair or underwear to buy.

The hypothesis holds some merit because, despite living a relatively austere life, I love to buy myself presents for Christmas (the only way to receive a gift at my age with three competing children) and I also like to obsessively think about what I should buy. Anecdotally, I have also observed that when most of these minimalist and essentialist experts reflect on their pasts, they evoke extreme and almost psychotic shopping or working behaviors. It is a curious connection.

During one of these long hours spent on such research, I discovered the famous Marie Kondo, also known as KonMari, a Japanese celebrity famous for her books and videos that help people organize their homes. In a curious twist, her customers, while initially saving time and avoiding the typical housekeeping hassles, end up requiring a consultant to find their socks. Curiously, wasting their precious time with Madame Kondo is an improvement for their stressful lives. Initially, they save some time by being lazy and untidy, but as the mess accumulates, the combinatorial explosion of the mess eventually require more time and space. At some point, the mess becomes unmanageable unless you call on KonMari to resolve the crisis.

In this case, it's not only trading living space for time but also exchanging present effort for future effort. A mess, if left unattended in your own home, will eventually need sorting. Either your survival instincts are triggered, or your neighbor's instincts are (and they call the police after detecting a nauseating odor seeping through the door).

Curiously, it seems that nowadays KonMari has opened up to embracing a messy home after having three kids. This evolution in her perspective highlights a fundamental truth: life is inherently messy, and our approaches to organizing it must be flexible.

In reflecting on minimalism, consumerism, time management, and the art of tidying up, I've come to realize that these are all different facets of the same core challenge: time and how our modern and efficient life consumes it. Whether it's deciding what to buy, how to organize our spaces, or how to spend our time, we're constantly balancing competing needs and desires. We are always optimizing. As the optimization accumulates, our time fades.

The irony is that in our quest for simplicity—be it through minimalism or perfect organization—we often create new complexities that consume our precious flow of time. My little obsession with minimalist videos, is a testament to this paradox—wasting time on videos instead of actual productive occupations. It's a reminder that the pursuit of perfection can sometimes lead us further from our goals.

In the end, perhaps the most valuable lesson as I've learned time and again, it's about listening more carefully to my wife, and perhaps, to other people, too. After all, sometimes the wisest advice comes not from celebrity organizers or minimalist gurus, but from those closest to us who understand our daily realities.

Communication versus Computation

Do you remember the 2011 15-M movement in Spain? Popular assemblies were spontaneously formed as unemployment rose after the 2008 debt crisis. These gatherings became a platform for collective decision-making and grassroots activism. The self-organization process of the street assemblies was very interesting; I had never seen anything similar. It was curious to observe the decision-making process of the assemblies where everybody could give their opinion. It seemed really slow, though. But is decision-making any faster in our current democracies? Is it faster within my family?

On a smaller scale at home, my kids struggle with the daily discussion about what movie or animated series to watch. Pokémon? The Sea Beast? Simon the Rabbit? Sometimes a decision is not reached, and a parent must descend from Mount Olympus in the kitchen and pause their coffee to decide. Sometimes the hot discussions and fights are settled as as Solomon might have done in Jerusalem: prohibiting TV for a day, or, more realistically, for some minutes.

A similar struggle happens with my wife when we try to decide on some controversial issues. Where should we look for a house? What kind of house? It has taken us a couple of years to come to a shared vision. Our ideal location is close to a small village, surrounded by forests and mountains, and near family—ideally in the beautiful Garrotxa region in Catalonia. However, reaching this shared understanding required many long and repetitive discussions. Sometimes I wonder, and most likely my wife does too, if it would be better to decide alone, without the other.

A similar thing happens at work. I have noticed that as the group gets larger, decisions require more and more time, not just in terms of one-on-one discussions, but also in terms of memos, presentations, documents, signatures, and so on. As the group gets larger, slow decision-making becomes the norm. It can be frustrating, too. I remember some discussions at work with a foreign delegation involving IT, business, and legal colleagues from several parts of the globe to integrate our systems. It was really slow; both teams walked through the discussions like cats in a minefield, and when a consensus was reached and the systems were finally integrated, it was considered a great success.

In the context of distributed systems, all these examples mirror the trade-off between computation and communication. The involvement of more people entails more communication, but fewer people tackling an equally difficult problem requires a deeper understanding of the situation by each individual—and, therefore, more computation. This trade-off appears in the context of remote API design, communication protocols, data encoding (whether plain text, binary, or compressed), client-side or server-side graphics rendering, service granularity, application partitioning between processes or threads, etc. As the number of subsystems or people involved increases, communication grows while computation is distributed, reducing the need for a centralized, all-knowing decision-maker. This balance between centralization and distribution, and the subsequent increase in communication and complexity, is fundamental, and the following sections will explore some of its consequences, including trends in computation, communication, and storage; parental and radiation-tolerant control; federalism; and the limits of centralization.

Computation, Communication, and Storage Trends

I find new computers or video consoles boring. They don't seem substantially better than the old ones. Nowadays, I only replace my computer or phone when they break, as the newer ones don't appear to offer significant improvements. In the past, a broken phone or computer used to be a reason for celebration; nowadays, it instead triggers feelings of guilt and prompts thoughts about wasted money. I don't believe this change is related to a personal or societal shift towards ecological consciousness, but rather, irrespective of what the advertisements say, upgrading a computer or phone has the dubious appeal of capital amortization, replacing the excitement of technological obsolescence once driven by exponential performance increases.

While CPU clock speeds peaked around 2004, other computing-related metrics have continued to grow exponentially. These include less glamorous metrics such as computations per chip per second or per dollar, memory capacity and bandwidth, and communication bandwidth have been doubling every 1.5 to 3 years over the last fifty years[125,166]. Computing power in terms of the number of transistors per dollar has been the fastest-growing, followed by communication bandwidth, memory, and finally system input/output. As explained anticipated by Richard Hamming in the *The Art of Doing Science and Engineering*[92], leveraging computation has been, therefore, the key to building future-proof systems (e.g., see the ever growing use of computing resources in embedded systems, telephones, search engines, cloud services, big data, and machine learning)

The differences in exponential growth rates create incentives to develop certain solutions. For example, the growth of computing power relative to memory and storage suggests that we can afford to cache less data and recompute results on the fly. Similarly, the growth in communication bandwidth relative to memory and storage indicates that we can request information from the network instead of storing it locally, and so on.

If the solution you provide aligns with the correct technology wave, it will self-improve without additional investment at an exponential rate. For example, years ago, JavaScript in the browser was expensive but was widely expected to rapidly improve. Nowadays, mobile applications requiring a nearly uninterrupted connection are poised to benefit as the available bandwidth keeps increasing. This means there may no longer be a need to store the data locally (e.g., documents, music, maps) if you can request it constantly, taking advantage of the growing communication capabilities.

But be careful, although communication bandwidth is improving exponentially, communication latency won't improve exponentially, and it is unlikely to even improve fractionally, as it has already reached a limit imposed by the speed of light. This means that memory access times and latency constraints are increasingly significant bottlenecks in certain applications, and therefore design and architecture choices minimizing these will likely be relatively beneficial. That is, some designs and architectural choices will be relatively beneficial in the medium and long-term including computations benefiting from data locality (e.g., content distribution networks, edge computing, caches and cache friendly algorithms minimizing main memory access, etc.); asynchronous communication (e.g., asynchronous languages); task decomposition (e.g., parallelizable tasks to maximize the use of computational resources while minimizing memory bottlenecks); and prioritizing algorithms that compute results incrementally or iteratively, avoiding the need for large memory allocations.

Parental and Radiation Tolerant Control

"Will you buy me a smartwatch? Luis has one, and he has games on it, and he can talk to his mother, too. Can it be pink?"

"A smartwatch?"

"Yes, a watch to talk to you or Mom."

"A smartwatch!? Corso, I'm talking to you right now, without needing a watch. Mom will be here in a few minutes after her walk with Patxi, and you can talk to her then or later."

"I know that. I don't want to talk to her. Why don't you get me a smartwatch?"

Just when the infant death rate is at historical minimums, we still try to minimize the remaining uncertainty (e.g. for the record mainly deaths by drowning and intoxication). It seems that parents, much like dictators, take pleasure in controlling their children through smartwatches, AirTags, phones, and Internet parental controls. Ironically, the reduced cost of communication is not fostering a more decentralized and free world but rather enabling more centralized control. It is curious that given the decentralized nature of the Internet protocols, a more centralized world is emerging instead [33].

---

[33]It seems that the global economy has become more monopolistic over the last century as well as during the first two decades of the twenty-first century, and IT appears to account for much of the growth in industry concentration. Modern IT has transformed industries by enhancing economies of scale and enabling more scalable production processes. IT investments allow firms to centralize control, optimize operations, and capture larger market shares, which contribute to industry consolidation and oligopolistic structures. IT has had a particularly strong influence since the 1970s, coinciding with the rise of dominant technology platforms and digital marketplaces having network effects with winner-take-all dynamics [24,129].

It is similar to the trendy removal of middle management. On one hand, we could conclude that the people in the field are more independent, but on the other hand, we could also conclude that people are more easily controlled by senior management, making the middle managers unnecessary. The control and monitoring of workers have become more centralized. In the case of software development, for example, a myriad of tools provide insights into the status of projects, source code quality, availability, security threats, and so on. Given the previous trends in communication, computation, and storage, the situation is likely to evolve in a similar direction.

For completely different reasons, a similar transformation was experienced by the distributed power supply control system of the Large Hadron Collider (LHC) between 2013 and 2018, the largest and most powerful particle accelerator in the world. For more than a decade, I worked there as one of the tens of thousands of engineers and physicists involved in building this engineering feat. Inside the accelerator, two high-energy particle beams, each narrower than the tip of a needle, race close to the speed of light, carrying the energy of a head-on collision with a truck before ultimately colliding. These particle beams are guided around the accelerator ring by a strong magnetic field maintained by superconducting electromagnets, which are powered by high-power and high-accuracy power supplies, controlled by a distributed control system where I worked.

During the first LHC run (2009–2013), it was discovered that future beam intensities could induce radiation levels high enough to affect the electronic control systems of the power supplies, rendering them unreliable. In other words, as the particle beam bends around the circular accelerator, synchrotron radiation is emitted with an intensity proportional to $O(E^4/r^2)$ where E is the particle energy and r is the radius of curvature of the particle trajectory. As the beam energy increases, this synchrotron radiation can eventually flip one or more bits in the computing systems that control the high-precision power supplies, causing malfunctions or crashes that may drive the beams out of their precise orbit.

To address this challenge, a new control strategy was designed and implemented. The most significant change involved relocating the regulation loop away from the embedded systems situated near the beams and magnets, enabling a more radiation-tolerant electronic design to be placed closer to the particle beam. Replacing embedded CPUs running software with FPGAs reduced the control electronics' radiation cross-section, thereby improving their radiation hardness[229].

This architectural change moved the computation of the regulation loop from the embedded systems close to the beam to the Linux servers that were previously used as relays to pass the set points and configuration to the embedded systems. This reduction in computing power requirements for the embedded systems resulted in an increase in the amount of information sent through the control chain to the middleware servers. This additional information, mainly measurements, was used to perform real-time regulation on the Linux servers. As a consequence of this change computation had to be moved to the Linux servers because more complex control algorithms were required to deal with the additional network delays and potential packet losses.

As in the case of smartwatches for children or the removal of middle management, this was a movement towards a more centralized system, moving computation from the embedded systems to the Linux middleware servers. Whereas previously it was possible to control the power converters without a middleware server, now the regulation depended on the remote servers; nothing functioned without them. The movement was enabled by the increased speed and computing power of the CPUs and by the increased speed and reliability of the communication networks. This new architecture required additional information and computing power in the Linux servers, effectively making them the new decision-makers of the control system.

Are you Spanish or Catalan?

"Are you Spanish or Catalan?" the boss of my boss of my boss asked me. I had been in the company for a week or two and found myself in a high-level meeting, without a suit, tie, or clue, being asked about my position on Catalonian independence. Why did it matter to her? Did my career depend on the answer?

The debate over the independence of Catalonia, in addition to its historical roots and animosities, revolves around the tension between a centralized state and a federal one (or for some a complete emancipation) within the field of Fiscal Federalism. This debate is analogous to the one between centralized and decentralized systems. Which is the better option?

The Decentralization Theorem in the context of Fiscal Federalism states that it is generally more efficient to make decisions as locally as possible, except in cases where there are cost savings by provisioning goods or services centrally, or when inter-jurisdictional externalities exist. In other words, centralization should be a fallback position. Where can the cost-savings from centralization arise? They can occur, for example, through economies of scale (e.g., better purchasing power of larger organizations, more efficient departments, etc.) and inter-jurisdictional externalities (e.g., avoiding tax rate competition between regions, preventing massive migration due to poor economic conditions, cost reductions associated with regulation homogenization, environmental regulations, etc.). In summary, the theorem suggests that the default option should be decentralization unless there is a compelling reason to centralize certain aspects.

Note the interesting perspective of the problem: a system should always be designed and built to be decentralized unless there is a need to centralize it for specific reasons (e.g., a centralized system could be more cost-effective, easier to secure, easier to apply common policies, and less prone to systematic failure modes, etc.). There should be good reasons to do otherwise [34]. This argument, rooted in economics, is somehow analogous to the argument made previously about the trade-off between centralized and decentralized control systems. As you may remember, centralization should be advocated when the number of subsystems is small and they are uncoupled, with a minimal uncertainty and delay. Given the complex and uncertain reality of many systems, only coupling seems to justify centralization[26].

As we have already mentioned, according to Yuval Harari, the author of the bestseller *Sapiens*[94], the pendulum of the centralized-decentralized trade-off might be swinging towards centralization. In the past, the five-year plans of the old Union of Soviet Socialist Republics (USSR) were technically infeasible, but nowadays, and even more so in the future, large centralized organizations may become more feasible due to the exponential improvements in computation and communication. The current technology seems to give a relative edge to future dictators and totalitarian regimes compared to

---

[34]For example, the empirical literature on the relation between Fiscal Federalism and economic growth shows widely mixed and inconclusive results in the relation [16]. This seems to indicate that both centralization or lack off are nuanced decisions.

libertarian ones.

Am I in favor of Catalonia's independence? Yes and no. Given the complexity mentioned above, it is clear that certain things should be centralized, while many others should be completely decentralized, and they are not. However, in that meeting with the boss, I didn't express my opinion; I wasn't sure if she genuinely cared, and more importantly, I wanted to keep my job.

Perfection is the Enemy of Good, Again

Although nobody likes to be bossed around, when we centralize, not only increases the amount of communication required to solve a problem, but it also fundamentally alters the problem itself. The dimensionality of the problem structure increases with the number of agents and subsystems. These new dimensions transform the problem, making it computationally hard or even intractable. In terms of problem complexity, optimizing with an increasing number of components or subsystems is equivalent to the complexity introduced when features such as non-determinism, nonlinearity, or delays are added to the system description. Centralizing decision-making can turn tractable distributed problems into intractable ones.

As is well-known decision-making within a group, where everyone's perspective is considered, can be significantly more demanding. Adding my wife, my kids, my brother and sister, my neighbor, my boss, and my dog changes the problem structure qualitatively. From a mathematical perspective, the structure of a decision-making process involving several people fundamentally alters the structure of the problem. Have you ever traveled with your partner? Or with your friends? Did you have conflicts or arguments during the trip? Are they still your friends after the trip?

The most important takeaway here is that centralizing decision-making inherently increases complexity. It requires far more computation than a decentralized approach and it can become intractable. If discussions within a group start failing, it is not necessarily our fault (nor that of our spouse, friends, or colleagues); it possibly is just a consequence of increasing the number of stakeholders, and therefore, the problem complexity.

This is another reason that justifies the use of heuristics, not merely as a clever technique, but as a practical solution to the intractable nature of complex problems involving several parties [26].

Perfection is the enemy of good.

Latency versus Throughput

One Monday morning during the time I was working on the Compact Muon Solenoid experiment, I arrived at the office and found my friend Ori exhausted. Recently, Ori had also become a colleague and joined the Level-1 Trigger team. For some miraculous reason, he had arrived early that day.

"How are you doing? You got here really early today," I said, jokingly, as the situation warranted a mention in the Almanac of extraordinary CERN events.

"Yeah," he replied evasively as I noticed a big cardboard box on the floor.

Suddenly, something clicked, and I asked, "Did you sleep in the office?"

Caught without an escape, half-ashamed yet oddly proud to be discovered doing something unusual, he said, "You know, in Japan, it is a sign of commitment to sleep in the office." Saying that knowingly, as he had spent his PhD days in Tokyo.

What is this obsession with being busy? Is it cultural, or is it limited to the companies I've worked for? People are busy—very busy—and we are proud of it. It seems that within our culture, not being busy is equated with being lazy, a sloth. As we have seen, everything has a cost. What, then, is the cost of being busy?

The goal of being busy often appears to be producing the maximum output per unit of time, increasing throughput as much as possible. In our culture, being busy is often considered equivalent to being productive or effective, and in some companies, it is even seen as a work ethic. However, what is the impact of producing more? Apart from the thermodynamic and ecological consequences of producing more (waste), being busy also affects the response time and the size of our work in progress queue. This relationship, however, does not behave as expected. Paradoxically, being busy also means being slow. Isn't that ironic?

Although the units of throughput and latency are different—one is the inverse of the other—these concepts may appear similar. Are they different representations of the same thing?

For example, fig. 4 illustrates the simplest model depicting the latency-throughput trade-off. The system takes τ seconds to process a request. Therefore, the latency is τ, and the throughput is $1/\tau$ requests per second. In this model, latency and throughput have an exact inverse proportionality relationship, like a perfect fluid flowing through a pipe. In the perfect fluid model, the speed of the fluid is proportional to the flow (i.e., speed multiplied by the pipe cross-sectional area). Unfortunately—and strangely—this simple relationship between latency and throughput (or speed and flow) does not hold in real-world scenarios.

Fluids could travel fast, but in a turbulent regime, the flow is disrupted. Similarly, cars on a road, packets in a network, and tasks in a project face comparable issues. A Lamborghini can get caught in a traffic jam, a fiber-optic connection might struggle to load a web page, and even top engineers fail to deliver projects on time.

In most situations, there is a trade-off between latency and throughput. They are not equivalent concepts, and one is not the inverse of the other. As we show in the next sections, as we get busier and produce more, the response time increases disproportionately, and latency and work in progress queue size grows explosively. This fundamental queueing theory trade-off will be the core of the next sections following a short exposition about the fundamental limit on latency (unlike throughput), and finally, the concept of bottleneck will be exposed again, but now in the light of queuing theory.

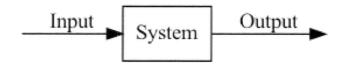

Figure 4: Simple input output representation of a system)

Haste Makes Waste, Again

"Who should we assign the new project to?" he asked.

"Well, people are quite overloaded. Nobody is free," I replied, fully aware he already knew the amount of work currently assigned.

After a moment he suggested, "What about Andres?"

"But, Andres is as overloaded as everybody else. On top of that, he is also learning the release management process, and he has recently assumed a major support role, too. Any additional load will have a disproportionate impact on his response time," I said, assuming that everyone knows about the latency-throughput trade-off.

"Marc, we are in a catch-22 situation. If we do not accept this project, the operations team won't be happy and they will complain again about our team's performance. However, Andres cannot break the SLA." On this last point, we agreed. I was not sure, though, if he was expressing the actual dilemma or giving an order, even if it was contradictory.

What happens if we add a first layer of uncertainty to the previously described perfect fluid latency-throughput model? We initially saw that throughput and latency are inversely proportional. Like liquid flowing through a pipeline, if it goes faster, then it takes less and less time to travel and the flow increases. Is this relationship maintained when we take into account randomness?

Welcome to Queuing Theory! Imagine that inputs can arrive at irregular times, and the time required to process or service each input might also vary unpredictably—in other words, the input inter-arrival rate λ and the processing time τ become random variables. In such a scenario, we might receive consecutive requests within a second or a day, and some inputs may have to wait in the queue until the preceding ones are served. As a result, the average service time and queue length increase, as described by Queuing Theory. Consequently, a request might be processed in half a minute, an hour, or even a day, depending on how many inputs have accumulated in the queue at a given time.

Queuing theory models these uncertainties and provides the best-known models for showing the trade-off between throughput and latency. These models help in understanding queues in supermarkets, airports, and computers networks. The typical model is decomposed into two subsystems: a queue and a server (see Figure fig. 5). The queue accumulates inputs waiting to be serviced, like customers waiting for the supermarket cashier, and the server processes inputs and dispatches them to their output.

A queuing system receives inputs randomly at an average rate of λ requests per second. The server takes an average time of τ seconds to serve a request. So, unlike the initial model, the input request rate, the output request rate, and the inverse of the service time do not necessarily exhibit proportional or inversely proportional values. If the average input rate and the service time are combined, we obtain the server utilization or efficiency expressed as $\lambda\tau$. For example, let's consider a supermarket cashier serving one customer in an average of 5 minutes (i.e. service time $\tau = 5$ minutes). If one customer arrives every 20 minutes, the cashier will be occupied $\lambda\tau = 5/20 = 0.25$, 25% of the time, and correspondingly the cashier will be idle, in average, for 75% of the time. If instead one customer arrives every 10 minutes, doubling the input rate, then the cashier will be occupied 50% of the time (i.e., $\lambda\tau = 5/10 = 0.5$).

The server, at full capacity, can serve one request every τ seconds[35]. In other words, the output rate, on average, cannot exceed $1/\tau$. Therefore, if the average input rate λ is higher than the average service rate $1/\tau$, the queue will grow indefinitely, and the queuing system is said to be unstable.

However, even when the input rate is below the $1/\tau$ threshold, the queue will still grow and shrink randomly due to uncertainties in both the input rate and the service time. These fluctuations affect the number of requests waiting in the queue (e.g., like traffic jams), and consequently the service time experienced by individual requests. This situation is analogous to a real fluid flowing through a pipe at increasing speed: friction between the fluid and the pipe eventually causes turbulent flow, undermining the predictability of the relationship between velocity and throughput. A turbulent fluid, like a busy employee, can move very fast—but unfortunately, not in a straight line.

As explained by Eliyahu M. Goldratt in *The Goal*[85], it is like a group of Boy Scouts walking through the woods. Some walk faster and some walk slower causing the queue length of scouts to grow and shrink as a function of the

---

[35]Note also that for a random variable X, it does not follow that $1/E[X] \neq E[1/X]$. This means that the average service time τ is not necessarily equal to the output rate of the queuing system μ.

Figure 5: Representation of a single server queue (source: wikipedia.org)

pace at which every individual walks. If at some point they need to walk over a difficult pass, then they will get all stuck in a long queue just before the pass. Afterward, it will be the opposite, and the group will spread out, with the faster ones ahead and the slower ones trailing behind. In this case, the equivalent of the throughput is the average speed of the group, and therefore the latency is instead determined by the slowest individual, the bottleneck.

The system throughput is measured by the system output rate, and as long as the average input rate λ is below the average service rate $1/\tau$, the throughput is also equal to λ (i.e., when the queuing system is said to be stable).

However, when I consider my personal workload, stability is not the norm. It's typical to observe an accumulation of proposed tasks and projects. My output rate has always been below the input rate. At work, particularly in certain roles, this condition of stability is never met[36]. The queue length continually grows, and we are always 100% busy.

What happens with the response time or latency of the system as the input rate grows? In 1961 Sir John Frank Charles Kingman published a formula showing that under very general conditions, the time we spend in the queue grows toward infinity as the average arrival time gets closer to the service rate. As we become busier, we experience a disproportionate increase in response

---

[36]Flow control, congestion control, and scheduling are different techniques that can be used to deal with such unstable situations and prevent the degradation of the network performance when the input traffic grows close or beyond the maximum capacity of the system[128,233]. In my personal experience, there aren't many managers who have made the connection between those network algorithms to deal with congestion and its possible applications to management (e.g. FIFO vs round-robin scheduling, additive increase/multiplicative decrease, slow start, random early detection, thresholds for the maximum work in progress,etc.).

time, and as we get close to 100 % utilization, the time it takes for certain tasks rapidly grows to infinity. That is, some tasks are never done. Does it resonate with your personal experience? An extremely slow task is never observed—because it never finishes.

This is the opposite of the relationship explained in the deterministic model. Becoming busier has a direct and explosive impact on latency.

For example, under the general conditions of the Kingman's model, if we work double (e.g., from being 50% idle to 25% idle, or from 25% idle to 12.5% idle, etc.), the latency is multiplied by two. Thus, as utilization increases and we get busier, latency rises dramatically, explosively approaching infinity. No wonder that experts like Tom De Marco, Eliyahu M. Goldratt, or Donald D. Reinertsten recommend maintaining slack in order to improve productivity. Even some companies have instituted the 30% slack policy not to improve the mental health of their workers, but to improve the speed of the organization.

Not only does the response time or latency grow exponentially with utilization, but also the queue size. As we get closer to the stability limit (i.e., $\lambda \approx 1/\tau$), the amount of work in progress and inventory accumulates—an accounting nightmare, especially for tangible production, as the work in progress is recorded in the balance sheets as an asset, but being unfinished and unsold, it does not have market value and entails an invisible accumulation of risk, and a cashflow hole, too.

It seems like a contradictory conclusion. As the system reaches its maximum flow (i.e., throughput), its latency grows to infinity, and it gets stuck. The faster the system appears to work, the slower it becomes in practice.

This should be a fundamental lesson for managers. Do all managers know? Or do they just observe their teams succumbing to overwork—falling ill, making mistakes, missing deadlines, seeing simple tasks take forever, requiring "all-hands-on-deck" or "war rooms" repeatedly, and having to be closely monitored to complete critical work?

As it is well known: Haste makes waste.

Faster! Faster!

"Faster! Faster!" She shouted while I spun her as fast as I could around me.

"Let's do it!"

"Faster!!" Jone laughed uncontrollably while twirling around me.

"Even more? Let's do it!!"

"FASTER!!"

"That's it! I can't go any faster! I can't!!" I stopped, feeling dizzy and close to losing her grip. My wife looked at me with a cold stare fully aware that I was close to my speed limit.

You can increase the throughput indefinitely, but not the speed. It is a fundamental limit in physics, and in the short and mid-term many processes and tasks cannot be made faster. Transporting microchips, phones, computers, or other items from China to Europe, writing a scientific paper or a book, going from Commugny to Geneva, cooking a paella, or building a house, a road, or a software system, all require a minimum amount of time. In the future, perhaps we will be able to do these things slightly faster, but never as fast as we might wish.

The minimum delay of a system is ultimately limited by the speed of light. In the early 20th century, Albert Einstein established the theory of special relativity, and with it, a limit to the speed at which all matter and energy, and hence all known forms of information in the universe, can travel. This speed is approximately 300,000 km/s, equivalent to 3 μs per kilometer, or 3 ns per meter. This sets an upper limit to the maximum computing and communication speeds, and therefore to latency.

I'm not aware of such a physical limitation for throughput, though at some point, attempting to produce more would surely become futile.

The Bottleneck

"Let's hire someone for one year or so to perform this small project. You can't imagine the constant grief I'm getting for this," she said. "This will allow us to deliver this non-critical piece of work that has turned into a political nightmare for me."

"Two years ago, it would have worked. But now, the bottleneck is our senior developers handling requirements, peer reviews, design discussions, security approvals, major architecture changes, and so on. Every time a junior developer joins the team, it requires more and more work from the senior ones. Adding another developer won't improve our flow," I said, showing the length of the queues at different phases of the development cycle.

What happens when we have a pipeline of several systems in series, one following another? Imagine a series of individual subsystems with average service times $\tau_1, \tau_2, ..., \tau_N$, respectively. The throughput will be determined by the slowest of the systems $1/\max(\tau_1, ..., \tau_N)$. While the latency increases linearly with the number of systems connected in series, while the throughput is determined by the slowest system—the bottleneck. Improving the capacity of non-bottleneck subsystems won't help because system throughput depends solely on the bottleneck. In fact, increasing the capacity of other subsystems can have the opposite effect: overloading the bottleneck with more tasks. According to Kingman's model, as the bottleneck's slack diminishes, end-to-end latency grows exponentially. Likewise, increasing the utilization of non-bottleneck subsystems makes them busier and more efficient, but without improving the bottleneck, the overall speed remains unchanged. Only the bottleneck matters.

Adding more junior (cheap) developers to a team where senior developers are the bottleneck does not help to improve throughput, and certainly not end-to-end latency. Instead, you should ask: How can I support these senior developers?

The stability of the pipeline, like in the case of a single system, will depend on the average input rate λ being smaller than the smallest of the service rates $1/\tau_i$, the bottleneck again. That is, the queue remains stable if and only if $\lambda < \min(1/\tau_1, ..., 1/\tau_N)$.

However, latency is a different beast. The total latency will be the sum of all service times and the sum of all queue waiting times. If any subsystem gets close to full utilization, or becomes overloaded, then the whole system will rapidly grind to a halt. It takes only one overloaded subsystem for latency to approach infinity. If you want to increase flow, then no subsystem should be overloaded, especially the slowest one.

In a chain of systems in series, the bottleneck must remain relatively idle to ensure optimal flow. If several subsystems—or individuals—are overloaded, the solution is to reduce their workload. This is paradoxical because, under heavy load, our instinct is to fully utilize the bottleneck. Instead, we should free up the bottleneck to improve flow.

A busy team benefits only if the added resources (e.g., people, money, training, computers, etc.) reduce the bottleneck's workload. This simple idea is rarely understood and even less frequently applied because it is paradoxical. Why should we reduce the load on our most valuable people? Instead, if someone is the bottleneck, we often demand more from them. Shame!

Efficiency Versus Thoroughness

"You are in a recurring pattern," my wife told me in a tone somewhere between concern and anger. "You must slow down. It doesn't make sense that you work at this intensity, having one discussion after another, helping one person and then another. You cannot be everywhere helping everybody." She is right. Over the last few months, I've felt the pressure mounting as I try to deal with more and more. It's not just that the tasks pile up and take longer, as predicted by queueing theory. This additional workload and stress might not be recognized by the company, mistakes, however, are. In this pressure-cooker environment, mistakes become not just more likely but almost inevitable. And how will senior management likely react to a busy engineer making mistakes? Most likely they won't praise him for trying to achieve more.

This reminds me that increasing utilization, efficiency, or throughput not only increases the end-to-end latency as predicted by queueing theory, but also degrades other metrics such as safety, quality, and reliability. As both people and systems become overloaded, there is a qualitative and quantitative degradation of service.

The efficiency-thoroughness trade-off (ETTO) is the principle that there is a trade-off between efficiency or effectiveness on one hand and thoroughness (e.g., safety assurance and human reliability) on the other. According to this principle, demands for productivity tend to reduce thoroughness, while demands for safety reduce efficiency. This trade-off is pervasive across industries and jobs, such as healthcare, aircraft maintenance, air traffic control, and so forth[102,124,161,247].

In other words, thoroughness faces diminishing returns with respect to efficiency. There is a sweet spot where increased efficiency, resource utilization, or throughput does not compensate for the qualitative degradation of service. If you want higher quality, you need somewhat "lazy" and inefficient people.

It is quite counter-intuitive how idleness seems to be the magic ingredient solving productivity, quality, safety, economic, and ecological issues, to name a few. I wonder if, like eating and consuming less, working less is another instance of a simple solution that everybody understands but nobody wants to implement.

In Praise of Idleness

> *Like most of my generation, I was brought up on the saying "Satan finds some mischief still for idle hands to do." Being a highly virtuous child, I believed all that I was told and acquired a conscience which has kept me working hard down to the present moment. But although my conscience has controlled my actions, my opinions have undergone a revolution. I think that there is far too much work done in the world, that immense harm is caused by the belief that work is virtuous, and that what needs to be preached in modern industrial countries is quite different from what always has been preached.*

Bertrand Russell, *In Praise of Idleness*, 1935.

Modern literature increasingly critiques the culture of overwork, from Tom de Marco's *Slack: Getting Past Burnout, Busywork, and the Myth of Total Efficiency*[163], or David Graeber's *Bullshit Jobs*[89]. Among these critiques, Bertrand Russell's still accurately describes the current state of our society. We are over-working, over-consuming, hyper-efficient, and consequently, past the point of diminishing returns. As in control systems, achieving maximum performance comes with a steep penalty.

In our rush to measure and optimize everything, we've confused efficiency, or how busy we are, with effectiveness, fulfillment, and happiness simply because it is easier to control the former. Efficiency can be easily measured with a wall clock. Unfortunately, what truly matters is the latter.

The solution is brutally simple, but it also seems impossible to implement due to the cultural constraints that deem idleness a sin.

For example, how did Einstein, while working full-time at the Bern Patent Office, find time to write his four groundbreaking papers in 1905 (i.e., on the photoelectric effect, Brownian motion, special relativity, and the equivalence of mass and energy)? Do you believe that Einstein was the model employee—working overtime, serving on several continuous improvement committees, examining more patents than any of his colleagues, and then at night working on several side projects?

Too Much and Too Little

During the pandemic, we were one of the fortunate families for whom the situation brought unexpected benefits. No more commuting meant more time for my family. My wife, kids, dog, and bank account all benefited from the change. We were also lucky to have a large garden and a nearby forest, which made the situation less challenging. However, despite being in a privileged position, we gradually grew tired of the lack of contact with friends and extended family over the course of almost two years. For most people, even an introvert like myself, having friends around is essential. Financial security, a fantastic partner, and wonderful kids alone are not enough. A fulfilling life requires a balanced combination of various elements.

Liebig's Law of the minimum, developed in agricultural science by Carl Sprengel and popularized by Justus von Liebig in the early 19th century, states that plant growth is determined not by the total abundance of nutrients but by the scarcest one, known as the limiting factor. In other words, some nutrients are non-interchangeable. Similarly, in life, thriving requires a balanced mix of essential elements: family, friends, health, and a meaningful occupation, among others. Just as plants cannot grow without their scarcest nutrient, a person cannot flourish if one critical aspect of life is missing. Growth—whether in plants or people—is not linear but depends on meeting a minimum threshold across multiple dimensions.

However, a criticism of Liebig's Law revolves around the fact that some organisms can adapt their strategies to collect nutrients by allocating more effort to scarce resources and less to abundant ones. That is, sometimes life sucks but we deal with it, somehow. Furthermore, at the community level, competition, coexistence, and evolutionary mechanisms can partially prevent Liebig's Law from holding true. The "minimum" is not fixed; rather, there is significant variation due to adaptation mechanisms.

Nonetheless, if certain nutrients are entirely absent, life cannot thrive.

An analogous but inverse phenomenon occurs when I visit my mother for more than a week. Too much of anything can be harmful. This aligns with one of the fundamental laws of toxicology:

> *Sola Dosis facit venenum*
>
> *Paracelsus, dritte defensio, 1538.*

Precisely, being my mother a blessing, sometimes it is too much.

The principle becomes more complex because harm could also arise not only from excessive single doses but also from the accumulation of small, repeated exposures over time. Subtle stressors—like lead in drinking water, plastic pollution, or even the constant noise of children—can quietly build until a breaking point is reached. In both life and toxicology, balance is key: too much of a good thing can become harmful, just as a nutrient in excess can poison rather than nourish.

This chapter explores different aspects of these fascinating non-linear relationships through some examples, including rate-limited chemical reactions, Eliyahu M. Goldratt's Theory of Constraints, the existence of free-riding and the paradoxical existence of cooperation, winner-take-all markets, and the theoretical, albeit unreal, trade-off between efficiency and inequality.

Rate-determining Chemical Reaction

"They are eating me alive," my wife told me on one of those days when there was no time for anything but logistics. Although she was no longer breastfeeding, they were metaphorically consuming all her energy and attention. I'm not sure if this is common, but I've noticed that my kids seem calmer when I engage in practical activities like cooking, cleaning, organizing, or looking for things. The moment I try to relax and take a break, an immediate and urgent request is triggered—a fight, a bump on the head (always the head), hunger or thirst, a request for toilet assistance, a keen observation about a flower, a fly, or a rock (to name just a few), or the quintessential urgency: a tantrum. It's as if their ability to enjoy life is directly tied to our capacity to keep up with them. We become the rate-determining reaction, the bottleneck, while they are like the endless substrate consuming our time and energy.

This parallels the concept of a rate-determining step in chemistry. It refers to the slowest step in a chemical reaction, which determines the overall rate of a multi-step reaction. It's like the neck of a funnel—the rate at which water flows through the funnel is dictated by the narrowest point, regardless of how much water you pour in. Similarly, in parenting, our attention—especially my wife's—is the limiting factor. It's the critical resource that determines how smoothly life flows for our kids, much like air or food sustains their physical well-being. Without her attention, everything grinds to a halt.

While the concept of a rate-determining step is essential in optimizing and understanding chemical processes, it offers little guidance when it comes to navigating the complexities of life with kids. Here, parenting often feels like trial and error, riddled with mistakes along the way. But, if attention is the air, the vitamins, the food—do not let them starve. Give them love and time [37].

The Theory of Constraints

"Dad, can you pick me up? I'm tired," Corso, like one of the Walkers in Stephen King's *The Long Walk*, said halfway back home after a picnic in the forest with Galo, Jone, Patxi, and, exceptionally, without my wife.

"But Corso, I'm carrying Galo on my back. I can't carry both of you," I replied, stating the obvious. Galo is four years old, and Corso is two years older. A backpack and a child in the back are enough for me.

"If you don't carry me, I'll stay here."

"Corso, it's raining, you're tired, but Galo is even more tired because he's only four. I'm also tired, but we're really close. Let's go," I tried to convince

---

[37]The scientific evidence is quite uncontroversial in this respect. Secure attachment of children to parents, built through attentive parenting, is linked to better emotional and social outcomes for children[69]. Parental engagement also significantly correlates with academic and behavioral outcomes, although external environmental factors also play a substantial role[68]. Finally, neglect, including emotional neglect—the flip side of parental attention—, severely impacts brain development and stress regulation, similarly to nutritional deprivation[105].

him.

"No, I'm not moving anymore," and we remained in the rain for 30 minutes before continuing the return home.

My kid was the bottleneck of our family parade. After a couple more hours, we arrived home, wet but happy as clams. Kids have this superpower. They completely reset their thoughts and feelings after a short pause. A day is a lifetime for them.

There's always a bottleneck. I kind of knew that, but I really understood the issue after reading Eliyahu M. Goldratt's The Goal[85]. In this book, Eliyahu M. Goldratt introduced the Theory of Constraints. Simply put, the Theory of Constraints affirms that the performance of a sufficiently complex organization is limited by one or, at most, a couple of its subsystems. These subsystems act as bottlenecks to the overall performance, and therefore, all efforts should be directed towards improving their flow. Trying to fix aspects that are not part of the system's bottleneck is useless, as it won't significantly improve the bottom line.

The basic idea seems obvious, and it is convergent with what we have previously explained about queueing theory and the maximum flow optimization problem: improving the bottleneck is the only thing that truly matters to enhance flow. However, identifying and improving the bottleneck is far from straightforward. Incorrectly identifying the bottleneck is like over-watering a plant when, in fact, it lacks nitrogen. If nitrogen is the bottleneck, no matter how much water is provided, the plant won't grow but will instead drown.

In addition to its agricultural roots, the Theory of Constraints can be traced back to various fields, including operational research, mathematical programming, queuing networks, system dynamics, and statistical process control. In a deterministic situation, the maximum flow of a network is equal to the total flow through the minimum cut, which represents the network bottleneck(s). However, as we have observed, the deterministic case can be extended to include statistical fluctuations, such as non-deterministic traffic (e.g., computer networks, road traffic, supermarket queues, factory lines, etc.) and non-deterministic service times (e.g., link bandwidth, factory subprocess, rate of idea generation, etc.). The deterministic maximum flow becomes an upper bound in the stochastic case, and new behaviors emerge that limit the flow, including network congestion, meta-stability, cascading failures, thrashing, and queues associated with traffic and link variability.

The underlying idea remains constant: systems of interconnected components always have a bottleneck. Although it can be shifted or adjusted in size, there is always one, though not necessarily always the same. Consequently, there is always a maximum possible flow determined by the bottleneck. Improving anything other than the bottleneck does not enhance the overall flow significantly.

Free Riding

"What is the price of the fine?"

"Not much, but the shame you could feel is far more expensive. Imagine you are on the bus surrounded by people while they ask you for the ticket. If you do not have your ID card with you, they will call the police, too," I explained patiently. It was not the first time I had explained the likely outcome of free riding in Geneva's public transport.

"But so far, I have never been asked for the ticket. So, even if they catch me, I will pay far less, including the fine." Logical, but still wrong.

"Sure," I replied without further arguing.

The fact is that people in Switzerland (and anywhere else) actually pay for their tickets, mostly. Why do people pay for them? Or, in more general terms, why do people cooperate and help each other? Why don't people act egoistically all the time?

From a certain perspective, my friend was right. Why should we pay for the ticket if we can be parasites of the system and get a free ride? Paradoxically, it turns out that most people everywhere pay for their tickets (with more or less free riders). Why do some countries settle on more or less free riders, on cheaper or more expensive tickets and fines? Why do all countries eventually settle on a mostly cooperative equilibrium (even with barriers, controls, and so on)[38]? Unless you talk with an economist, it seems that we are wired to

---

[38]Unlike the mainstream approach to modeling economic interactions, which often assumes purely self-interested agents, humans, like bees or monkeys, exhibit a high degree of characteristically cooperative behavior. A comprehensive summary of empirical evidence from laboratory experiments and field studies regarding human cooperative interactions

cooperate, even in the most stressful and life-endangering situations [39].

There are two types of rationality: the rationality found in most books and the rationality derived from evolution and the filtering effect of time (also known as the Lindy effect). This second rationality evaluates any kind of behavior, including selfish, cooperative, and altruistic ones, by looking beyond the theory and the immediate present and the individual. Although this may seem somewhat esoteric compared to maximizing profit, it becomes very rational when the survival of a family, tribe, or species is at stake. The Homo Economicus rationality does not consider these other scales of the survival process [40]. These theoretical hominids, if they ever existed, were wiped out a long time ago by the perhaps less intelligent but more cooperative primates.

How is it that these non-competitive behaviors remain in the population? Most likely, parasites and selfish behaviors have an edge in the race for survival when surrounded by their cooperative conspecifics.

But then, why do families, tribes, villages, and countries exist? Why are disabled people taken care of and have been cared for throughout history?[41] Why do we have kids? More to the point, why did I have kids?

A similar paradox arises when I think about exporting the good aspects, and only the good aspects, of Switzerland to Spain. I live in Switzerland, undoubtedly a country with its defects but with many virtues as well. Schools are well organized and equipped, people are polite, pedestrians are respected by drivers, houses are built to last, infrastructure is abundant and well maintained, public transport is efficient, timely, and affordable, citizens vote directly for all new laws, and economic indicators are excellent, among other

---

and their underlying mechanisms can be found in [183].

[39]Intriguingly, immersing oneself in traditional economic theories, which are deeply entrenched in self-interest, appears to promote more self-centered behavior among those who study them [76,146].

[40]Despite prevailing economic textbooks suggesting otherwise, modern behavioral economics widely acknowledges that many individuals frequently deviate from strict rational utility maximization exemplified by the classic Homo Economicus [50,205]. Equally interesting and somewhat shameful is the fact that wealthy individuals have been proved to be less ethical, fair, generous, charitable, trusting, and helpful compared to their poorer counterparts [58,173,174].

[41]Although it is somewhat paradoxical in our chrematistic society, cooperation is common in non-human animals, plants, and micro-organisms. Evolution, the ultimate Lindy filter has proven cooperation to be rational [59,96,239].

things. Why haven't the good parts of Switzerland been copied in other countries?

An explanation for this lack of convergence can be derived from the inverse of the Law of the Minimum and the Theory of Constraints. A country, organization, or process can be considered as a chain of interconnected subsystems. To replicate such a system, it is not enough to replicate some individual processes; all of them need to perform at their minimum level. Although copying each individual part may seem relatively easy, it becomes extremely difficult to do it for the whole system. Switzerland cannot be replicated by simply reducing unemployment, creating chocolate factories, or making drivers more respectful. Hopefully it is just a matter of time and thoughtful effort.

It is the coordinated composition of its parts that makes it exceptional. And this coordination is possible among rational individuals precisely because, depending on the definition, rationality can encompass more than just individualistic aims.

Messi, Jordan, Brad Pitt, and Steve Jobs

"Messi, Jordan, Brad Pitt, and Steve Jobs all deserve their salaries. They are the best and they worked really hard, harder and smarter than anybody else. What does 'too much' mean anyway?" Dariusz began a discussion during a coffee break. The conversation began with an observation about interns earning one zero less than the staff. Do interns generate ten times less value? Dariusz was young, exceptionally bright, and had extensive expertise in embedded systems and electronics for his age. He was also an intern. Despite his talents, he was one of the least-paid team members. However, he defended large salary disparities among the team members, possibly envisioning himself swiftly ascending the salary ladder in the future.

If one zero is already challenging to justify, what about six or more? Is anyone's time worth six or more figures more than another person's? Who deserves a billion[42]? Why should some people live with less than $1 a day?

---

[42]Although it is well-known that the role of talent and hard work plays in the acquisition of wealth, it is sometimes less discussed how significant a role is played by chance and the initial conditions of the individual on the acquisition of wealth [30,177]. Given that talent

Paracelsus' Law of toxicology does not seem to have an analogy for money. Do the huge wealth and income disparities make sense? Yet, this is the state of affairs in the world, and it is widely believed that a more equal world would be less efficient.

In 1975, Arthur Okun influenced a generation of economists with the publication of *Equality and Efficiency: The Big Trade-off* [165]:

> *The money must be carried from the rich to the poor in a leaky bucket. Some of it will simply disappear in transit, so the poor will not receive all the money that is taken from the rich.*

In this way, Arthur Okun summarized a well-known, to him, problem: taxes will be inefficiently redistributed to the poor by state bureaucrats, hurting the market economy—a more fair and efficient redistributive system. That is, redistributive policies via taxes and regulation cause private profits to fall below the social ones. The profit leaks out in various forms of economic activity, distorting incentives and leading to sub-optimal outcomes and efficiency losses. According to common Economics wisdom, that's why policies aimed at improving equality come at a cost in terms of lower efficiency. Of course, this is just one aspect of redistribution, and it does not consider the case where equality is achieved, for example, by having salaries more evenly distributed.

The controversy surrounding this subject remains open, and it's not clear whether such a trade-off exists or if it is exactly the opposite[43]. As Robert Barro pointed out:

> *Evidence from a broad panel of countries shows little overall relation between income inequality and rates of growth and investment. For growth, higher inequality tends to retard growth in poor countries and encourage growth in richer places. The Kuznets*

---

likely has a Gaussian or quasi-Gaussian distribution, it is available to many individuals, at least 50% of the population. However, it is actually luck and initial conditions that determine the final outcome for these top 1% performers.

[43]There is substantial evidence showing there is no such relation between inequality and efficiency[15,22,55]. In fact, more unequal societies appear bad for almost everyone within them—the well-off as well as the poor. Almost every modern social and environmental problem—health, lack of community life, violence, drugs, obesity, mental illness, long working hours, big prison populations—is more likely to occur in a less equal society [243]. While solutions may sometimes be simple, our entrenchment in the status-quo often prevents progress.

curve—whereby inequality first increases and later decreases during the process of economic development—emerges as a clear empirical regularity. However, this relation does not explain the bulk of variations in inequality across countries or over time.

Isn't it intriguing? Something so ingrained in our meritocratic culture could be mistaken. Why might this tenet of our modern societies be so prevalent?

Winner-take-all Markets

"Will you come to the football match?"

"I'm busy." I didn't want to initiate a rant about the astronomical salaries of certain players, my meager interest in beer, the issue of not being able to hear anyone in a crowd, or my unusual aversion to football.

"You shouldn't work so much." Well, I was really referring to my family, but the best excuses are the ones that are handed to you.

I wonder why overworking or watching a match with a beer is socially acceptable, but relaxing in a café while engrossed in a dense book is considered unusual, and even reprehensible if you have children. Regardless, I wish I could.

How is it that certain football players or CEOs receive these enormous remunerations? Every year a new star seems to further increase the ceiling of what is achievable. I wonder how they feel when they look at their teammates or assistants, fully aware of the stark differences.

There are markets where a small number of top performers take the lion's share of the total rewards. This payoff structure has long been prevalent in entertainment and professional sports, but it has recently penetrated into other fields: law, journalism, consulting, investment banking, corporate management, design, fashion, and even academia.

These markets are extraordinarily unequal. But are they equally efficient? Are these top earners really worth their salary?

In sports we have Michael Lewis's account in *Moneyball: The Art of Winning an Unfair Game*[134], and in business the impact of CEO changes on a company's performance is a well-studied case as well. A cursory review of existing meta-analyses and reviews appears to indicate that the variability in CEO performance is uncorrelated with pay differences, exogenous CEO changes (i.e., due to death, health issues, or retirements), and successions[70,201,230]. Instead, performance seems to correlate with firm size, the origin of the CEO (i.e., insiders perform better than outsiders), and the change itself (a change typically has a negative short-term impact on performance and behaves as a non-minimum phase system). Isn't it peculiar that these remuneration disparities still exist and many people believe they're fair?

Although the market structure produces these winner-take-all outcomes, those salaries might not necessarily be the optimal ones. Given the evidence, we should, at least, view them with a degree of skepticism as the market for CEOs does not seem to be efficient.

The Dawn of Everything

"Marc, let's grab a coffee and leave the slaves working," Daniel told me jokingly.

"Slaves?" I've always been slow to catch on to jokes.

"Man! The interns! They are so badly paid yet they do the same job," he said with crystalline clarity. It had never occurred to me that, in the past, I was also paid four times less for doing more or less the same job. How is it possible? Am I really four times more productive than my colleagues? If I work one day a week, and they work all week long, will I produce roughly the same?

If there is such a fundamental trade-off between efficiency and inequality, it must be scale-dependent, because the concept doesn't even make sense when discussing the issue within a family or team. What will happen if a team member earns a thousand times more than you? It might hold some merit at the country or regional level (although as we saw in the previous section, the evidence is not conclusive and often suggests the opposite), but it absolutely doesn't apply when someone is sleeping on the streets. On a team scale, I instinctively feel it's ethically dubious to withhold salary information, even when the differences are small.

A historically grounded perspective on inequality is explored in *The Dawn of Everything: A New History of Humanity* by David Graeber and David Wengrow[90]. Why do we accept inequality as a necessary byproduct of civilization, when archaeological evidence doesn't support it?

What is your gut reaction when you encounter poverty? It's something I find hard to stomach, and it fills me with guilt. Is it just me, or is it an instinctual reaction of all human beings, cultivated from generations of survival? I believe I'm not alone, as I frequently observe people consciously averting their gaze and distancing themselves from the homeless. Is it because we despise poverty, or because it stirs guilt within us? The fact that our bodies react suggests that something is deeply wrong—much like our instinctive fear of snakes and spiders, the vertigo that grips us near a cliff, or the nausea triggered by the stench of rotten food. It's as if our evolutionary journey is hardwired to sound an alarm when faced with extreme inequality, and perhaps, there are good reasons.

Once, I traveled to Los Angeles with my wife, and I distinctly remember a large, barefoot man pushing a supermarket cart near Hollywood Boulevard (where dreams are made—and broken). It made me wonder whether the concept for *The Walking Dead* comic originated from a visit to the suburbs of a renowned U.S. city[117]. The 'walkers' versus the healthy individuals shielded by shops, fences, and guards—the pervasive pandemic named poverty feels eerily analogous to Robert Kirkman's comic book fantasy.

Why do we, as a society, accept the possibility of individuals without a home or shoes? Would we tolerate such disparities within our own families? Why is it that historical records show disabled individuals, evidently well-fed, in lavish burials? Why does our society permit someone to amass a billion dollars? Why does someone need a billion dollars? And what does a billion dollars even represent, anyway?

Opportunity Cost

"Dad, I want to buy a pink rabbit, a chocolate egg, and a Pikachu!" Corso exclaimed.

"Sure, but tonight the Tooth Fairy brought you 5 francs, not 100. It's not your birthday either."

"100. . . " he thought and continued: "How much are 100 francs?"

"You have just one coin and you have to choose," I replied.

"But, no! I will buy all the things with my coin!"

"Sure," I said, thinking perhaps it wasn't the best time to introduce the concept of Opportunity Cost to my son.

It is well known in economics that a price does not contain information by itself but only in relation to other prices. For example, two prices, like the price of corn and rice, can be combined in a ratio, p_{corn}/p_{rice}. The ratio of prices represents a trade-off between two decisions (buying corn versus buying rice). This ratio tells us the quantity of rice we must sacrifice to get one unit of corn. A price is meaningless except in relation to other prices.

Corn and rice may seem somewhat academic, but have you ever thought about the combined salary spent on a meeting? What is the cost of a meeting? Does the meeting pay off? You just need to multiply the number of people by their hourly salary. A typical meeting with 10 people for 1 hour can easily cost between \$100 (e.g., McDonald's employees) and \$1,000 (e.g., Google's engineers). In many cases, free time seems like a better alternative to a meeting.

Curiously, it seems more likely for highly paid workers to have meetings than those at the bottom of the pyramid. Sometimes, there are good reasons to meet regularly with your entire team, but it is still surprising to see the numbers.

This notion of economic trade-off can be generalized in the context of decision-making using the concept of opportunity cost. The opportunity cost of a decision is the benefits lost by choosing one alternative instead of another

How is this notion relevant for decision-making? What is the difference between choosing the decision with the highest absolute benefit and choosing the decision with the highest benefit minus opportunity cost? They are exactly the same; the main difference is that, by definition, the not-chosen opportunities are not observed, and opportunity costs can be easily overlooked if one is not careful. Understanding the potential missed opportunities foregone by choosing one investment over another allows for better decision-making. It is a bit like inverting the decision process: instead of thinking about the benefits of the chosen decision, we think about the benefits of the ones not chosen [44].

Unlike finding the profit for a given project, finding the opportunity cost is an open problem because it involves finding the second-best alternative. It requires creative effort to determine the opportunity cost of a decision. The profit, on the other hand, which is benefits minus costs, can be at least estimated; it is a known unknown, while the opportunity cost involves the determination of an unknown unknown.

It is, indeed, a highly thought-provoking concept. Neither Corso nor my boss enjoys making choices—especially when confronted with what they stand to lose, their opportunity cost.

This chapter will explore some of its applications, including the concept of sunk cost, the expression of opportunity cost as a delay, expertise and the limitations of judging it, my lack of clear priorities, the false dichotomy of the work-life balance and the sources of happiness, and finally, the interpretation of opportunity cost as an heuristic, like Charles Munger's inversion, to improve our decisions.

---

[44]*Thinking, Fast and Slow* by Daniel Kahneman synthesizes decades of research in psychology and behavioral economics to explore the strengths and weaknesses of human decision-making.

Opportunity Cost is not a Sunk Cost

"What would you do if you were in your twenties again?" we frequently ask each other. Today, I answered: "I would have spent less time training for the decathlon. Why didn't I travel more?" For different reasons, Bego orbits around the same thought: time. I wonder if all parents follow similar mental trajectories at times.

I do not regret the past as I have always tried to do my best in each moment. Equally importantly, I do not know if I could be better off. It is an absurd but recurrent conversation. We cannot change the past, the time just flows.

A sunk cost seems to trigger an analogous mental mechanism. While we regret a past investment or decision, we keep holding onto it; sometimes, we even say we are too invested. Dwelling on a past mistake does nothing to improve your present. Sunk costs have an irrational psychological effect on humans leading to an escalation of commitment toward suboptimal decisions. Sunk costs negatively affect the decision-making process, and they should not be taken into account. Instead, decisions should be guided by opportunity costs. Unfortunately, it is often overshadowed by the feeling of a sunk cost; failure overwhelms us. Sunk costs are like chains anchoring us to the past, clouding our view of the present.

For example, if we bought a laptop in the past for \$2,000, and its current market value is \$400, its sunk cost is \$1,600. The \$1,600 is lost, and it should not be factored into future decisions. However, we could (irrationally) argue that it does not make sense to buy a better laptop for \$600 (effectively just \$200 after selling our old computer) because we have already invested so much in the previous one.

Judging by popular press accounts and everyday observations, one might argue that there is a tendency to become locked into escalation situations, that is, to throw good money (or resources) after bad. This tendency was most graphically described by George Ball during the early days of the Vietnam War[113]:

> *The decision you face now is crucial. Once large numbers of U.S. troops are committed to direct combat, they will begin to take heavy casualties in a war they are ill equipped to fight in a non-cooperative if not downright hostile countryside. Once we suffer*

large casualties, we will have started a well-nigh irreversible process. Our involvement will be so great that we cannot—without national humiliation—stop short of achieving our complete objectives. Of the two possibilities, I think humiliation would be more likely than the achievement of our objectives—even after we have paid terrible costs.

Another highly cited example of sunk costs is the Concorde project, a French-British turbojet-powered supersonic passenger airliner that was operated from 1976 until 2003. The initial program cost estimate of £70 million met huge overruns and delays, with the program eventually costing £1.3 billion. Already in 1971, an official British document expressed a very clear understanding of the concept of sunk costs and cautioned against falling for the sunk-cost fallacy [190]:

Concorde is a commercial disaster. It should never have been started. On 30 November, 1971, it had cost the British Government an irrecoverable £350 million. If continued, development and production will cost us at least £475 million more (£392 million present value) from 1971-75. Concorde will make little money for its manufacturers and precious little, if anything, for the airlines who buy it. The total liability to the United Kingdom alone could be about £550 million excluding the written off £350 million mentioned above.

[...] The decision whether or not to abandon Concorde must start from where we are now-much of the milk is already spilt.

Still, the decision was made to continue with its development and operation. It is tragically funny because the author above was overly optimistic.

However, sunk costs are also part of our evolutionary heritage. It is likely that they are survival mechanisms. What is their value? As explained by Robert B. Cialdini in his book *Influence*[41], one of the best psychology books I have ever read, our irrational perception of sunk costs seems to be a side effect of our tendency to seek internal consistency, which is typically a great trait—except when you are wrong.

Cost of Delay

"In the old days with the Mainframe, we would ask a developer for a change, and it would be in production within a few hours. Now, it is so slow... " The senior manager raised the issue while talking about the past, his running shoes, and the long list of unsatisfied requests waiting to be implemented.

It is shameful to realize that the new is not always better.

As we have explained, time is a pivotal concept, whether in software, product development, or the production of goods and services. It is obvious that getting a product to the customer earlier is better than later. But why? Because the earlier deliver to the customer, the earlier your investment is converted into a stream of value, and more importantly, the earlier you get feedback. So, time can be seen as an opportunity cost associated with launching new products, buying a house or stocks in a bullish market, fixing a problem that causes recurring issues, maintaining and storing inventories, etc. In these cases, the opportunity cost of time is called the "Cost of Delay".

Do you know your Cost of Delay? If you do not know it, you do not know much about the value you are generating. What happens if you delay delivery by a month? How much do you lose?

In *Principles of Product Development Flow*, Don Reinertsen speaks extensively about it [186]. The Cost of Delay is the money lost per day that the product is not delivered. That is, if the product is not delivered because it is in transit, in process, not assembled or tested, or not sold, then we lose money. The Cost of Delay is not just the added development cost of the people, machines, storage, and real estate used, but also the lost revenue.

What can be done to reduce the cost of delay? As we have explained before, trying to get busier—increasing our efficiency—just slows us down by increasing the work in progress and reducing the quality of our work. So, what else can we do? As explained by D. Reinertsen, there are several strategies to reduce the cost of delay. First, the batch size can be reduced (never increased to reduce latency!). As the batch size is reduced, some value is realized earlier, and direct and indirect economic gains are made (i.e., increased cash flow, reduced inventory, increased market share, early feedback, etc.). Second, the number of tasks done in parallel can be reduced. Limiting parallel tasks minimizes the cost of delay caused by task-switching inefficiencies. Third, the different tasks can be prioritized to maximize output value. Finally, the different tasks in a sequence can be synchronized to the same cadence, reducing the delay associated with the statistical fluctuations of the individual steps.

In the old days, it seems that the batch size was one, and given the time they spent on coffee, it also seems they were relatively idle. They were masters at minimizing the Cost of Delay. Our generation is, in a way, very efficient, academically intelligent, slow, and somehow very stupid, too.

Are you an expert?

"You never hire people from those universities, I only choose people from the Grandes Écoles: Paris, La Sorbonne, Lyon, you know." This senior manager was referring to people graduating from certain exclusive French universities, the best of the best, the future leaders of French society, like him and unlike me. It would be funny if it weren't true, and not only in France. Is it classism, elitism, tribalism, or plain ignorance? Are the great works from Einstein, Feynman, Turing, Curie, Ramanujan, Darwin, to name a few only available in some exclusive universities? Is the intelligence lottery not blind to race, gender, income, and class? But, do we even know what is a better education? Is it a better income after the studies, better standardized scores, lower dropout rates or higher graduation rates, learner satisfaction, economic growth, research output? More importantly, does the decision to choose one institution or another based on any such information make sense? For example, in the restricted field of intelligence testing, IQ, people's variability seems to be partially determined by family genetic and economic influence [176], a bit over 50%. However, should we select an individual based on his or her family's intelligence test results and environment? Such a decision would be rational and not entirely stupid, but very much politically incorrect, even though we could easily measure these directly instead of using one of the previous surrogates. Unfortunately, we are constantly using unnecessary proxies for our decisions; race, age, personal style, height, good looks, and gender serve as typical biases of our judgment [45].

---

[45] All of these can be used to improve our odds in a forthcoming interview process or a sales pitch [41], but obviously, we should not use them to determine the selection of the best candidate.

I have interviewed hundreds of people for software development positions. I have been on the other side of the table, too. So far, the university of origin has never been relevant. It is not a data point even if you are proud of it. Am I jealous? Am I a lesser being coming from a lesser institution? I'm sure these kinds of interviews exist, fortunately I have not been present in any. Does status, university entry-level grades, or student debts convey a signal related to good candidates? It does not seem so, reality is both simpler and more complex. In a selection process, it seems that most of the information about the candidate future performance can be found in a simple intelligence test and a structured interview where all the candidates are asked the same questions to simplify the comparison [46]. Small projects, self-evaluation, previous experience on a similar job and so on are worse predictors and do not convey additional information. Don't you believe it? Just consider the analogous known difficulty in identifying real expertise from others or even ourselves [43,127,237].

If we are not able to judge ourselves, how can we pretend to judge others? In any case, all the above seems at odds with the long selection processes of some companies or the elitist points of views of some managers. Intelligence grows wherever it pleases. Can you extract a signal when there is none? What is the cost of these lengthy processes? The cost can be estimated by the time spend by the people performing all these evaluations, the direct cost, plus the delay and the corresponding lost value, the cost of delay, the opportunity cost of not hiring someone. Every month we do not hire a necessary person is an additional month of project delay.

Priorities

"Marc, you do not have your priorities straight." That's my wife's motto. I typically overwork for the sake of companies that do not care about my well-being. Don't get me wrong. The people you work with typically care to some degree, but for the most part, it is not in their power to help you

---

[46]According to the research in selection methods the best combination of methods is a General Mental Ability test and a structured interview [202]. It is interesting to note the lack of ingenuity of this combination of methods as well as its little predictive power. If your company has a large cost of delay, it could pay off to just select someone at random after some basic testing. At least it will reduce the certain hiring cost and it will create an unbiased process.

personally or professionally when there is a problem. At the end of the day, when your life goes south, only your family and close friends will lend you a hand.

According to my wife, I do not know what is most important. She is usually right on these fuzzy matters. However, I seem to know exactly what the most important professional task I should be doing at any given moment is. Isn't it surprising? Where does this dissonance come from? Why do we care so much about the companies we work for? Companies are not people, so they cannot care, even if your CEO tells you so in a glorious memorandum. Evidence seem to clearly indicate that long work hours is significantly correlated with poorer physical and mental health, reduced job satisfaction, and worse family relationships[7,51,151,212].

A priority list, the one that I use professionally but not personally, is a way to establish which tasks have more value. Even if we do not evaluate each decision numerically, listing all possible tasks and sorting them qualitatively is equivalent to using the opportunity cost of the alternatives.

The mystery still remains. Why do work priorities overshadow the ones in our personal life? Perhaps it's because we structure our time around work first, by establishing the 9-to-5 work hours and then structuring our lives around the bits and pieces that remain.

Work-Life Balance

"Look, my colleagues know that I do not respond to emails between six and eight PM. I have a family, you know!" said Jean Pierre, an intelligent and funny physicist, friend, and proud parent, who told me during one of our gossip/detox discussions over coffee.

"So, your colleagues know that if they send an email at any other time, you will respond. Right?" I replied with my eyes wide open, trying to convey a message. I was taken aback by the implications of his words. I felt a bit ashamed, realizing I don't work as hard—and I don't even want to pretend I do.

"Family is the most important. Otherwise, I do not get to see my kid," he continued as if he had derived an irrefutable logic—certainly a different logic than mine. I guess my telepathic signals were not strong enough.

I have spent close to 40 years realizing that the people who really care about you are your family, and a very small number of friends, sometimes one, sometimes two. It is obvious that I won't be remembered, even for a week, for spending a night fixing a bug, a weekend deploying the latest release, some holidays developing a new library for a web user interface, or finishing my workday late to polish a document. If I'm lucky, someone will thank me, but they will most likely also thank me and pay my salary anyway.

Work-life balance is the term used to describe the trade-off faced by individuals when choosing between personal and professional activities. An additional hour of work means one hour less for our families and personal interests, its opportunity cost.

In the last century, the demographic transition that began with modern industrialization has consolidated and, among other things, has reduced extended families to their bare minimum. Almost no one lives with cousins, aunts, parents, and grandparents under the same roof. Women also began to work outside their homes—and according to popular wisdom, liberating themselves from the burden of household chores. However, although the number of work hours per salaried person has more than halved in the past century[131], the reality is that now both parents often work outside the home. In some cases, a single parent—typically a woman, due to cultural norms or divorce—must manage the entire household while holding down an outside job, effectively juggling two jobs instead[101,217]. So, in practice, I wonder if these changes have shifted the balance even further towards the work part of the work-life trade-off.

For example, what is the percentage of time overworked individuals spend with their kids as quality time? What does it mean, quality time? Does it mean enjoying every minute we spend with them, a week of holidays together at a resort, Saturday and Sunday lunches and dinners, or the sacred breakfast?

The work-life balance is about time, values, and how much we are willing to compromise with our family and friends for additional income or professional recognition, sometimes neither. Over the past century, although as individuals we work home less time, society has shifted its focus from time with family to time at work. What did we gain? What di we lose?

What Makes Us Happy?

"You have not seen your friends for a long time. Do you even call them?" my mother exclaimed after a discussion about our rare visits to Girona.

"Yes, I haven't seen many of them for a long time. I do my best, but family and work come first," I replied, attempting to justify a behavior that didn't feel right.

"Excuses."

Looking for your old friends or extended family, especially your mother, instead of exclusively taking care of your wife, children, and job closely resembles the famous work-life balance we discussed earlier. Either you spend time on one or the other; it seems impossible to keep a balance. My accounts always seem to be in the red.

I struggle with maintaining a work-life balance. How can I keep up with the demands of a happy life? Am I happy? Do I work too much or too little? Should I call my mom or my old friends more often? Apart from the certainty that I should call my mother more often, how should we choose between these seemingly contradictory goals?

Research on happiness shows that factors like health, marriage, work, and social relationships have the strongest impact on our well-being. Interestingly, other elements —like age, income (beyond a certain level), social class, religion, ethnicity, personality, welfare system, gender, and even hours worked— don't have a clear-cut effect once those key factors are accounted for[10,54].

This suggests that the divide between professional and personal time might be a false dichotomy. There is no such thing as work-life balance. Maximizing happiness requires minimizing work (not the same as an occupation). Work should be a means of achieving a minimum income to enable the real goals. It should be considered in the same category as eating or sleeping, a constraint to happiness. However, once that minimum is reached, we should shift the focus to health, marriage, occupation, and social relationships. Family, friends, community — while keeping ourselves in good health.

This makes me think about the famous dilemma from Charles Darwin whether to marry or remain single [81]. He expressed his thoughts to a friend in a letter in the following way:

Marry

Children (if it Please God); Constant companion (& friend in old age); object to be beloved & played with, better than a dog anyhow; Home & someone to take care of house; Charms of music & female chit-chat; These things good for one's health, but terrible loss of time.

Not Marry

Freedom to go where one liked; choice of Society & little of it; Conversation of clever men at clubs; Not forced to visit relatives & to bend in every trifle; to have the expense & anxiety of children; perhaps quarrelling; loss of time; cannot read in the Evenings; fatness & idleness; anxiety & responsibility; less money for books; if many children forced to gain one's bread.

Unexpectedly, given the above points, he concluded that marriage was the best option, and after a short time, he married her cousin Emma Wedgwood and had 10 children. Even more surprising is the fact that Darwin, the man who feared losing time due to marriage, once he was married, spent almost 40 years doing experiments observing earthworms. That's a time-management feat for a parent of ten children. Perhaps he was not really attending to typical house chores with the utmost diligence.

In other words, is work-life balance a real dilemma, or just an excuse for arriving late at home while letting your partner shower and feed the children?

I'm not always following my own advice, though.

Opportunity Cost, Inversion, and Framing

"I want to marry Naia. I love her better than Sofia." Galo told me after an exciting day during his first school year.

"I thought that you liked both." I said remembering our last discussion about the five year old beauties.

"I don't like Sophia anymore. She told me that my drawing was super ugly!" he confirmed with an almost angry face.

"But, did you ask Naia? Unless she agrees, you cannot marry her," I explained.

"It is a secret! Don't tell anybody!! I don't want to tell her, otherwise she might prefer Louise." With Louise being the incarnation of evil, it was certainly something to avoid.

A similar analysis of future scenarios was raised by my wife. Being the most analytical of us both, she asked during a discussion about buying and renovating an old homestead near Santa Pau: "What is the worst thing that can happen?"

The old house situated in La Garrotxa, in the north of Catalonia, requires a full renovation, including the roof, walls, floors, installations, kitchen, bathrooms, etc. Although we have some savings, we will have to incur debt to afford the purchase and the renovation. So, she pointedly asked if it would still be a good decision if something bad and unexpected happened.

Since we spend most of our holidays in Spain near our families, fear the volatility of stock markets, and find Swiss house prices completely out of reach, investing in such a house seems like a sensible choice. This will make good use of our savings, and we will stop throwing money away on renting holiday homes—our best alternative. The decision makes sense from an opportunity cost perspective.

However, are there other ways to look at this problem? Some chapters ago, I explained Charles Munger's inversion heuristic. Inverting the housing problem will requires us to look for the most affordable, beautiful, and risk-free house near our families. Galo, instead, according to Charles Munger, should look for the best way to express his love. However, none of us has taken this approach. Are we wrong? Is Charles Munger's Inversion perspective the only alternative approach to these problems?

In the context of Robust Decision Making, two common methods stand out. Bego and Galo lean towards the MaxMin approach, which seeks to maximize benefits in the worst-case scenario (e.g., should I declare my love if Louise might embarrass me? Should we buy a house if a future financial setback puts us at risk?). Another method is minimizing future regret, a strategy many of us follow: How will I feel in five years if I don't take this step? Will I regret not buying the house or expressing my feelings?

But, is it useful to frame the problem from one or more different perspectives?

Absolutely. As popularized by Daniel Kahneman in Thinking, Fast and Slow [109], people reach different decisions depending on the point of view used. From a naive perspective, it may seem unnecessary to consider different points of view. Since reality is unique, the best solution should also be unique, and therefore, changing one's perspective would make no difference to the conclusion. Unfortunately, we are computationally and information-limited beings. That is, we are real beings, not Gods, and therefore, sometimes using different frames of reference allows for a simpler understanding of certain problems. For some complex problems, like getting married or going into debt, the worst-case scenario of losing your job for a year is especially relevant; for others, like investing in a startup, the best-case scenario is more important; and for others, like climate change, precaution given the unknowns and risks could be more meaningful.

Breadth or Depth

"For Christmas, I want Santa to bring me a Clue, a unicorn-shaped Stabilo, a Nintendo Switch, a phone like yours or a tablet, one of these fluffy pink cats with unicorn horns, Pokémon cards, and... wait..." Corso relentlessly listed his unrealistic Christmas expectations.

Hearing that, Galo said: "I want the small cute pink teddy bear we saw the other day."

"Nothing else?" I said, surprised and proud, especially given my unfulfilled minimalist aspirations with a family of five and a dog.

"No, pleeease. Only the cute pink teddy bear, pleaaaase!"

Irrespective of my personal preferences regarding the different Christmas wish lists, it is surprising how different the approaches are to happiness. At first glance, both are equally valid. One spreading attention and money over an unending list of presents, the other narrowing the selection to a single present.

Just as Corso's broad wish list contrasts with Galo's single request, I've found that people also differ in their professional approaches—some spread their focus widely, while others concentrate deeply on one area. I, for example, relate more to Corso's approach in my career. At some point in my life, I realized that I wasn't—and could not be—a specialist. From my mother's perspective, I might be a hyper-specialist, but from my own viewpoint, I, regrettably, don't see myself as one. I'm not a data scientist, an architect, a database administrator, a developer, an artificial intelligence expert, an embedded systems programmer, a compiler guru, a front-end or back-end expert, a full-stack developer, a technical lead, or engineering manager. I understand the fundamentals of various fields within computer science, but I don't perceive myself as an expert in any of them. Does this perspective result from my professional career, or is it a natural inclination?

Why do some people gravitate towards breadth rather than depth? What strengths and weaknesses do each approach have? Who will be happier, Corso or Galo, with their presents? Traditionally in the past, regarding skills, I imagine that people followed a more breadth-like approach; they knew how to cook, harvest and hunt, perform home and tool repairs, or even build them, raise children, and take care of the elderly. This diversity made families and tribes more robust to the loss of their beloved members.

In the same way that an object's breadth and depth are inversely related for a given mass, our attention also has limits. It can be spread thin across many tasks or concentrated intensely on one. It can be focused or diffused. It can be expanded but made thinner. Focused attention is powerful, allowing me to read a science textbook in the middle of daily chaos, but it's also extremely fragile, as I zone out and cannot hear my children fighting over the pink pencil or the last teddy bear from the déchetterie.

In a business context, the depth and breadth strategies are analogous to the vertical and horizontal growth strategies, respectively. Vertical growth, like human specialization, allows a more efficient transformation of inputs into outputs. This strategy is meant to control the whole supply chain, reducing uncertainty and transaction costs through the synchronization of supply and demand across the supply chain. The Bell System, Carnegie Steel, Alibaba, ExxonMobil, Royal Dutch Shell, and British Petroleum are prime examples of vertical growth. Vertical growth is deep specialization in a product line and market. However, the strategy also has drawbacks, including higher complexity in coordinating activities across the supply chain, rigidity due to the increased costs of switching suppliers and products, and weakened incentives at the bottom of the supply chain since demand is guaranteed. It's a powerful but potentially rigid organizational structure. Vertical integration, like a chain of non-redundant components linked in series, is fragile, too. As we noted earlier, if the number of non-redundant components in series increases, the probability that any of them will fail also increases exponentially because all the components must function simultaneously—a single failure stops the flow through the chain.

Contrarily, horizontal growth, a breadth strategy, involves the acquisition of business activities operating at the same level of the value chain in similar or different industries, allowing for expansion. Instances of horizontal growth include Standard Oil's acquisition of approximately 40 other refineries and HP's acquisition of Compaq. A horizontal growth strategy has its advantages, including increased market power through economies of scale in distribution and demand for certain resources. The disadvantages include increased organizational complexity due to the diversification of product lines and the constant pruning and expansion of the product lines to keep pace with market preferences. While constantly evolving, horizontal growth seems more robust than vertical growth because non-productive branches can be pruned without shutting down the whole business.

Just as businesses can choose between vertical or horizontal growth, the natural world also mirrors these strategies through specialist and generalist species. When environmental conditions change, the former, like the lovely koala or panda, perish, while the latter, generalists like humans, rats, and cockroaches, survive. Note that both approaches, as expected by the No Free Lunch Theorem for Search and Optimization, have proven successful over evolutionary history. Specialization, with its small niche, faces reduced competition from other species. Generalists, instead, find resources in different niches but face competition from both other generalists and specialists.

The trade-off between breadth and depth, analogous to the one between generalists and specialists, is the focus of this last chapter, and several examples will be explored, including the defense-in-depth strategy with Russia as a paradigmatic example; the breadth-first and depth-first search strategies and their adaptation to different problem structures; and finally, the envelope or pincer tactic and its n-dimensional generalization.

Defense in Depth

I was eighteen years old and had just arrived in Barcelona to study Telecommunications Engineering and continue my career as a professional decathlete. On my first day of training with my Apollonian pals, Quim—my new coach after 10 years with Lucero—shouted, "If you want to talk during training, you can pack your belongings and go back to Girona." Compared to the laughs and chit-chat with Lucero, his cold words triggered something inside me. I felt ashamed and furious, with teary eyes, ready to leave. Looking back, I realize I felt trapped—but I wasn't. I would have been true to myself by leaving the training session at that point and continuing my decathlete career with another, kinder coach. Yet, I stayed—and I regret it.

I admire authentic people. They have what I lack—an instinctive and genuine response to the wild emotional currents of daily lives. However, only a quick and finely tuned intelligence can ride these torrents. A quick response can easily overshoot; unnecessarily running from fear, getting angry, or acting stupidly is a likely outcome of a fast reaction. Still, authentic people speak, feel, think, and even dress as they see fit, unburdened by the facades most adults wear. It's as though they can distinguish what truly matters amidst the noise. The rest of us, including myself, resemble onions, layered with thoughts, excuses, and fears. Do I even know why I act or think the way I do[188]? I have my reasons, but are they authentic motivations, or merely justifications meant to safeguard something at my core, buried beneath layer upon layer of defenses?

My emotional defenses and the layers of my personality have deepened with time, but I still feel fragile, like a child—again and again. I have adopted a defense-in-depth strategy to guard what feels like a helpless core.

"Defense in Depth" is a traditional military concept currently applied across a range of fields, including the nuclear and chemical industries, information and communication technology, transportation, and many others. This strategy slows down the progression of an attack against a target by utilizing multiple, independent layers of protection or defense. Each layer is designed to compensate for the potential failure of one or more defenses, ensuring that risks remain manageable. The term originated within the military as a defensive strategy intended to protect civilian populations while maintaining the effectiveness of defense installations (e.g., moats, curtain walls, lookout towers, etc.).

However, safeguarding the core (e.g., the king, nuclear reactor, computers and databases) often implies the relative insecurity of the non-core elements, such as their surroundings and the larger population. What is left unprotected? Commoners are exposed, with only the king under protection.

Defense in Depth may appear theoretically sound, but in practice, additional layers of defense often add complexity, making systems more challenging to comprehend and defend. A famous example in Computer Science is Donald Knuth's analysis of a "super-random number generator," which attempted to combine multiple methods for random number generation into a single complex algorithm. Paradoxically, this approach produced no randomness at all [123].

Just as in military strategy, where each layer is designed to protect the core, in life, we often construct emotional layers to shield our most vulnerable selves. These defenses, like a fortress, are meant to keep us safe but can also isolate us. As we age, layers upon layers of thoughts are added until even we no longer understand why we think or act in certain ways. In adults, this defense mechanism, while protective, often leads to isolation and fragility. Children are undoubtedly more authentic. Who hasn't felt the refreshing sincerity of children, as evoked in The Emperor's New Clothes fable?

Imagine a soul so vast that, even if punctured at one point or another, the overall damage would be negligible. Such a person would rather occasionally leap into an empty swimming pool and break a bone or two than never swim again. Such a person wouldn't feel ashamed to disagree, say no to an unfair or impossible request, or fail to give a correct answer to a difficult question. Such a person wouldn't be afraid to freely express their opinion on a delicate issue.

I have some friends close to this ideal, and I certainly know a country: Russia.

Russia

Will I ever be able to walk from my home to Moscow? Given my current circumstances, it seems impossible. Perhaps when I'm older and no longer able to run or walk as I can now, I'll have more time. It's one of those improbable promises I made to myself the day my friend Eduardo, now far away, recounted the misfortunes of Napoleon's soldiers and the later Führer's futile attempts to reach the Russian capital. They found desolation, cold, and hunger instead of the expected glory[47]. My plan doesn't involve invading Russia, but rather simply walking across the country, staying in hotels, and paying for hot meals with my credit card.

Russia is immense—the largest country in the world. It's twice the size of the United States or China, five times the size of India, and twenty-five times the size of the UK. Despite its vastness, Russia has only around 144 million

---

[47]I highly recommend the legendary diagram of the French Army in the Russian Campaign 1812-1813 as shown in Edward Tufte *The Visual Display of Quantitative Information*[231].

inhabitants, making it the world's largest country by landmass and one of the least densely populated.

As explained by Tim Marshall in *Prisoners of Geography*[145], Russia has never been successfully invaded from the direction of Poland, partly due to its strategic depth and partly because people simply don't desire it. By the time an army reaches Moscow, it typically suffers from unsustainably long supply lines—a mistake Napoleon made in 1812 and one that Hitler repeated in 1941. This historical fact gives the dream of journeying into the depths of Mother Russia an allure similar to that of El Camino, though for different and less spiritual reasons. Will Eduardo and I ever find the time and energy to embark on this path?

Strategic depth, as defined in military literature, refers to the distance between the front lines or battle sectors and the industrial core areas, capital cities, heartlands, and other key population or military production centers of the combatants. In this case, it's not the number of defense layers that matter, but the sheer distance.

What's the most fatal error one could commit when attacking Russia? Launching a land invasion. And the most disastrous defense strategy for Russia? Concentrating all forces in a single location.

Perhaps a more relevant question is: Why has anyone ever sought to conquer Russia? Weren't they comfortable at home?

Depth or Breadth First Search

"Did you know there are millions of light switch types and brands? I never imagined deciding on a light switch could consume so much of my time," Laura, my wife's friend, half-jokingly told her after detailing the nerve-wracking complexities of her home renovation project. Without skipping a beat, she added, "And did you know I can buy a kitchen extractor hood with Wi-Fi? Why does an extractor hood even need Wi-Fi?"

When choosing among various options, what's the better strategy? Should you delve deeply into each option, one by one (similar to a depth-first search in computer science, where you focus on one path at a time, thoroughly evaluating each before moving on)? Or should you gather a little information about each product (similar to a breadth-first search)?

As suggested by the No Free Lunch Theorem in Optimization and Search, both methods could lead to an optimal solution, depending on the context.

For instance, when searching for a flight, the search engine usually provides a list of flights sorted by price, while other attributes (departure/arrival times, airline, seat location, aircraft model, baggage fees, flexibility, in-flight meal options, etc.) are not even shown. However, when an investor decides on a particular opportunity, they often seek as much information as possible about that specific option, a strategy that Warren Buffett is known for employing. In this latter case, it is more important to avoid missing critical information than to repeatedly choose, unsuccessful, targets.

So, which search strategy is optimal? The answer depends on the nature of the payoff function and the distribution of attributes for each option. A depth-first search strategy, where you thoroughly review each alternative, is better when each factor is highly uncertain and has a significant impact on the payoff (e.g., lacking critical business information could make the difference between profit and loss). On the other hand, a breadth-first search, where you review one factor across all options, is more suitable when uncertainty is lower, and one attribute is predominantly important (e.g., price for commodities like switches and airplane tickets, or durability and energy efficiency for an extractor hood, not the Wi-Fi in any case.)

Starting a Campfire

Some of my most cherished memories are linked to fire. There was a fire in Narderans with Jero and Bego, where we laughed until our sides ached when Jero accidentally burned his hand with the stove while patiently explaining, "Don't touch the stovepipe like that, or you'll get burned." There was also a fire during a campervan trip with my wife and kids. Another fire was burning by the Allondon River, where my children played during a Sunday picnic. And, of course, there were the countless times I toasted bread in my parents' fireplace as a child.

Although I'm uncertain why fire tends to yield such vivid memories, I do know how to start one.

A campfire is essentially a chemical reaction. The fire converts wood into various gases and radiates heat in the process. To initiate this reaction, we typically use small twigs instead of large logs. This approach increases the surface-area-to-volume ratio, maximizing the exposed surface area for the initial reaction and boosting the amount of oxygen in contact with the wood. It's a breadth-first strategy.

Ants Swarming and the Battle of Cannae

It was a fool's game, even for a pair of pre-teen brothers. The idea was to place our hands on an ant nest and let the ants swarm up to our wrists, forearms, shoulders, and, eventually, our necks. Inevitably, the pain from the bites or the unsettling sensation of being covered by tiny insects would force us to surrender, running away and shouting. We competed with each other to see who would last longer: "One, two, three, four!" The ants didn't follow a single direct path; instead, they moved chaotically, unaware of their enemy's nature or location, yet inexorably finding ways to attack us.

The ants behaved like an old school military strategy famously recorded in one of the deadliest battles of our distant past, the Battle of Cannae. I had assumed that modern warfare methods and larger populations would lead to higher casualty counts, but as it turns out, the Battle of Cannae is one of the bloodiest single-day battles in history. This conflict took place in the summer of 216 BC near the ancient village of Cannae in Apulia, Italy. An estimated 50,000 to 90,000 Roman soldiers died in a single day at the hands of the Carthaginians and their allies. Not only is it notorious for its carnage, but it also stands as a seminal example of strategic innovation, showcasing the Carthaginians' use of the double envelopment or pincer tactic. This strategy involves surrounding and subsequently overcoming the enemy. The U.S. and coalition forces employed a similar tactic in 1991 during Operation Desert Storm in Kuwait. In both instances, the defeated army had expected a simple frontal attack. Much like a fire kindled by twigs, these battles were won through an expansive, breadth-oriented attack.

The envelopment tactic involves encircling the enemy. This strategy can be effective even for relatively smaller armies due to the mathematics of surface-to-perimeter ratios. As a surface expands, its perimeter grows at a slower rate relative to the surface area. When the perimeter grows linearly, the surface area grows quadratically. For example, if one soldier occupies one square meter, then four soldiers are needed to surround one Roman (a ratio of four Carthaginians to one Roman), eight soldiers to surround four Romans (a ratio of two Carthaginians to one Roman), and sixteen soldiers to surround sixteen Romans (the tipping point, a one-to-one ratio). Eventually, 1,024 soldiers could theoretically surround 65,536 Romans, achieving a ratio of one Carthaginian to sixty-four Romans.

This is analogous to the growth of the volume-to-surface ratio in three-dimensional objects, which explains the relatively large feet of elephants, the rapid heartbeat and high calorie expenditure of rodents and hummingbirds, and the tremendous relative strength of ants.

This mathematical relation that expresses the relationship between surface area and volume as volume increases explains why ants can swarm easily over our bodies and how the Separatist spaceships were able to blockade Naboo in Star Wars before its invasion. However, as the number of dimensions increases, this tactic becomes less effective. In higher dimensions, most of the hyper-volume is located close to the hyper-surface surrounding it. Thus, as the number of dimensions increases, it becomes harder—if not impossible—to surround the enemy, as the enemy always resides on the higher dimension surface.

On a more positive note, as explained by R. Hamming, this property of hyper-surfaces suggests that finding a solution to a multi-dimensional problem is somewhat like a battle: by encircling the problem, you can capture the solution. Since most of the solution space lies on the hyper-surface, the optimal solution will likely be at one of the extremes of one or more dimensions. As the dimensionality of the solution space grows, the extremes are likely to contain the optimal solution [92].

Further Reading

We are like dwarfs sitting on the shoulders of giants. We see more, and things that are more distant, than they did, not because our sight is superior or because we are taller than they, but because they raise us up, and by their great stature add to ours.

John of Salisbury, Metalogicon, 1159.

You might classify me as a dilettante, a hobbyist, or an enthusiastic textbook reader. Regardless of the label, my goal has been to effectively communicate my love for learning. To that end, below you can find some references to deepen the study of the subjects I've discussed.

None of the references below offer quick and easy learning paths. There is no "21-day recipe" for mastering physics, nor a series of video lectures for beginners hoping to learn mathematics in a month. The world is vast and complex. While a few extraordinary minds might achieve such feats, I am not one of them. I believe that for most people, the journey to knowledge is long and challenging, akin to climbing a mountain or embarking on a lengthy trek on foot. Yet, it is deeply fulfilling. The references below provide a cost-effective introduction to the subjects I am passionate about. I believe that, instead of getting lost in today's information overload, the reader could take the fast lane to understanding by studying these materials.

The best book that covers fundamentals across disciplines is Richard W. Hamming's *The Art of Doing Science and Engineering* [92]. Although the book demands an understanding of undergraduate-level mathematics and physics to be fully appreciated, it is the finest general engineering book I have ever read. The best undergraduate mathematics textbooks I have encountered are *Mathematics: Its Content, Methods and Meaning* [6] and David G. Luen-

265

berger's *Introduction to Dynamic Systems* [137]. For computer science, the best general introduction to the subject is *The Nature of Computation* from Christopher Moore and Stephan Martens [152], *Security Engineering* by Ross Anderson provides broad overview of the security landscape associated with computers [9], *Algorithms* from Sanjoy Dasgupta[48] and the classic *Programming Pearls* from Jon Bentley both offer a very good overview of fundamental algorithms and data structures[21], and finally, *Designing Data-Intensive Applications* from Martim Kleppmann as the best introduction to distributed computing[121]. For probability, I enjoyed the slightly more advanced *Information theory, inference and learning algorithms* by David J. C. MacKay [140] and *Probability theory: The logic of science* by Edwin T. Jaynes[106]. For signal processing, Alan Oppenheim and Roland Schafer's *Discrete-Time Signal Processing* is highly recommended[167]. Lastly, for control theory, Karl J. Astrom and Richard M. Murray's *Feedback Systems* offers a comprehensive introduction to the subject, with numerous multi-disciplinary examples[14].

In physics, without a doubt, the *Feynman Lectures on Physics* are the best undergraduate textbooks on the subject[71]. In biology, I have thoroughly enjoyed the vivid imagery of *The Machinery of Life* and Uri Alon's *An Introduction to Systems Biology*, which provides a good overview of several molecular mechanisms amenable to the engineer's eye. A general introduction with the *Molecular Biology of the Cell* or Campbell's *Biology* is also a good starting point.

Guesstimation[238] and again *The Art of Insight in Science and Engineering*[92] offer excellent introductions to science and engineering through the study of Fermi problems.

My absolute favorite history book is the two-volume *Sources of World History* by Mark A. Kishlansky [118]. Why read a history book when you can read instead the original texts? In second place, *The Lessons of History* by Will and Ariel Durant offers a succinct summary of their down-to-earth observations about world history [60]. Durant's lessons should be used as a calibrated B.S. detector.

Many cultural anthropology textbooks are worth reading, and most introductory undergraduate textbooks will suffice. I appreciated *Cultural Anthropology* by Marvin Harris[95]. As far as I can tell, anthropology is well-grounded in observations, even though some theories and conclusions can be debatable. It provides an excellent way to familiarize oneself with the human diversity surrounding us.

Economics is a contentious subject, and most textbooks should be approached with a critical mindset. Avoiding them might even be beneficial. Regrettably, economics textbooks often prioritize theory based on unrealistic assumptions over real-world observations. The books closest to this ideal are *Microeconomics: Behavior, Institutions, and Evolution* by Samuel Bowles[29], *Networks, Crowds, and Markets* by David Easley and Jon Kleinberg[61], the controversial *Debt: the First 5,000 Years* from David Graeber[88], and the *Statistical consequences of fat tails* by Nassim Taleb[226]. I acknowledge that many people might disagree with this viewpoint, but I have not found anything better.

For a broad approach to the biological processes influencing human behavior, I would recommend Robert Sapolsky's *Behave: The Biology of Humans at Our Best and Worst*[198], the fascinating *Influence: The Psychology of Persuasion* from Robert B. Cialdini[41], and Charles Munger's observations *The Psychology of Human Misjudgment* (although I would love to find a serious in-depth scientific review of Charles Munger's thoughts on the subject)[156].

References

[1]   Abadi D. Replication and the latency-consistency tradeoff 2011.
[2]   Abbass AA, Kisely SR, Town JM, Leichsenring F, Driessen E, De Maat S, et al. Short-term psychodynamic psychotherapies for common mental disorders. Cochrane Database of Systematic Reviews 2014.
[3]   Adams J. Cars, cholera, cows, and contaminated land: Virtual risk and the management of uncertainty. In: Adams J, editor. What risk?: Science, politics and public responses, UCL Press; 1999, p. 285–303.
[4]   Aggarwal CC, Hinneburg A, Keim DA. On the surprising behavior of distance metrics in high dimensional space. Database theory—ICDT 2001: 8th international conference london, UK, january 4–6, 2001 proceedings 8, Springer; 2001, p. 420–34.
[5]   Akahito A. The amateur scientist: How to build a Planck-mass accelerator in your solar system. Scientific American 1989;260:112–5.
[6]   Aleksandrov AD, Lavrent'ev MA, et al. Mathematics: Its content, methods and meaning. Courier Corporation; 1999.
[7]   Allen TD, Herst DE, Bruck CS, Sutton M. Consequences associated with work-to-family conflict: A review and agenda for future research. Journal of Occupational Health Psychology 2000;5:278.
[8]   Allum N. What makes some people think astrology is scientific? Science Communication 2011;33:341–66.
[9]   Anderson RJ. Security engineering: A guide to building dependable distributed systems. John Wiley & Sons; 2021.
[10]   Argyle M. Causes and correlates of happiness. 1999.
[11]   Arrow KJ. A difficulty in the concept of social welfare. Journal of Political Economy 1950;58:328–46.
[12]   Astrom KJ, Murray RM. Feedback systems: An introduction for scientists and engineers 2008.

[13]   Åström KJ, Wittenmark B. Computer-controlled systems: Theory and design. Courier Corporation; 2013.

[14]   Åström KJ, Murray R. Feedback systems: An introduction for scientists and engineers. Princeton university press; 2021.

[15]   Barro RJ. Inequality and growth in a panel of countries. Journal of Economic Growth 2000;5:5–32.

[16]   Baskaran T, Feld LP, Schnellenbach J. Fiscal federalism, decentralization, and economic growth: A meta-analysis. Economic Inquiry 2016;54:1445–63.

[17]   Beacham J, Zimmermann F. A very high energy hadron collider on the moon. arXiv Preprint arXiv:210602048 2021.

[18]   Begon M, Townsend CR. Ecology: From individuals to ecosystems. John Wiley & Sons; 2021.

[19]   Bellman R. Curse of dimensionality. Adaptive Control Processes: A Guided Tour Princeton, NJ 1961;3.

[20]   Benhabib J, Bisin A. Skewed wealth distributions: Theory and empirics. Journal of Economic Literature 2018;56:1261–91.

[21]   Bentley J. Programming pearls: Little languages. Communications of the ACM 1986;29:711–21.

[22]   Berg A, Ostry JD, Tsangarides CG, Yakhshilikov Y. Redistribution, inequality, and growth: New evidence. Journal of Economic Growth 2018;23:259–305.

[23]   Bernerth J, Beus JM, Helmuth CA, Boyd TL. Team size and performance: A meta-analytic investigation. Academy of management proceedings, vol. 2021, Academy of Management Briarcliff Manor, NY 10510; 2021, p. 12271.

[24]   Bessen J. Industry concentration and information technology. The Journal of Law and Economics 2020;63:531–55.

[25]   Björklund A, Finnveden G. Recycling revisited-life cycle comparisons of global warming impact and total energy use of waste management strategies. Resources, Conservation and Recycling 2005;44:309–17.

[26]   Blondel VD, Tsitsiklis JN. A survey of computational complexity results in systems and control. Automatica 2000;36:1249–74.

[27]   Bohr MT, Young IA. CMOS scaling trends and beyond. Ieee Micro 2017;37:20–9.

[28]   Bostrom N. Existential risks: Analyzing human extinction scenarios and related hazards. Journal of Evolution and Technology 2002;9.

[29]   Bowles S. Microeconomics: Behavior, institutions, and evolution. Princeton University Press; 2003.

[30]   Bowles S, Gintis H. The inheritance of inequality. Journal of Economic Perspectives 2002;16:3–30.

[31]   Braguinsky S, Yavlinsky G. Incentives and institutions: The transition to a market economy in russia. Princeton University Press; 2000.

[32]   Brembs B, Button K, Munafò M. Deep impact: Unintended consequences of journal rank. Frontiers in Human Neuroscience 2013:291.

[33]   Brewer E. CAP twelve years later: How the" rules" have changed. Computer 2012;45:23–9.

[34]   Brilliant SS, Knight JC, Leveson NG. Analysis of faults in an n-version software experiment. IEEE Transactions on Software Engineering 1990;16:238–47.

[35]   Brooks Jr FP. The mythical man-month: Essays on software engineering. Addison-Wesley; 1975.

[36]   Cable D, Vermeulen F. Why CEO pay should be 100% fixed. London Business School Review 2016.

[37]   Carlson JM, Doyle J. Highly optimized tolerance: A mechanism for power laws in designed systems. Physical Review E 1999;60:1412.

[38]   Cerpa N, Verner JM. Why did your project fail? Communications of the ACM 2009;52:130–4.

[39]   Chandra TD, Griesemer R, Redstone J. Paxos made live: An engineering perspective. Proceedings of the twenty-sixth annual ACM symposium on principles of distributed computing, ACM; 2007, p. 398–407.

[40]   Christopher H, Hood C. Gaming in targetworld: The targets approach to managing british public services. Public Administration Review 2006;66:515–21.

[41]   Cialdini RB, Cialdini RB. Influence: The psychology of persuasion. Collins New York; 2007.

[42]   Cian C, Koulmann N, Barraud P, Raphel C, Jimenez C, Melin B. Influences of variations in body hydration on cognitive function: Effect of hyperhydration, heat stress, and exercise-induced dehydration. Journal of Psychophysiology 2000;14:29.

[43]   Cramer RJ, Brodsky SL, DeCoster J. Expert witness confidence and
        juror personality: Their impact on credibility and persuasion in the
        courtroom. Journal of the American Academy of Psychiatry and the
        Law Online 2009;37:63–74.

[44]   Dagsvik JK, Jia Z, Vatne BH, Zhu W. Is the pareto–lévy law a
        good representation of income distributions? Empirical Economics
        2013;44:719–37.

[45]   Daniel K. Thinking, fast and slow. 2017.

[46]   Daniels GS. The "average man"? Air Force Aerospace Medical Research
        Lab Wright-Patterson; 1952.

[47]   Darwin C. On the origin of species by means of natural selection, or
        the preservation of favoured races in the struggle for life. John Murray,
        London; 1859.

[48]   Dasgupta S, Papadimitriou CH, Vazirani U. Algorithms. McGraw-Hill,
        Inc.; 2006.

[49]   Dean G, Kelly IW. Is astrology relevant to consciousness and psi?
        Journal of Consciousness Studies 2003;10:175–98.

[50]   DellaVigna S. Psychology and economics: Evidence from the field.
        Journal of Economic Literature 2009;47:315–72.

[51]   Demerouti E, Bakker AB, Leiter M. Burnout and job performance:
        The moderating role of selection, optimization, and compensation
        strategies. Journal of Occupational Health Psychology 2014;19:96.

[52]   Dennett DC. Intuition pumps and other tools for thinking. WW
        Norton & Company; 2013.

[53]   Dewar R. Information theory explanation of the fluctuation theorem,
        maximum entropy production and self-organized criticality in non-
        equilibrium stationary states. Journal of Physics A: Mathematical and
        General 2003;36:631.

[54]   Dolan P, Peasgood T, White M. Do we really know what makes us
        happy? A review of the economic literature on the factors associ-
        ated with subjective well-being. Journal of Economic Psychology
        2008;29:94–122.

[55]   Dollar D, Kleineberg T, Kraay A. Growth, inequality and social welfare:
        Cross-country evidence. Economic Policy 2015;30:335–77.

[56]   Domingos P. A few useful things to know about machine learning.
        Communications of the ACM 2012;55:78–87.

[57] Doyle JC, Alderson DL, Li L, Low S, Roughan M, Shalunov S, et al. The "robust yet fragile" nature of the internet. Proceedings of the National Academy of Sciences 2005;102:14497–502.

[58] Dubois D, Rucker DD, Galinsky AD. Social class, power, and selfishness: When and why upper and lower class individuals behave unethically. Journal of Personality and Social Psychology 2015;108:436.

[59] Dugatkin LA. Cooperation among animals: An evolutionary perspective. Oxford University Press, USA; 1997.

[60] Durant W, Durant A. The lessons of history. Simon; Schuster; 2012.

[61] Easley D, Kleinberg J, et al. Networks, crowds, and markets: Reasoning about a highly connected world. Cambridge university press Cambridge; 2010.

[62] Eckhardt DE, Caglayan AK, Knight JC, Lee LD, McAllister DF, Vouk MA, et al. An experimental evaluation of software redundancy as a strategy for improving reliability. IEEE Transactions on Software Engineering 1991;17:692–702.

[63] Einstein A. On the method of theoretical physics. Philosophy of Science 1934;1:163–9.

[64] England J. Every life is on fire: How thermodynamics explains the origins of living things. Hachette UK; 2020.

[65] Enns RH. It's a nonlinear world. Springer; 2011.

[66] Esmaeilzadeh H, Blem E, St. Amant R, Sankaralingam K, Burger D. Dark silicon and the end of multicore scaling. Proceedings of the 38th annual international symposium on computer architecture, 2011, p. 365–76.

[67] Eterno JA, Silverman EB. The crime numbers game: Management by manipulation. crc Press; 2017.

[68] Fan X, Chen M. Parental involvement and students' academic achievement: A meta-analysis. Educational Psychology Review 2001;13:1–22.

[69] Fearon RP, Bakermans-Kranenburg MJ, Van IJzendoorn MH, Lapsley A-M, Roisman GI. The significance of insecure attachment and disorganization in the development of children's externalizing behavior: A meta-analytic study. Child Development 2010;81:435–56.

[70] Fee CE, Hadlock CJ, Pierce JR. Managers who lack style: Evidence from exogenous CEO changes. Available at SSRN 1805028 2011.

[71] Feynman RP. Feynman lectures on physics: Electrical and magnetic behavior. Volume 4. Addison-Wesley; 1918-1988.

[72]   Fischer P, Krueger JI, Greitemeyer T, Vogrincic C, Kastenmüller A, Frey D, et al. The bystander-effect: A meta-analytic review on bystander intervention in dangerous and non-dangerous emergencies. Psychological Bulletin 2011;137:517.

[73]   Flyvbjerg B. Top ten behavioral biases in project management: An overview. Project Management Journal 2021;52:531–46.

[74]   Flyvbjerg B, Gardner D. How big things get done: The surprising factors that determine the fate of every project, from home renovations to space exploration and everything in between. Signal; 2023.

[75]   Flyvbjerg B, Skamris Holm MK, Buhl SL. What causes cost overrun in transport infrastructure projects? Transport Reviews 2004;24:3–18.

[76]   Frank RH, Gilovich T, Regan DT. Does studying economics inhibit cooperation? Journal of Economic Perspectives 1993;7:159–71.

[77]   Garvin DA. How google sold its engineers on management. Harvard Business Review 2013;91:74–82.

[78]   Gigerenzer G, Brighton H. Homo heuristicus: Why biased minds make better inferences. Topics in Cognitive Science 2009;1:107–43.

[79]   Gigerenzer G, Todd PM, ABC Research Group the. Simple heuristics that make us smart. Oxford University Press; 1999.

[80]   Gilbert S, Lynch N. Brewer's conjecture and the feasibility of consistent, available, partition-tolerant web services. Acm Sigact News 2002;33:51–9.

[81]   Glass B. The correspondence of charles darwin. Volume 2: 1837-1843 1988.

[82]   Glass RL. Short-term and long-term remedies for runaway projects. Communications of the ACM 1998;41:13–5.

[83]   Glass RL. Facts and fallacies of software engineering. Addison-Wesley Professional; 2002.

[84]   Goldratt EM. Critical chain: A business novel. 1997.

[85]   Goldratt EM, Cox J. The goal: A process of ongoing improvement. 1985.

[86]   Gonzales L. Deep survival: Who lives, who dies, and why: True stories of miraculous endurance and sudden death. WW Norton & Company; 2003.

[87]   Gopinathan P, Pichan G, Sharma V. Role of dehydration in heat stress-induced variations in mental performance. Archives of Environmental Health: An International Journal 1988;43:15–7.

[88]   Graeber D. Debt: The first 5,000 years, updated and expanded. Melville House; 2014.

[89]   Graeber D. Bullshit jobs: A theory. Simon & Schuster; 2018.

[90]   Graeber D, Wengrow D. The dawn of everything: A new history of humanity. Penguin UK; 2021.

[91]   Green MW, Rogers PJ, Elliman NA. Dietary restraint and addictive behaviors: The generalizability of tiffany's cue reactivity model. International Journal of Eating Disorders 2000;27:419–27.

[92]   Hamming RR. The art of doing science and engineering: Learning to learn. CRC Press; 1997.

[93]   Hamming RW. The unreasonable effectiveness of mathematics. The American Mathematical Monthly 1980;87:81–90.

[94]   Harari Y. Sapiens: A brief history of humankind. Random House; 2014.

[95]   Harris M. Cultural anthropology. Allyn & Bacon; 2006.

[96]   Heil M, Karban R. Explaining evolution of plant communication by airborne signals. Trends in Ecology & Evolution 2010;25:137–44.

[97]   Heitz RP. The speed-accuracy tradeoff: History, physiology, methodology, and behavior. Frontiers in Neuroscience 2014;8:150.

[98]   Hellerstein JM, Alvaro P. Keeping CALM: When distributed consistency is easy. arXiv Preprint arXiv:190101930 2019.

[99]   Hendricks KB, Singhal VR. Does implementing an effective TQM program actually improve operating performance? Empirical evidence from firms that have won quality awards. Management Science 1997;43:1258–74.

[100] Hendricks KB, Singhal VR. The long-run stock price performance of firms with effective TQM programs. Management Science 2001;47:359–68.

[101] Hochschild A. The second shift: Working families and the revolution at home. Penguin Books; 2012.

[102] Hollnagel E. The ETTO principle: Efficiency-thoroughness trade-off: Why things that go right sometimes go wrong. CRC Press; 2017.

[103] Horgan J, Boyle MJ. A case against "critical terrorism studies." Critical Studies on Terrorism 2008;1:51–64.

[104] Hubbard DW. How to measure anything: Finding the value of intangibles in business. John Wiley & Sons; 2014.

[105] Hughes K, Bellis MA, Hardcastle KA, Sethi D, Butchart A, Mikton C, et al. The effect of multiple adverse childhood experiences on health: A systematic review and meta-analysis. The Lancet Public Health 2017;2:e356–66.

[106] Jaynes ET. Probability theory: The logic of science. Cambridge university press; 2003.

[107] Jones CI. Pareto and piketty: The macroeconomics of top income and wealth inequality. Journal of Economic Perspectives 2015;29:29–46.

[108] Jones SR. Was there a hawthorne effect? American Journal of Sociology 1992;98:451–68.

[109] Kahneman D. Thinking, fast and slow. Farrar, Straus and Giroux 2011.

[110] Kaki G, Priya S, Sivaramakrishnan KC, Jagannathan S. Mergeable replicated data types. Proc ACM Program Lang 2019;3. https://doi.org/10.1145/3360580.

[111] Kauffman LH. Laws of form-an exploration in mathematics and foundations ROUGH DRAFT 2005.

[112] Kemps E, Tiggemann M, Grigg M. Food cravings consume limited cognitive resources. Journal of Experimental Psychology: Applied 2008;14:247.

[113] Kenworthy E, Butterfield F, Smith H, Sheehan N. The pentagon papers: The secret history of the vietnam war, as published by the new york times 1971.

[114] Kerr NL, Tindale RS. Group performance and decision making. Annu Rev Psychol 2004;55:623–55.

[115] Kim G, Behr K, Spafford K. The phoenix project: A novel about IT, DevOps, and helping your business win. IT Revolution; 2014.

[116] Kim G, Humble J, Debois P, Willis J, Forsgren N. The DevOps handbook: How to create world-class agility, reliability, & security in technology organizations. IT Revolution; 2021.

[117] Kirkman R. The walking dead. Image Comics; 2003.

[118] Kishlansky MA. Sources of world history: Readings for world civilization. Wadsworth Publishing Co Inc; 2011.

[119] Kitano H. Biological robustness. Nature Reviews Genetics 2004;5:826–37.

[120] Klass OS, Biham O, Levy M, Malcai O, Solomon S. The forbes 400 and the pareto wealth distribution. Economics Letters 2006;90:290–5.

[121]   Kleppmann M. Designing data-intensive applications 2019.

[122]   Knuth DE. 3:16: Bible texts illuminated. A-R Editions; 1991.

[123]   Knuth DE. Art of computer programming, volume 2: Seminumerical algorithms. Addison-Wesley Professional; 2014.

[124]   Kontogiannis T, Malakis S. Remaining safe by working at the edge of compliance and adaptation: Reflective practices in aviation and air traffic control. Theoretical Issues in Ergonomics Science 2013;14:565–91.

[125]   Koomey J, Berard S, Sanchez M, Wong H. Implications of historical trends in the electrical efficiency of computing. IEEE Annals of the History of Computing 2011;33:46–54.

[126]   Koopman P, DeVale J. Comparing the robustness of POSIX operating systems. Digest of papers. Twenty-ninth annual international symposium on fault-tolerant computing (cat. No. 99CB36352), IEEE; 1999, p. 30–7.

[127]   Kruger J, Dunning D. Unskilled and unaware of it: How difficulties in recognizing one's own incompetence lead to inflated self-assessments. Journal of Personality and Social Psychology 1999;77:1121.

[128]   Kurose JF, Ross KW. Computer networking: A top-down approach. Pearson 2022.

[129]   Kwon SY, Ma Y, Zimmermann K. 100 years of rising corporate concentration. American Economic Review 2024;114:2111–40.

[130]   Landau ID, Zito G. Digital control systems: Design, identification and implementation. vol. 130. Springer; 2006.

[131]   Landes DS. The unbound prometheus: Technological change and industrial development in western europe from 1750 to the present. 2nd ed. Cambridge: Cambridge University Press; 2003.

[132]   Leichsenring F, Rabung S. Effectiveness of long-term psychodynamic psychotherapy: A meta-analysis. Jama 2008;300:1551–65.

[133]   Levine M. Wells fargo opened a couple million fake accounts. Bloomberg View Retrieved September 2016;9:2016.

[134]   Lewis M. Moneyball: The art of winning an unfair game. W. W. Norton & Company; 2003.

[135]   Little RJ, Rubin DB. Statistical analysis with missing data. John Wiley & Sons; 2019.

[136]   Livingston MS. High-energy accelerators 1954.

[137]   Luenberger DG. Introduction to dynamic systems: Theory, models, and applications 1979.

[138] Lum C, Kennedy LW, Sherley AJ. The effectiveness of counter-terrorism strategies: Campbell systematic review summary. Campbell Systematic Reviews 2006;2:1–50.

[139] M. M. Seron J. H. Braslavsky, Graham C. Fundamental limitations in filtering and control 2011.

[140] MacKay DJ. Information theory, inference and learning algorithms. Cambridge university press; 2003.

[141] Mandelbrot BB, Hudson RL. The (mis)behavior of markets: A fractal view of risk, ruin, and reward. Basic books; 2004.

[142] Mandelbrot BB. The fractal geometry of nature. New York: W. H. Freeman; Company; 1982.

[143] Mao A, Mason W, Suri S, Watts DJ. An experimental study of team size and performance on a complex task. PloS One 2016;11:e0153048.

[144] Markowitz H. Portfolio selection. Journal of Finance 1952;7:77–91.

[145] Marshall T. Prisoners of geography: Ten maps that tell you everything you need to know about global politics. Temas de Actualidad En El Mediterráneo 2018:84.

[146] Marwell G, Ames RE. Economists free ride, does anyone else?: Experiments on the provision of public goods, IV. Journal of Public Economics 1981;15:295–310.

[147] Maxwell JC. On governors. Proceedings of the Royal Society of London 1868:270–83.

[148] Mayer J, Khairy K, Howard J. Drawing an elephant with four complex parameters. American Journal of Physics 2010;78:648–9.

[149] McC S. Brooks' law repealed. IEEE Software, November/December 1999.

[150] McCarney R, Warner J, Iliffe S, Van Haselen R, Griffin M, Fisher P. The hawthorne effect: A randomised, controlled trial. BMC Medical Research Methodology 2007;7:30.

[151] Michel JS, Kotrba LM, Mitchelson JK, Clark MA, Baltes BB. Antecedents of work–family conflict: A meta-analytic review. Journal of Organizational Behavior 2011;32:689–725.

[152] Moore C, Mertens S. The nature of computation. Oxford University Press; 2011.

[153] Moore G. The chasm: Marketing and selling high-tech products to mainstream customer 1991.

[154] Morrison SJ, Price HE, Geiger CG, Cornacchio RA. The effect of conductor expressivity on ensemble performance evaluation. Journal of Research in Music Education 2009;57:37–49.

[155] Muller J. The tyranny of metrics. Princeton University Press; 2018.

[156] Munger CT. The psychology of human misjudgment. Remarks, Harvard Law School, Cambridge, MA 1995.

[157] Munger CT. Poor charlie's almanack: The wit and wisdom of charles t. munger. Donning Company Publishers; 2005.

[158] Murphy A. A colossal failure of common sense: The inside story of the collapse of lehman brothers. Journal of Applied Finance 2010;20:145–8.

[159] Nakamoto S. Bitcoin: A peer-to-peer electronic cash system 2008.

[160] Narayanan A, Clark J. Bitcoin's academic pedigree: The concept of cryptocurrencies is built from forgotten ideas in research literature. Queue 2017;15:20–49.

[161] Nathanael D, Tsagkas V, Marmaras N. Trade-offs among factors shaping operators decision-making: The case of aircraft maintenance technicians. Cognition, Technology & Work 2016;18:807–20.

[162] Nauta B. 1.2 racing down the slopes of moore's law. 2024 IEEE international solid-state circuits conference (ISSCC), vol. 67, IEEE; 2024, p. 16–23.

[163] Newton T. Slack: Getting past burnout, busywork, and the myth of total efficiency. Henry Holt; Company; 2018.

[164] Nichols SL, Berliner DC. Collateral damage: How high-stakes testing corrupts america's schools. Harvard Education Press; 2007.

[165] Okun AM. Equality and efficiency: The big tradeoff. Brookings Institution Press; 1974.

[166] Oliveira SF, Fürlinger K, Kranzlmüller D. Trends in computation, communication and storage and the consequences for data-intensive science. High performance computing and communication & 2012 IEEE 9th international conference on embedded software and systems (HPCC-ICESS), 2012 IEEE 14th international conference on, IEEE; 2012, p. 572–9.

[167] Oppenheim AV. Discrete-time signal processing. Pearson; 1999.

[168] Orlitzky M, Hirokawa RY. To err is human, to correct for it divine: A meta-analysis of research testing the functional theory of group decision-making effectiveness. Small Group Research 2001;32:313–41.

[169] Parasuraman R, Manzey DH. Complacency and bias in human use of automation: An attentional integration. Human Factors 2010;52:381–410.

[170] Parkinson CN. Parkinson's law, or the pursuit of progress. 1958.

[171] Pease M, Shostak R, Lamport L. Reaching agreement in the presence of faults. Journal of the ACM (JACM) 1980;27:228–34.

[172] Pfeffer J, Salancik G. External control of organizations—resource dependence perspective. Organizational behavior 2, Routledge; 2015, p. 355–70.

[173] Piff PK, Kraus MW, Côté S, Cheng BH, Keltner D. Having less, giving more: The influence of social class on prosocial behavior. Journal of Personality and Social Psychology 2010;99:771.

[174] Piff PK, Stancato DM, Côté S, Mendoza-Denton R, Keltner D. Higher social class predicts increased unethical behavior. Proceedings of the National Academy of Sciences 2012;109:4086–91.

[175] Pires JC, Conant GC. Robust yet fragile: Expression noise, protein misfolding, and gene dosage in the evolution of genomes. Annual Review of Genetics 2016;50:113–31.

[176] Plomin R, DeFries JC, Knopik VS, Neiderhiser JM. Top 10 replicated findings from behavioral genetics. Perspectives on Psychological Science 2016;11:3–23.

[177] Pluchino A, Biondo AE, Rapisarda A. Talent versus luck: The role of randomness in success and failure. Advances in Complex Systems 2018;21:1850014.

[178] Price HE, Chang EC. Conductor and ensemble performance expressivity and state festival ratings. Journal of Research in Music Education 2005;53:66–77.

[179] Priest G. Doubt truth to be a liar. Clarendon Press; 2005.

[180] Priest G. In contradiction. Oxford University Press, USA; 2006.

[181] Proctor RN, Schiebinger L. Agnotology: The making and unmaking of ignorance 2008.

[182] Puri HS. Perilous interventions: The security council and the politics of chaos. New Delhi: HarperCollins; 2016.

[183] Rand DG, Nowak MA. Human cooperation. Trends in Cognitive Sciences 2013;17:413–25.

[184] Ratcliff R, Smith PL, Brown SD, McKoon G. Diffusion decision model: Current issues and history. Trends in Cognitive Sciences 2016;20:260–81.

[185] Raymond ES. The cathedral and the bazaar: Musings on linux and open source by an accidental revolutionary. O'Reilly; 1999.

[186] Reinertsen DG. The principles of product development flow: Second generation lean product development. Celeritas Pub; 1997.

[187] Reinhardt B. Why does DARPA work? 2020.

[188] Rhodes RE, Dickau L. Experimental evidence for the intention–behavior relationship in the physical activity domain: A meta-analysis. Health Psychology 2012;31:724.

[189] Rodriguez D, Sicilia M, Garcia E, Harrison R. Empirical findings on team size and productivity in software development. Journal of Systems and Software 2012;85:562–70.

[190] Rotschild L. Memorandum by the head of the central policy review staff 1971.

[191] Rumelt RP. Good strategy bad strategy: The difference and why it matters. Crown Business; 2011.

[192] Russell B. In praise of idleness. Harper's Magazine 1932.

[193] Rydning DR-JG-J, Reinsel J, Gantz J. The digitization of the world from edge to core. Framingham: International Data Corporation 2018;16:1–28.

[194] Saez E. Income and wealth inequality: Evidence and policy implications. Contemporary Economic Policy 2017;35:7–25.

[195] Sagan SD. The problem of redundancy problem: Why more nuclear security forces may produce less nuclear security. Risk Analysis: An International Journal 2004;24:935–46.

[196] Sagan SD. The limits of safety: Organizations, accidents, and nuclear weapons. Princeton University Press; 1993.

[197] Samoradnitsky G, Taqqu MS. Stable non-gaussian random processes: Stochastic models with infinite variance. Chapman; Hall/CRC; 1994.

[198] Sapolsky RM. Behave: The biology of humans at our best and worst. Penguin; 2018.

[199] Sassaman L, Patterson ML, Bratus S, Shubina A. The halting problems of network stack insecurity. USENIX; Login 2011;36:22–32.

[200] Savva CS, Theodossiou P. The risk and return conundrum explained: International evidence 2018.

[201] Schepker DJ, Kim Y, Patel PC, Thatcher SM, Campion MC. CEO succession, strategic change, and post-succession performance: A meta-analysis. The Leadership Quarterly 2017;28:701–20.

[202] Schmidt FL, Oh I-S, Shaffer JA. The validity and utility of selection methods in personnel psychology: Practical and theoretical implications of 100 years... Fox School of Business Research Paper 2016:1–74.

[203] Schrodinger E. What is life?: The physical aspect of the living cell 1946.

[204] Science UPO of, Technology. Carbon footprint of electricity generation 2011.

[205] Sent E-M. Behavioral economics: How psychology made its (limited) way back into economics. History of Political Economy 2004;36:735–60.

[206] Seryi A. Unifying physics of accelerators, lasers and plasma. Taylor & Francis; 2016.

[207] Shalev-Shwartz S, Ben-David S. Understanding machine learning: From theory to algorithms. Cambridge university press; 2014.

[208] Shapiro M, Preguiça N, Baquero C, Zawirski M. Conflict-free replicated data types. Stabilization, safety, and security of distributed systems: 13th international symposium, SSS 2011, grenoble, france, october 10-12, 2011. Proceedings 13, Springer; 2011, p. 386–400.

[209] Shedler J. The efficacy of psychodynamic psychotherapy. American Psychologist 2010;65:98.

[210] Smil V. How the world really works: A scientist's guide to our past, present and future. Penguin UK; 2022.

[211] Smil V. How the world really works: A scientist's guide to our past, present and future. Viking; 2022.

[212] Sparks K, Cooper C, Fried Y, Shirom A. The effects of hours of work on health: A meta-analytic review. Managerial, occupational and organizational stress research, Routledge; 2018, p. 451–68.

[213] Spolsky J. Joel on software. Sharp Microbility; 2004.

[214] Strogatz S. Sync: The emerging science of spontaneous order. Hyperion; 2003.

[215] Strogatz SH. Nonlinear dynamics and chaos: With applications to physics, biology, chemistry, and engineering. CRC press; 2018.

[216] Sull DN, Eisenhardt KM. Simple rules: How to thrive in a complex world. Houghton Mifflin Harcourt; 2015.

[217] Sullivan O, Gershuny J, Robinson JP. Stalled or uneven gender revolution? A long-term processual framework for understanding why change is slow. Journal of Family Theory & Review 2018;10:263–79.

[218] Sutter H. The free lunch is over: A fundamental turn toward concurrency in software. Dr Dobb's Journal 2005;30.

[219] Suzuki S. Zen mind, beginner's mind. New York: Weatherhill; 1970.

[220] Taleb NN. Fooled by randomness: The hidden role of chance in life and in the markets. Random House trade paperback edition; 2001.

[221] Taleb NN. The black swan: The impact of the highly improbable. Random house; 2007.

[222] Taleb NN. The bed of procrustes: Philosophical and practical aphorisms. Random House; 2010.

[223] Taleb NN. Antifragile: Things that gain from disorder. Random House trade paperback edition; 2012.

[224] Taleb NN. Skin in the game: Hidden asymmetries in daily life. Random House; 2018.

[225] Taleb NN. How much data do you need? An operational, preasymptotic metric for fat-tailedness. International Journal of Forecasting 2019;35:677–86.

[226] Taleb NN. Statistical consequences of fat tails: Real world preasymptotics, epistemology, and applications. STEM Academic Press; 2020.

[227] Tertrais B. "On the brink"—really? Revisiting nuclear close calls since 1945. The Washington Quarterly 2017;40:51–66.

[228] Thompson NC, Spanuth S. The decline of computers as a general purpose technology. Communications of the ACM 2021;64:64–72.

[229] Todd B, Dinius A, King Q, Uznanski S. Radiation tolerant power converter controls. Journal of Instrumentation 2012;7:C11012.

[230] Tosi HL, Werner S, Katz JP, Gomez-Mejia LR. How much does performance matter? A meta-analysis of CEO pay studies. Journal of Management 2000;26:301–39.

[231] Tufte ER, Graves-Morris PR. The visual display of quantitative information. vol. 2. Graphics press Cheshire, CT; 1983.

[232] United Nations Environment Programme. Food waste index report 2024: Think eat save: Tracking progress to halve global food waste. Nairobi, Kenya: United Nations Environment Programme; 2024.

[233] Varghese G, Xu J. Network algorithmics: An interdisciplinary approach to designing fast networked devices. Morgan Kaufmann; 2022.

[234] Villalobos P, Sevilla J, Besiroglu T, Heim L, Ho A, Hobbhahn M. Machine learning model sizes and the parameter gap. arXiv Preprint arXiv:220702852 2022.

[235] Viscusi WK. The lulling effect: The impact of child-resistant packaging on aspirin and analgesic ingestions. The American Economic Review 1984;74:324–7.

[236] Viswanathan GM, Raposo E, Da Luz M. Lévy flights and superdiffusion in the context of biological encounters and random searches. Physics of Life Reviews 2008;5:133–50.

[237] Wathen CN, Burkell J. Believe it or not: Factors influencing credibility on the web. Journal of the American Society for Information Science and Technology 2002;53:134–44.

[238] Weinstein L. Guesstimation 2.0: Solving today's problems on the back of a napkin. Princeton University Press; 2012.

[239] West SA, Griffin AS, Gardner A, Diggle SP. Social evolution theory for microorganisms. Nature Reviews Microbiology 2006;4:597–607.

[240] Wickström G, Bendix T. The" hawthorne effect"—what did the original hawthorne studies actually show? Scandinavian Journal of Work, Environment & Health 2000:363–7.

[241] Wiener EL, Curry RE. Flight-deck automation: Promises and problems. Ergonomics 1980;23:995–1011.

[242] Wigner EP. The unreasonable effectiveness of mathematics in the natural sciences. Mathematics and science, World Scientific; 1990, p. 291–306.

[243] Wilkinson R, Pickett K, Cato MS. The spirit level. Why more equal societies almost always do better 2009.

[244] Wohlleben P. The secret network of nature: The delicate balance of all living things. Random House; 2018.

[245] Wolpert DH, Macready WG. No free lunch theorems for optimization 1996.

[246] Woolley AW, Chabris CF, Pentland A, Hashmi N, Malone TW. Evidence for a collective intelligence factor in the performance of human groups. Science 2010;330:686–8.

[247] Xiao T, Sanderson P, Clayton S, Venkatesh B. The ETTO principle and organisational strategies: A field study of ICU bed and staff management. Cognition, Technology & Work 2010;12:143–52.

[248] A new textiles economy: Redesigning fashion's future. Ellen Mcarthur Foundation; 2017.

[249] Pulse of the fashion industry 2019. Boston Consulting Group; 2019.

[250] Materials market report 2024. Testile Exchange; 2024.